STAR WARS

THE HIGH REPUBLIC

THE HEART OF DRENGIR

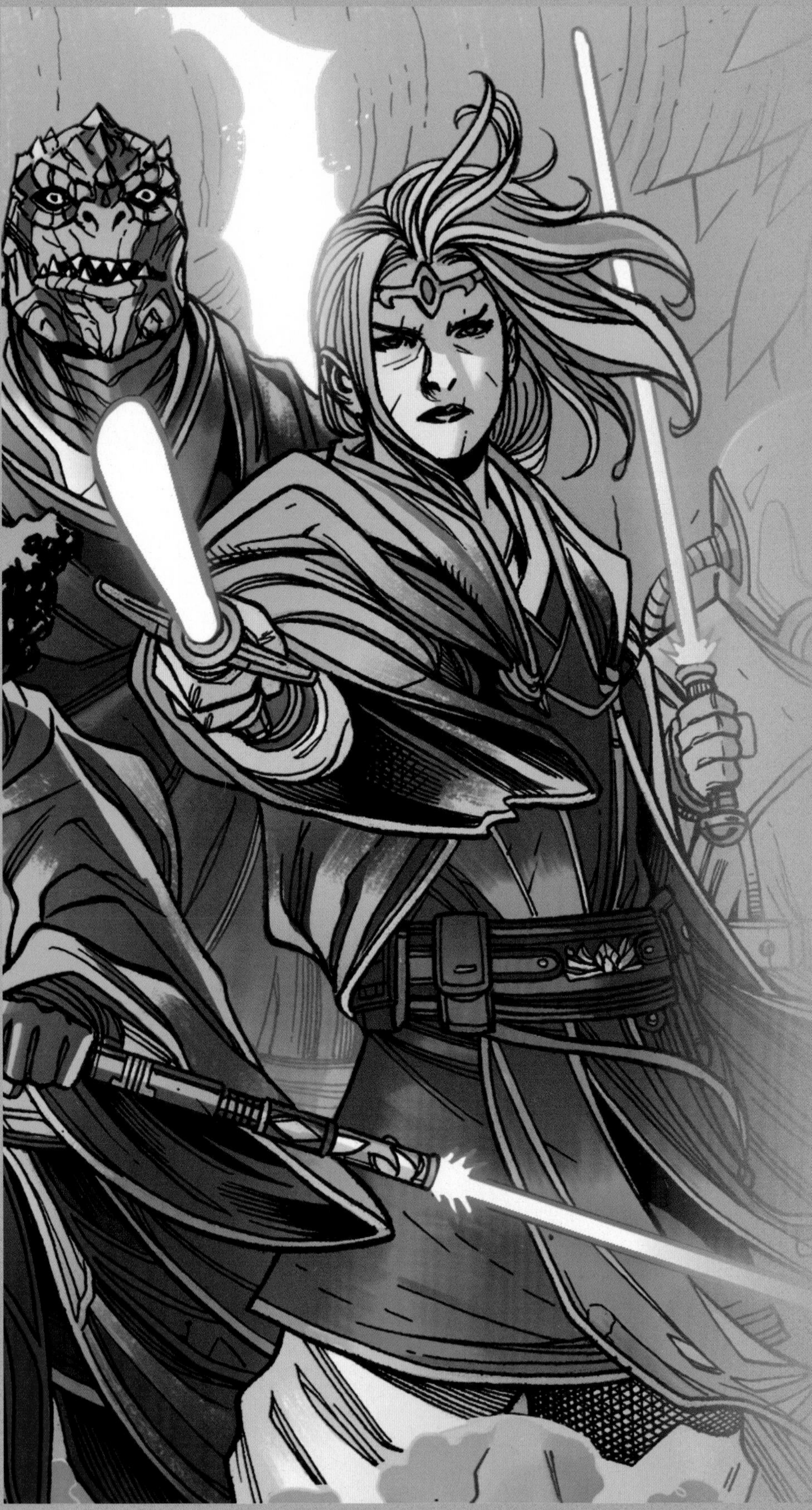

STAR WARS
THE HIGH REPUBLIC

THE HEART OF DRENGIR

Writer
CAVAN SCOTT

Pencilers
GEORGES JEANTY (#6-7, #10) & **ARIO ANINDITO** (#8-9)

Inkers
KARL STORY (#6-7), **MARK MORALES** (#8-9) & **GEORGES JEANTY** (#10)
with **VICTOR OLAZABA** (#9), **SEAN PARSONS** (#9) & **MARC DEERING** (#9)

Color Artists
ANNALISA LEONI (#6-8), **RACHELLE ROSENBERG** (#9) &
CARLOS LOPEZ (#10)

Letterers
VC's JOE CARAMAGNA (#6), **ARIANA MAHER** (#7-9) & **TRAVIS LANHAM** (#10)

Cover Art
PHIL NOTO

Timeline Design
CARLOS LAO

Assistant Editors
TOM GRONEMAN &
DANNY KHAZEM

Editor
MARK PANICCIA

Collection Editor **JENNIFER GRÜNWALD**
Assistant Editor **DANIEL KIRCHHOFFER**
Assistant Managing Editor **MAIA LOY**
Assistant Managing Editor **LISA MONTALBANO**
VP Production & Special Projects **JEFF YOUNGQUIST**
Book Designer **ADAM DEL RE**
SVP Print, Sales & Marketing **DAVID GABRIEL**
Editor in Chief **C.B. CEBULSKI**

For Lucasfilm:
Senior Editor **ROBERT SIMPSON**
Creative Director **MICHAEL SIGLAIN**
Art Director **TROY ALDERS**
Lucasfilm Story Group **MATT MARTIN**
PABLO HIDALGO
EMILY SHKOUKANI
JASON D. STEIN
Lucasfilm Art Department **PHIL SZOSTAK**

STAR WARS: THE HIGH REPUBLIC VOL. 2 — THE HEART OF DRENGIR. Contains material originally published in magazine form as STAR WARS: THE HIGH REPUBLIC (2021) #6-10. First printing 2021. ISBN 978-1-302-93142-1. Published by MARVEL WORLDWIDE, INC., a subsidiary of MARVEL ENTERTAINMENT, LLC. OFFICE OF PUBLICATION: 1290 Avenue of the Americas, New York, NY 10104.

Printed in Canada. KEVIN FEIGE, Chief Creative Officer; DAN BUCKLEY, President, Marvel Entertainment; JOE QUESADA, EVP & Creative Director; DAVID BOGART, Associate Publisher & SVP of Talent Affairs; TOM BREVOORT, VP, Executive Editor; NICK LOWE, Executive Editor, VP of Content, Digital Publishing; DAVID GABRIEL, VP of Print & Digital Publishing; JEFF YOUNGQUIST, VP of Production & Special Projects; ALEX MORALES, Director of Publishing Operations; DAN EDINGTON, Managing Editor; RICKEY PURDIN, Director of Talent Relations; JENNIFER GRÜNWALD, Senior Editor, Special Projects; SUSAN CRESPI, Production Manager; STAN LEE, Chairman Emeritus. For information regarding advertising in Marvel Comics or on Marvel.com, please contact Vit DeBellis, Custom Solutions & Integrated Advertising Manager, at vdebellis@marvel.com. For Marvel subscription inquiries, please call 888-511-5480. **Manufactured between 10/1/2021 and 11/2/2021 by SOLISCO PRINTERS, SCOTT, QC, CANADA.**

10 9 8 7 6 5 4 3 2 1

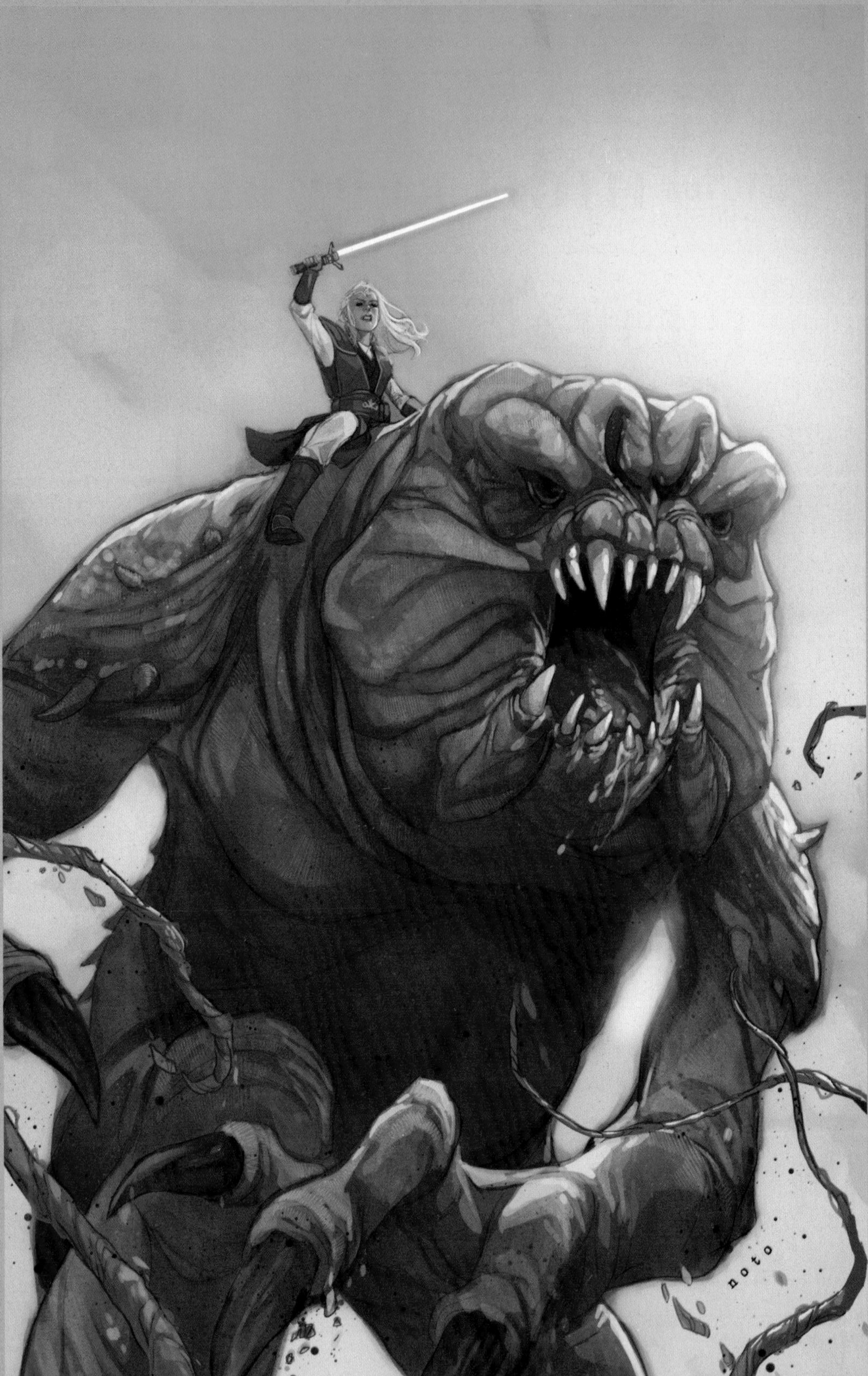

6 | THE GALAXY UNITES

STAR WARS
TIMELINE

THE HIGH REPUBLIC

FALL OF THE JEDI

THE PHANTOM MENACE

ATTACK OF THE CLONES

THE CLONE WARS

REVENGE OF THE SITH

REIGN OF THE EMPIRE

THE BAD BATCH

SOLO: A STAR WARS STORY

AGE OF REBELLION

REBELS

ROGUE ONE: A STAR WARS STORY

A NEW HOPE

THE EMPIRE STRIKES BACK

RETURN OF THE JEDI

THE NEW REPUBLIC

THE MANDALORIAN

RISE OF THE FIRST ORDER

RESISTANCE

THE FORCE AWAKENS

THE LAST JEDI

THE RISE OF SKYWALKER

THE HIGH REPUBLIC
HEART OF THE DRENGIR

The Drengir assault on Starlight Beacon and Sedri Minor was stopped thanks to an uneasy alliance between the Jedi and the Hutts.

Jedi Keeve Trennis' desperate gambit to help stop the attack paid off...but may have cost the life of her former master Sskeer.

Now a much greater conflict is about to test Keeve and the Jedi like never before.

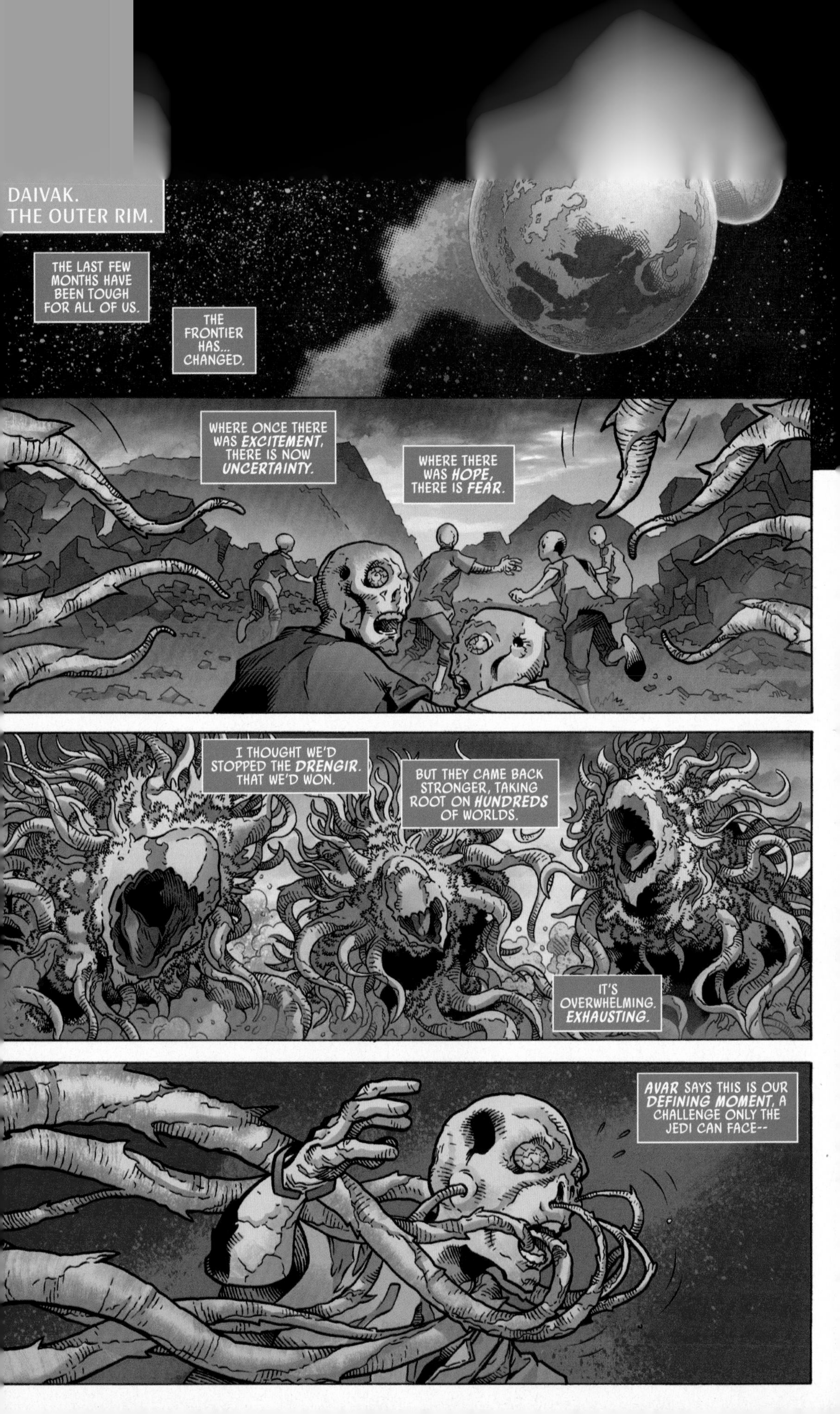
DAIVAK.
THE OUTER RIM.
THE LAST FEW MONTHS HAVE BEEN TOUGH FOR ALL OF US.
THE FRONTIER HAS... CHANGED.
WHERE ONCE THERE WAS *EXCITEMENT*, THERE IS NOW *UNCERTAINTY*.
WHERE THERE WAS *HOPE*, THERE IS *FEAR*.
I THOUGHT WE'D STOPPED THE *DRENGIR*. THAT WE'D WON.
BUT THEY CAME BACK STRONGER, TAKING ROOT ON *HUNDREDS* OF WORLDS.
IT'S OVERWHELMING. *EXHAUSTING*.
AVAR SAYS THIS IS OUR *DEFINING MOMENT*, A CHALLENGE ONLY THE JEDI CAN FACE--

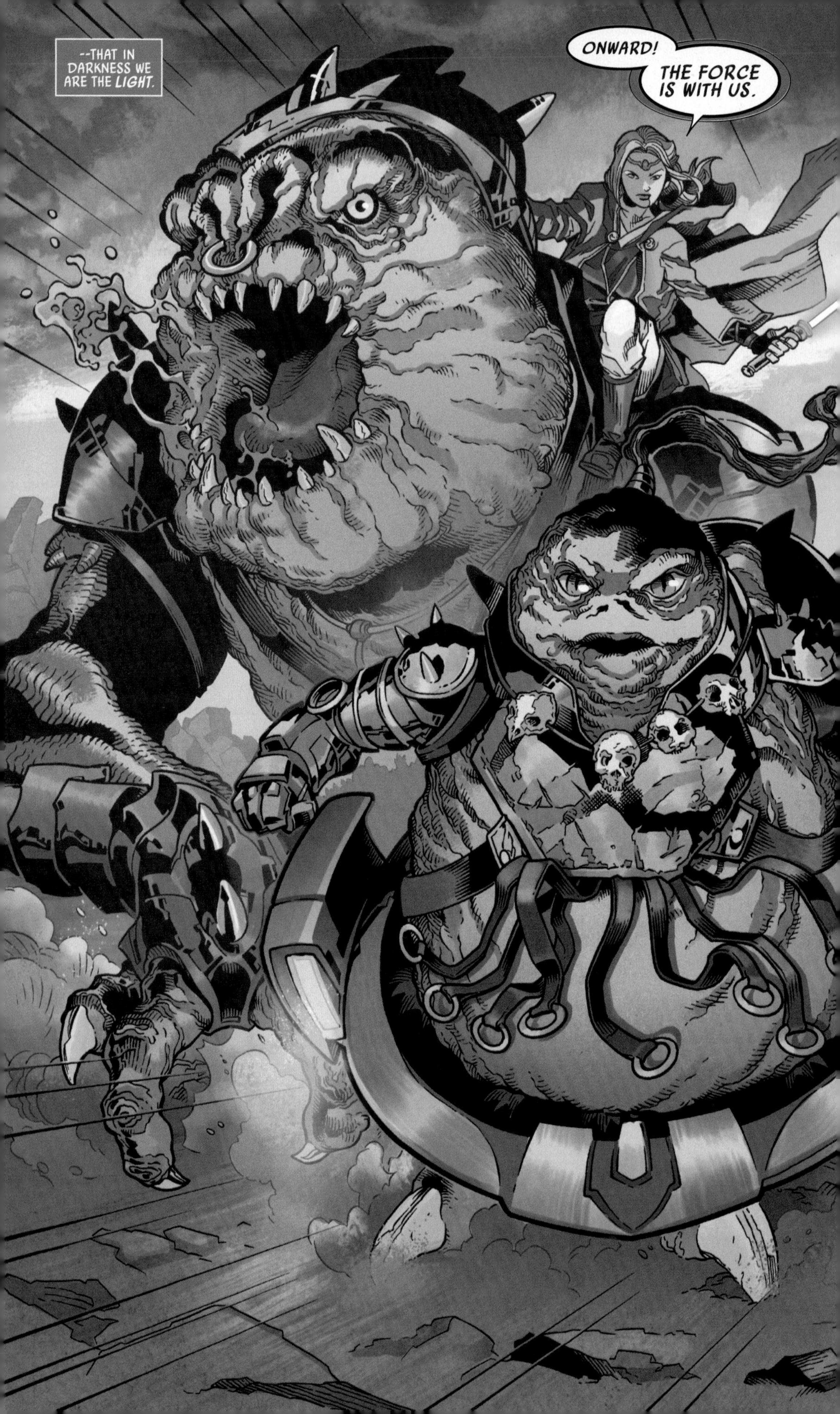
--THAT IN DARKNESS WE ARE THE LIGHT.
ONWARD!
THE FORCE IS WITH US.

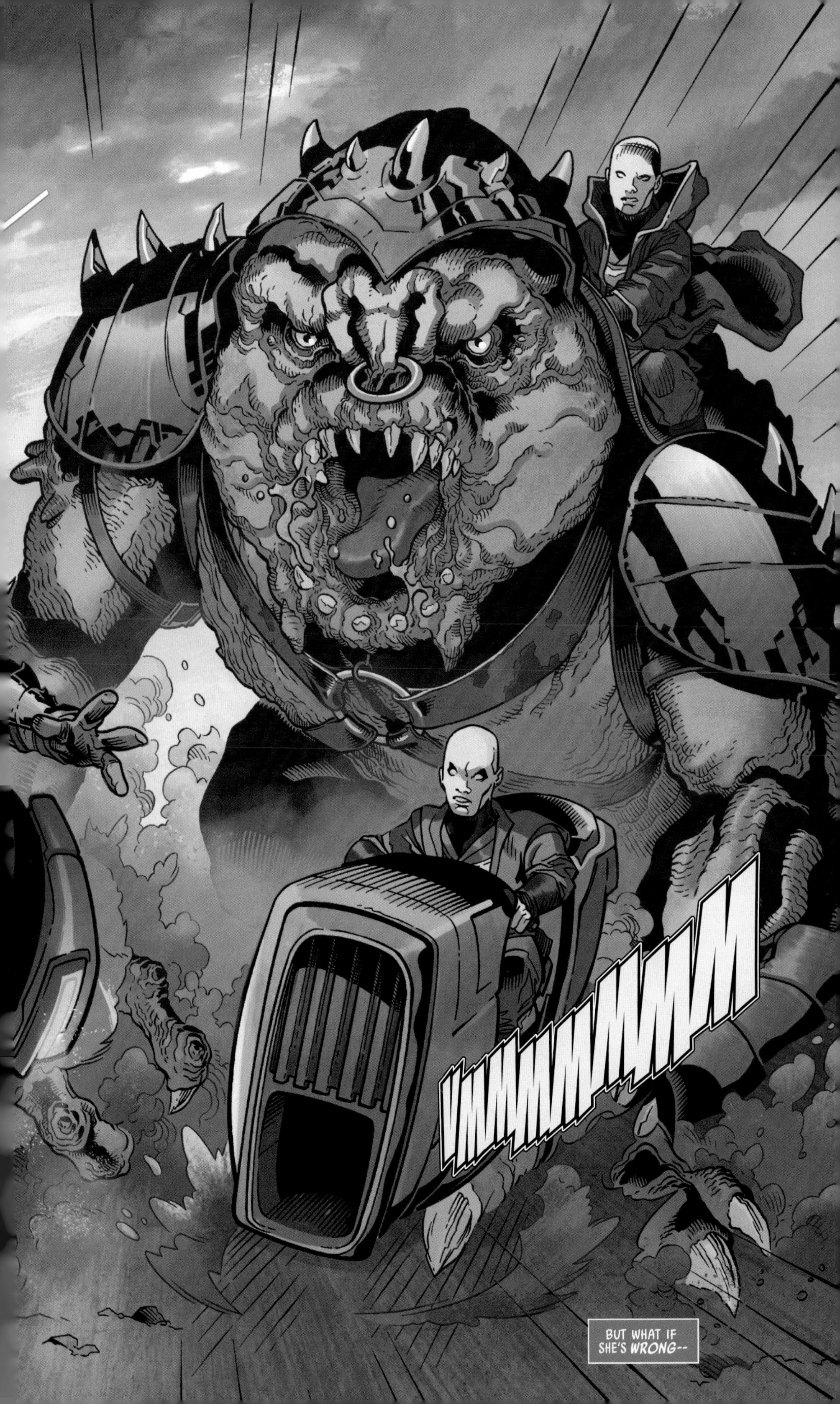
VMMMMMMMM
BUT WHAT IF SHE'S WRONG--

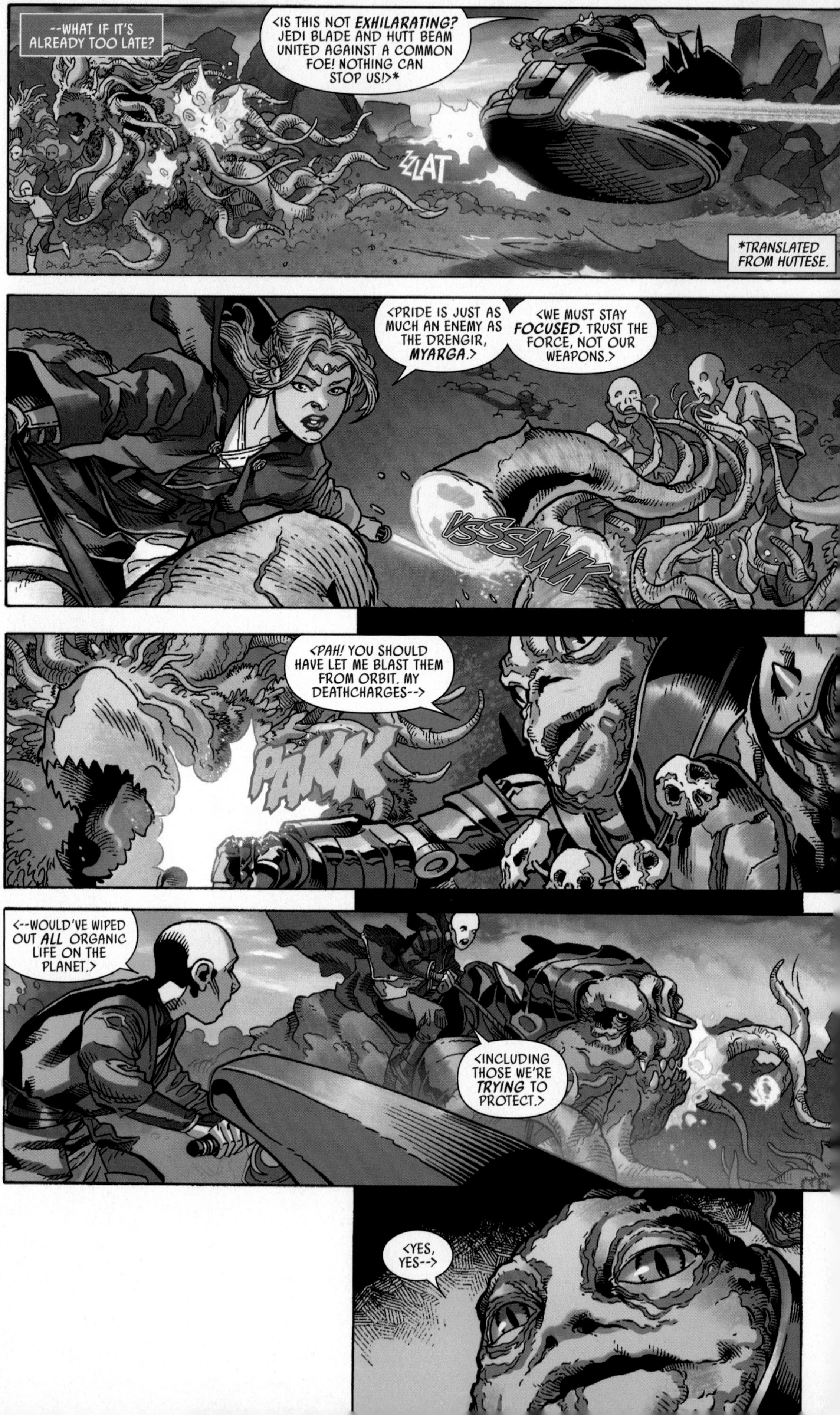
--WHAT IF IT'S ALREADY TOO LATE?
<IS THIS NOT EXHILARATING? JEDI BLADE AND HUTT BEAM UNITED AGAINST A COMMON FOE! NOTHING CAN STOP US!>*
ZZLAT
*TRANSLATED FROM HUTTESE.
<PRIDE IS JUST AS MUCH AN ENEMY AS THE DRENGIR, MYARGA.>
<WE MUST STAY FOCUSED. TRUST THE FORCE, NOT OUR WEAPONS.>
VSSSNNK
<PAH! YOU SHOULD HAVE LET ME BLAST THEM FROM ORBIT. MY DEATHCHARGES-->
PAKK
<--WOULD'VE WIPED OUT ALL ORGANIC LIFE ON THE PLANET.>
<INCLUDING THOSE WE'RE TRYING TO PROTECT.>
<YES, YES-->

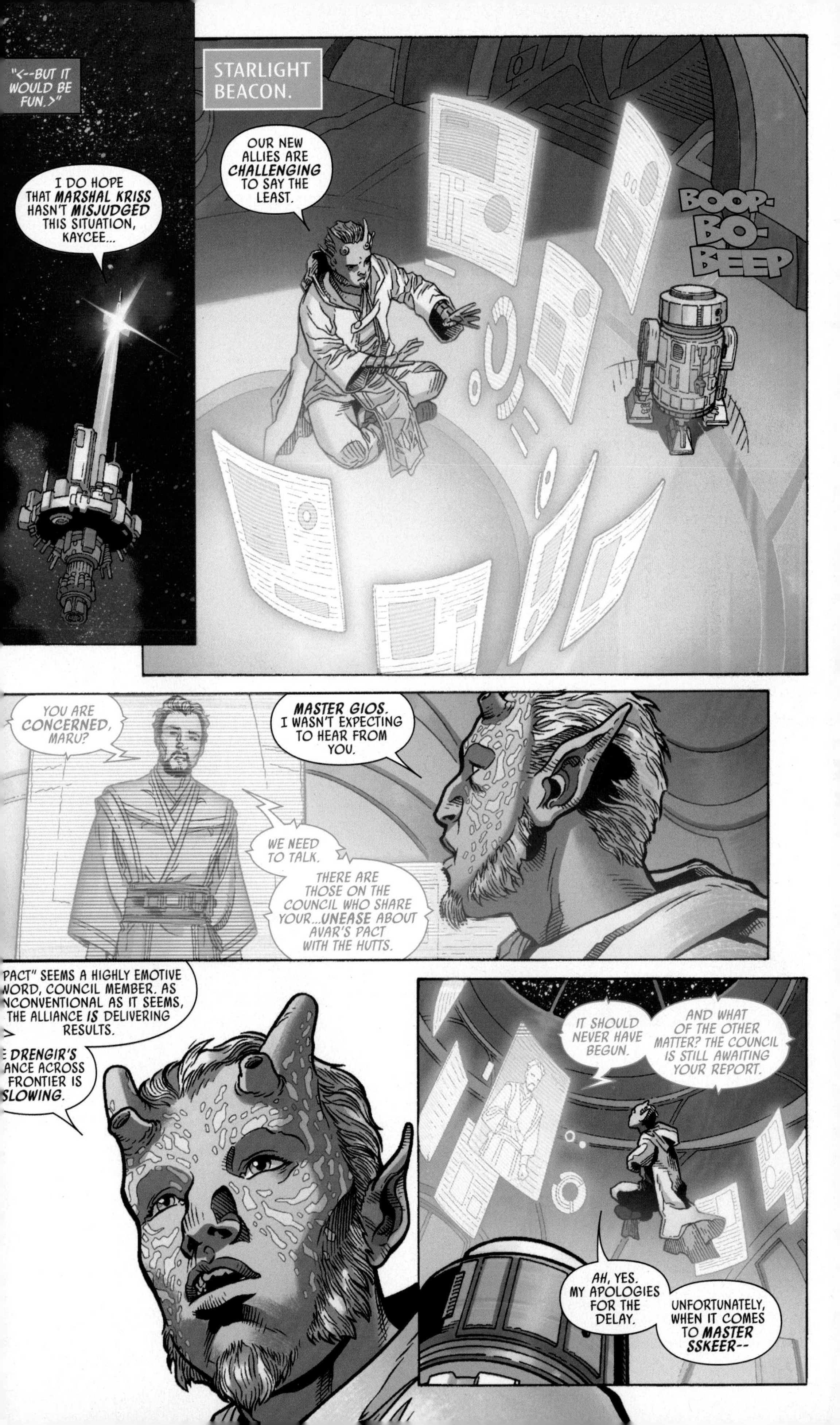
"<--BUT IT WOULD BE FUN.>"
STARLIGHT BEACON.
I DO HOPE THAT MARSHAL KRISS HASN'T MISJUDGED THIS SITUATION, KAYCEE...
OUR NEW ALLIES ARE CHALLENGING TO SAY THE LEAST.
BOOP-BO-BEEP
YOU ARE CONCERNED, MARU?
MASTER GIOS. I WASN'T EXPECTING TO HEAR FROM YOU.
WE NEED TO TALK.
THERE ARE THOSE ON THE COUNCIL WHO SHARE YOUR...UNEASE ABOUT AVAR'S PACT WITH THE HUTTS.
"PACT" SEEMS A HIGHLY EMOTIVE WORD, COUNCIL MEMBER. AS UNCONVENTIONAL AS IT SEEMS, THE ALLIANCE IS DELIVERING RESULTS.
DRENGIR'S ANCE ACROSS FRONTIER IS SLOWING.
IT SHOULD NEVER HAVE BEGUN.
AND WHAT OF THE OTHER MATTER? THE COUNCIL IS STILL AWAITING YOUR REPORT.
AH, YES. MY APOLOGIES FOR THE DELAY.
UNFORTUNATELY, WHEN IT COMES TO MASTER SSKEER--

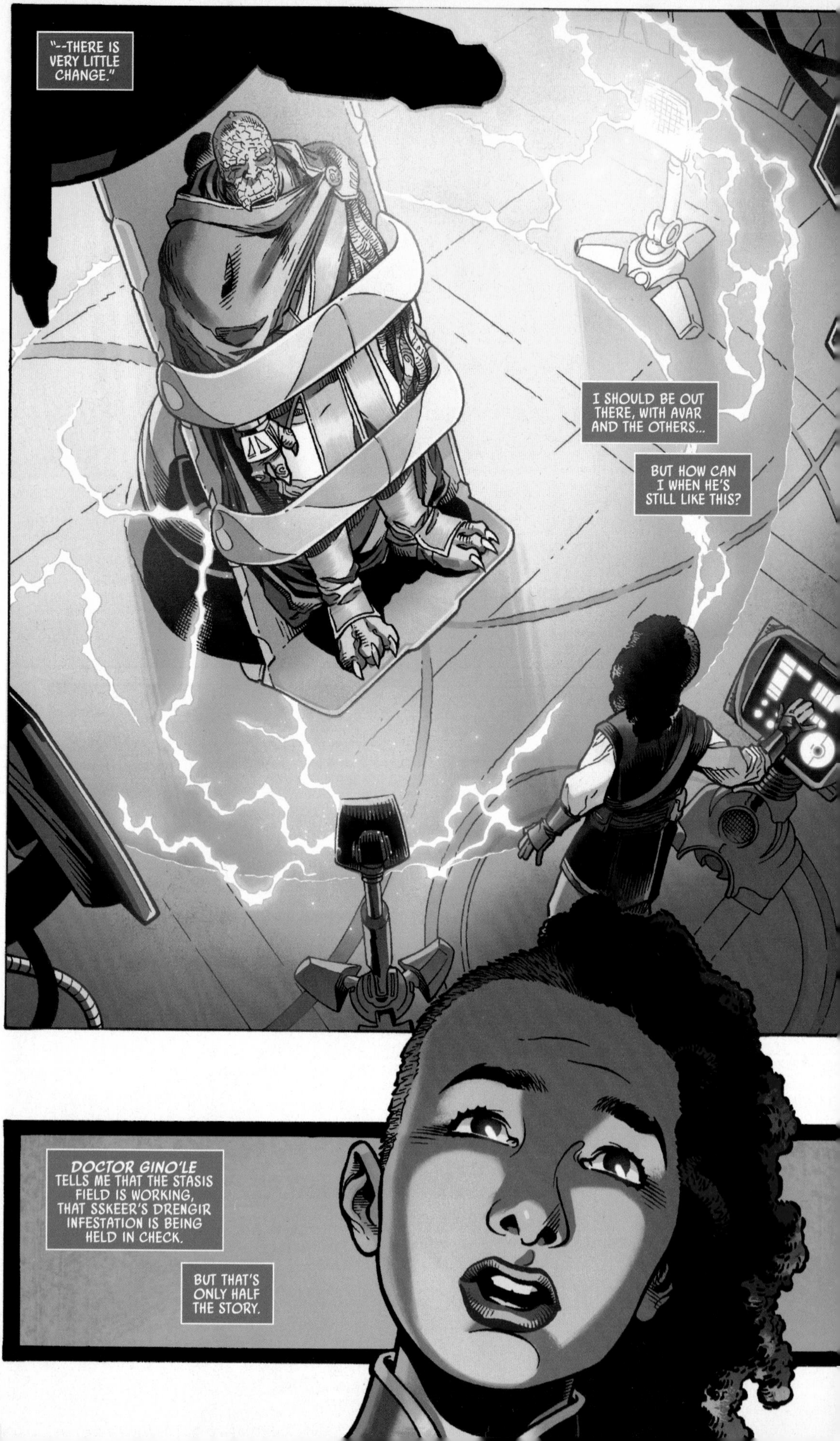
"--THERE IS VERY LITTLE CHANGE."
I SHOULD BE OUT THERE, WITH AVAR AND THE OTHERS...
BUT HOW CAN I WHEN HE'S STILL LIKE THIS?
DOCTOR GINO'LE TELLS ME THAT THE STASIS FIELD IS WORKING, THAT SSKEER'S DRENGIR INFESTATION IS BEING HELD IN CHECK.
BUT THAT'S ONLY HALF THE STORY.

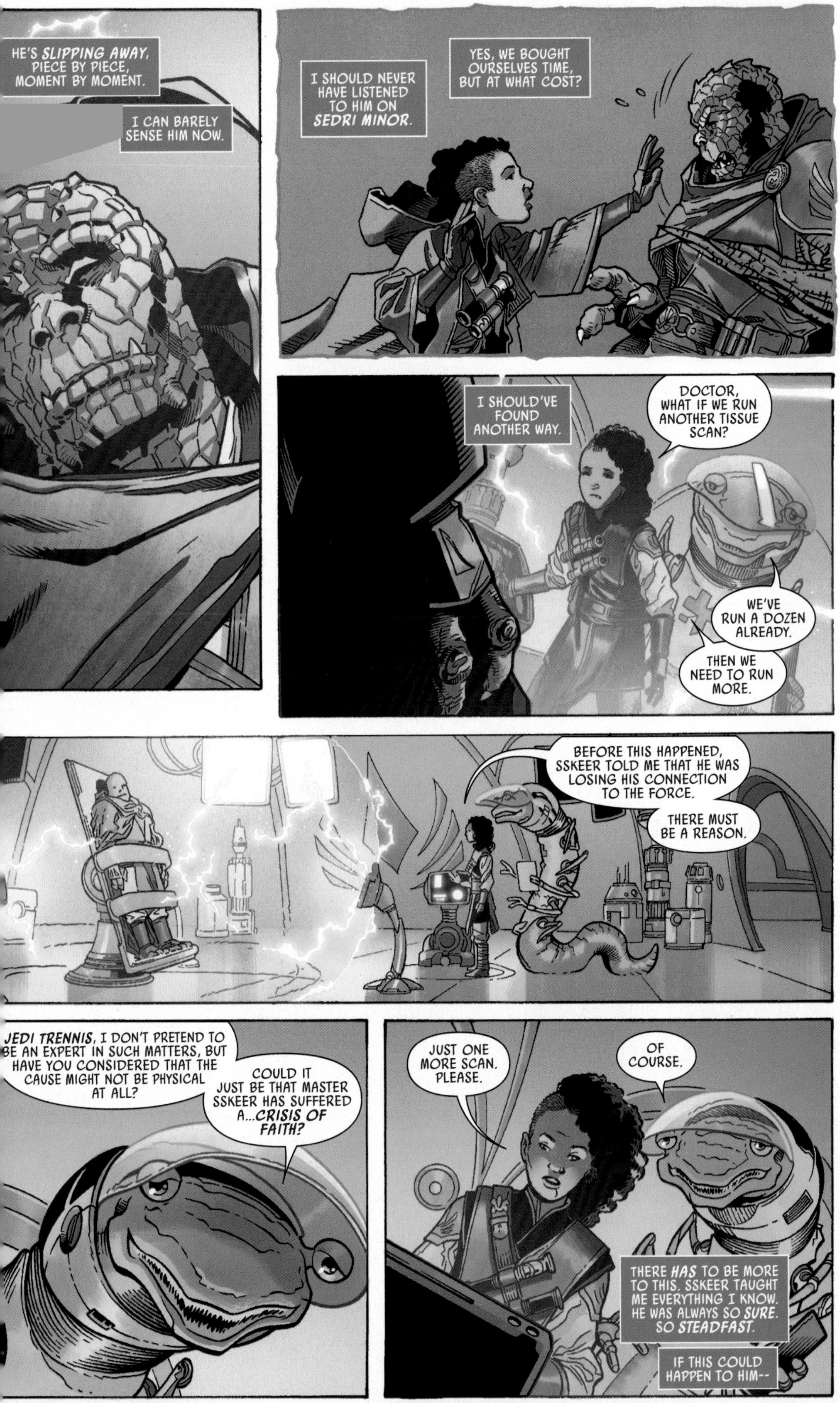

HE'S SLIPPING AWAY, PIECE BY PIECE, MOMENT BY MOMENT.
I CAN BARELY SENSE HIM NOW.
I SHOULD NEVER HAVE LISTENED TO HIM ON SEDRI MINOR.
YES, WE BOUGHT OURSELVES TIME, BUT AT WHAT COST?
I SHOULD'VE FOUND ANOTHER WAY.
DOCTOR, WHAT IF WE RUN ANOTHER TISSUE SCAN?
WE'VE RUN A DOZEN ALREADY.
THEN WE NEED TO RUN MORE.
BEFORE THIS HAPPENED, SSKEER TOLD ME THAT HE WAS LOSING HIS CONNECTION TO THE FORCE.
THERE MUST BE A REASON.
JEDI TRENNIS, I DON'T PRETEND TO BE AN EXPERT IN SUCH MATTERS, BUT HAVE YOU CONSIDERED THAT THE CAUSE MIGHT NOT BE PHYSICAL AT ALL?
COULD IT JUST BE THAT MASTER SSKEER HAS SUFFERED A...CRISIS OF FAITH?
JUST ONE MORE SCAN. PLEASE.
OF COURSE.
THERE HAS TO BE MORE TO THIS. SSKEER TAUGHT ME EVERYTHING I KNOW. HE WAS ALWAYS SO SURE. SO STEADFAST.
IF THIS COULD HAPPEN TO HIM--

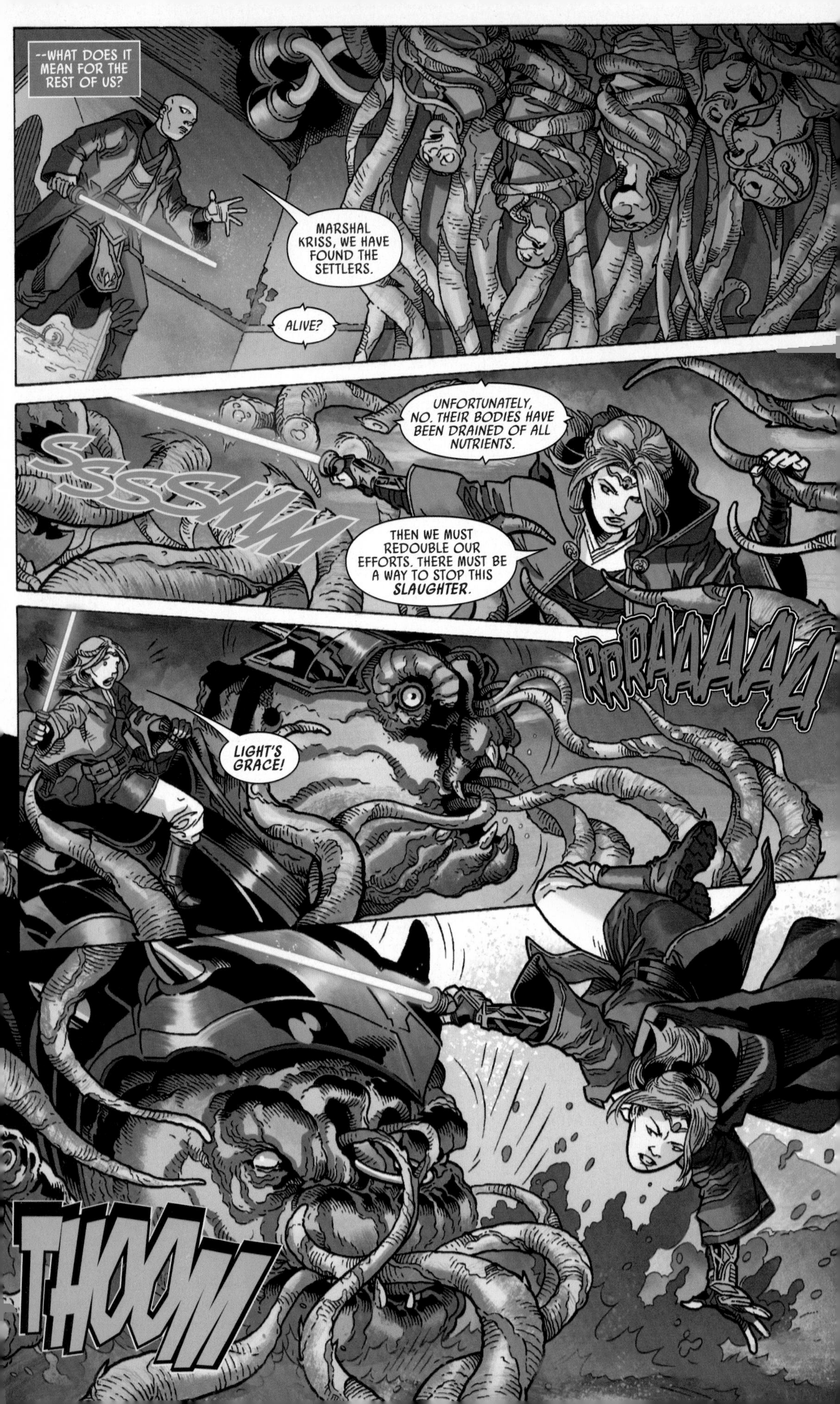
--WHAT DOES IT MEAN FOR THE REST OF US?
MARSHAL KRISS, WE HAVE FOUND THE SETTLERS.
ALIVE?
SSSSMM
UNFORTUNATELY, NO. THEIR BODIES HAVE BEEN DRAINED OF ALL NUTRIENTS.
THEN WE MUST REDOUBLE OUR EFFORTS. THERE MUST BE A WAY TO STOP THIS SLAUGHTER.
RRRAAAAAA
LIGHT'S GRACE!
THOOM

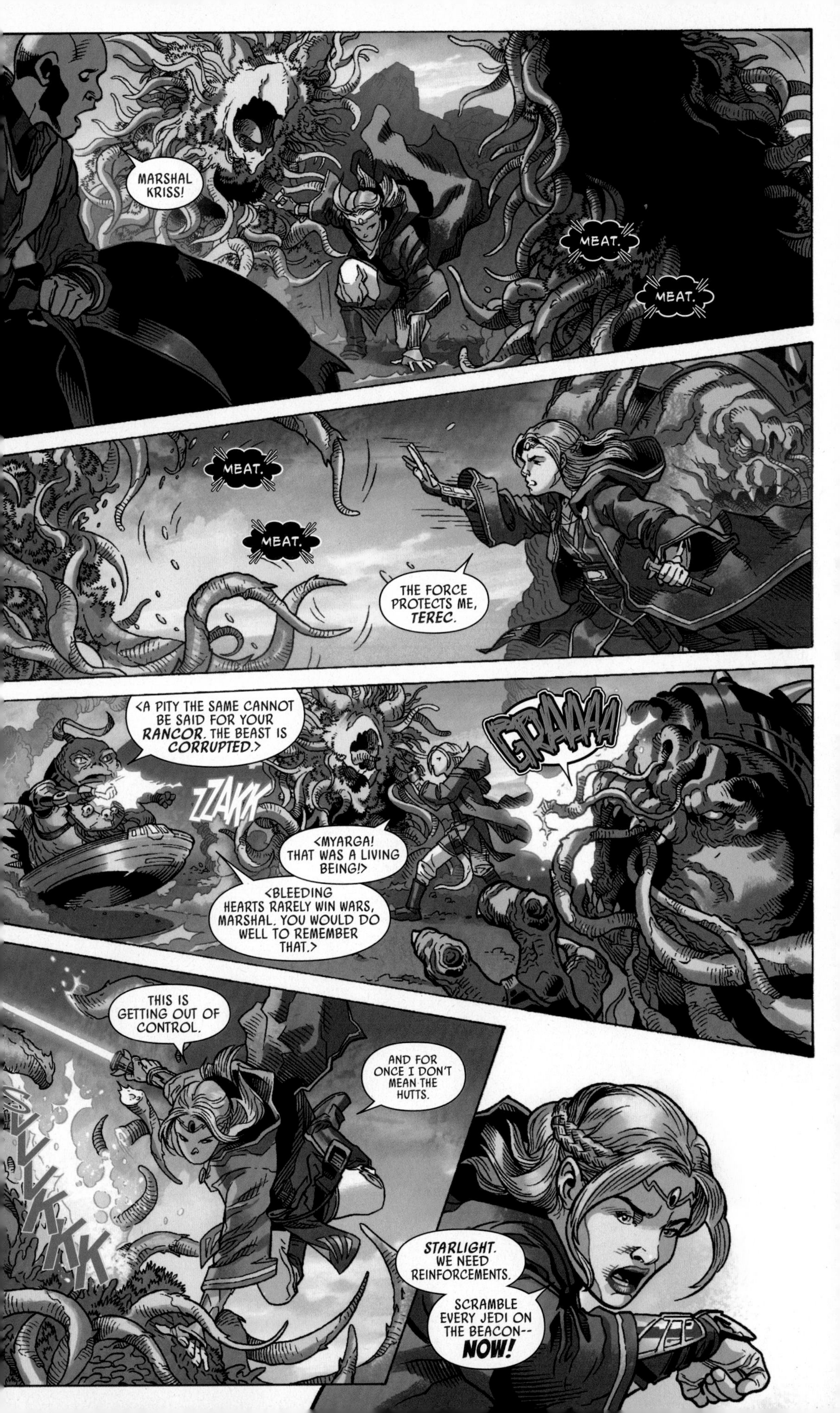
MARSHAL KRISS!
MEAT.
MEAT.
MEAT.
MEAT.
THE FORCE PROTECTS ME, TEREC.
<A PITY THE SAME CANNOT BE SAID FOR YOUR RANCOR. THE BEAST IS CORRUPTED.>
GRAAAAA
ZZAKK
<MYARGA! THAT WAS A LIVING BEING!>
<BLEEDING HEARTS RARELY WIN WARS, MARSHAL. YOU WOULD DO WELL TO REMEMBER THAT.>
THIS IS GETTING OUT OF CONTROL.
AND FOR ONCE I DON'T MEAN THE HUTTS.
SSLLKKKK
STARLIGHT. WE NEED REINFORCEMENTS.
SCRAMBLE EVERY JEDI ON THE BEACON-- NOW!

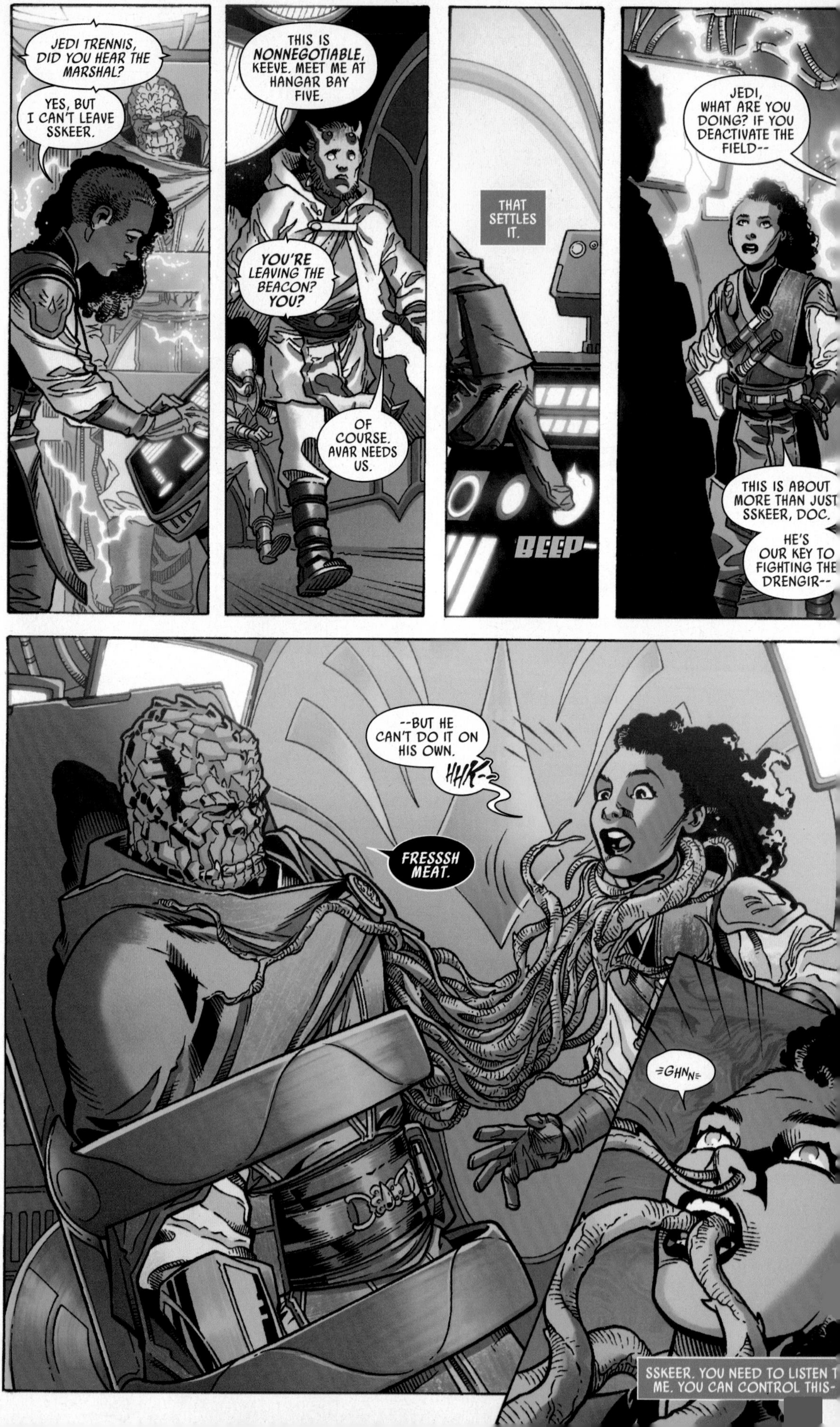

JEDI TRENNIS, DID YOU HEAR THE MARSHAL?
YES, BUT I CAN'T LEAVE SSKEER.
THIS IS NONNEGOTIABLE, KEEVE. MEET ME AT HANGAR BAY FIVE.
YOU'RE LEAVING THE BEACON? YOU?
OF COURSE. AVAR NEEDS US.
THAT SETTLES IT.
BEEP-
JEDI, WHAT ARE YOU DOING? IF YOU DEACTIVATE THE FIELD--
THIS IS ABOUT MORE THAN JUST SSKEER, DOC.
HE'S OUR KEY TO FIGHTING THE DRENGIR--
--BUT HE CAN'T DO IT ON HIS OWN.
HHK--
FRESSSH MEAT.
GHNN
SSKEER. YOU NEED TO LISTEN T ME. YOU CAN CONTROL THIS-

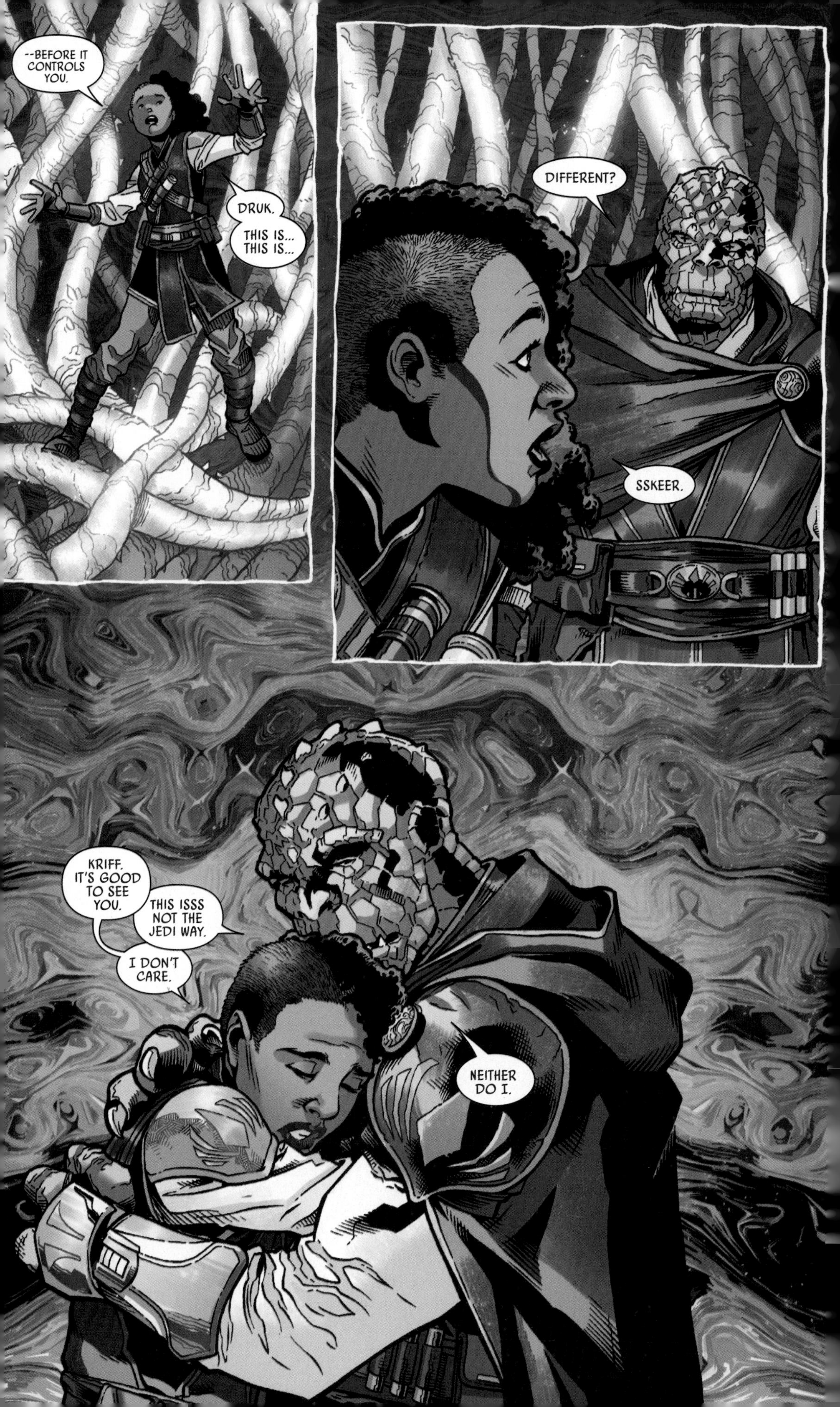
--BEFORE IT CONTROLS YOU.
DRUK.
THIS IS... THIS IS...
DIFFERENT?
SSKEER.
KRIFF. IT'S GOOD TO SEE YOU.
THIS ISSS NOT THE JEDI WAY.
I DON'T CARE.
NEITHER DO I.

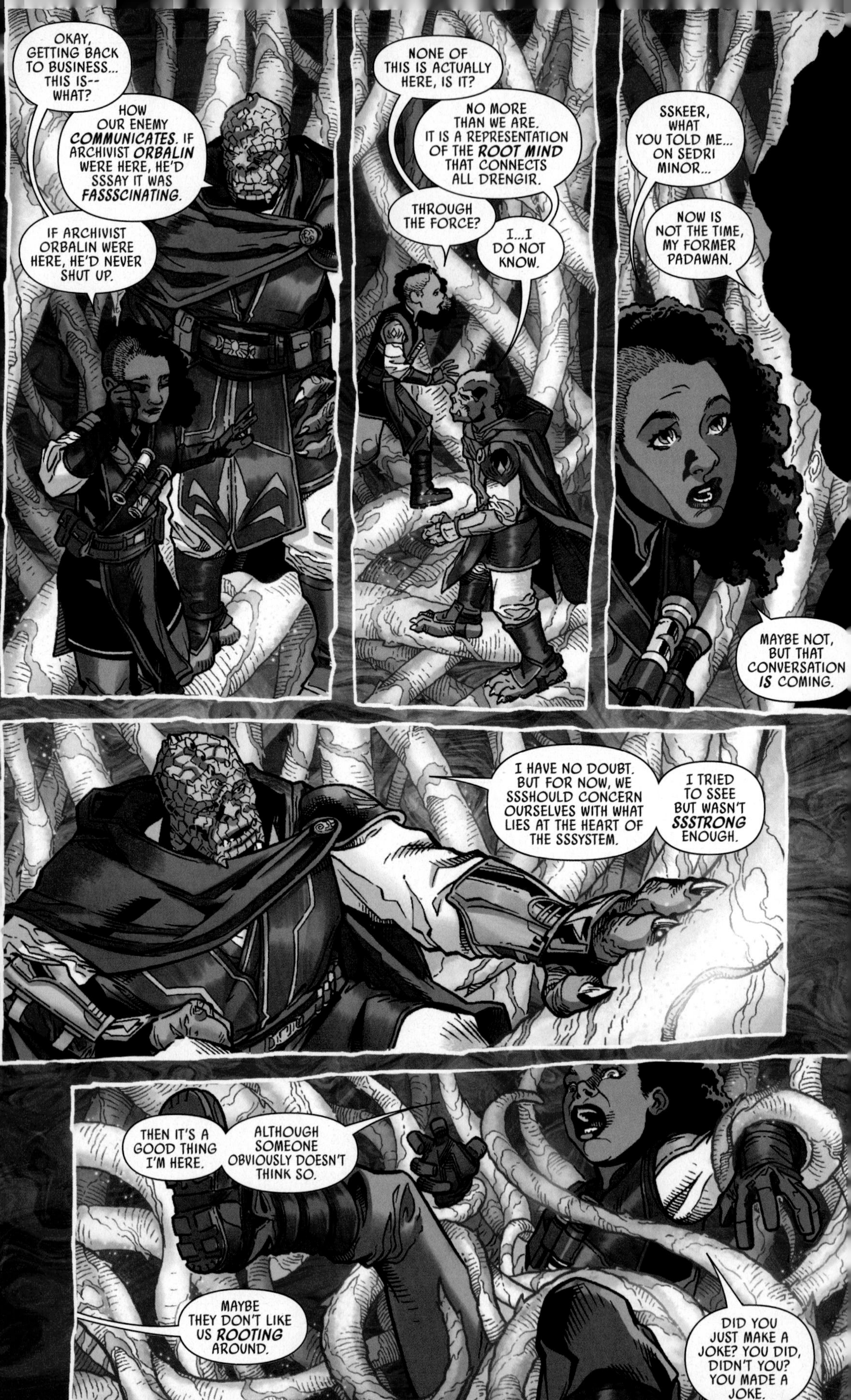
OKAY, GETTING BACK TO BUSINESS... THIS IS-- WHAT?
HOW OUR ENEMY **COMMUNICATES**. IF ARCHIVIST **ORBALIN** WERE HERE, HE'D SSSAY IT WAS **FASSSCINATING**.
IF ARCHIVIST ORBALIN WERE HERE, HE'D NEVER SHUT UP.
NONE OF THIS IS ACTUALLY HERE, IS IT?
NO MORE THAN WE ARE. IT IS A REPRESENTATION OF THE **ROOT MIND** THAT CONNECTS ALL DRENGIR.
THROUGH THE FORCE?
I...I DO NOT KNOW.
SSKEER, WHAT YOU TOLD ME... ON SEDRI MINOR...
NOW IS NOT THE TIME, MY FORMER PADAWAN.
MAYBE NOT, BUT THAT CONVERSATION **IS** COMING.
I HAVE NO DOUBT. BUT FOR NOW, WE SSSHOULD CONCERN OURSELVES WITH WHAT LIES AT THE HEART OF THE SSSYSTEM.
I TRIED TO SSEE BUT WASN'T **SSSTRONG** ENOUGH.
THEN IT'S A GOOD THING I'M HERE.
ALTHOUGH SOMEONE OBVIOUSLY DOESN'T THINK SO.
MAYBE THEY DON'T LIKE US **ROOTING** AROUND.
DID YOU JUST MAKE A JOKE? YOU DID, DIDN'T YOU? YOU MADE A JOKE.

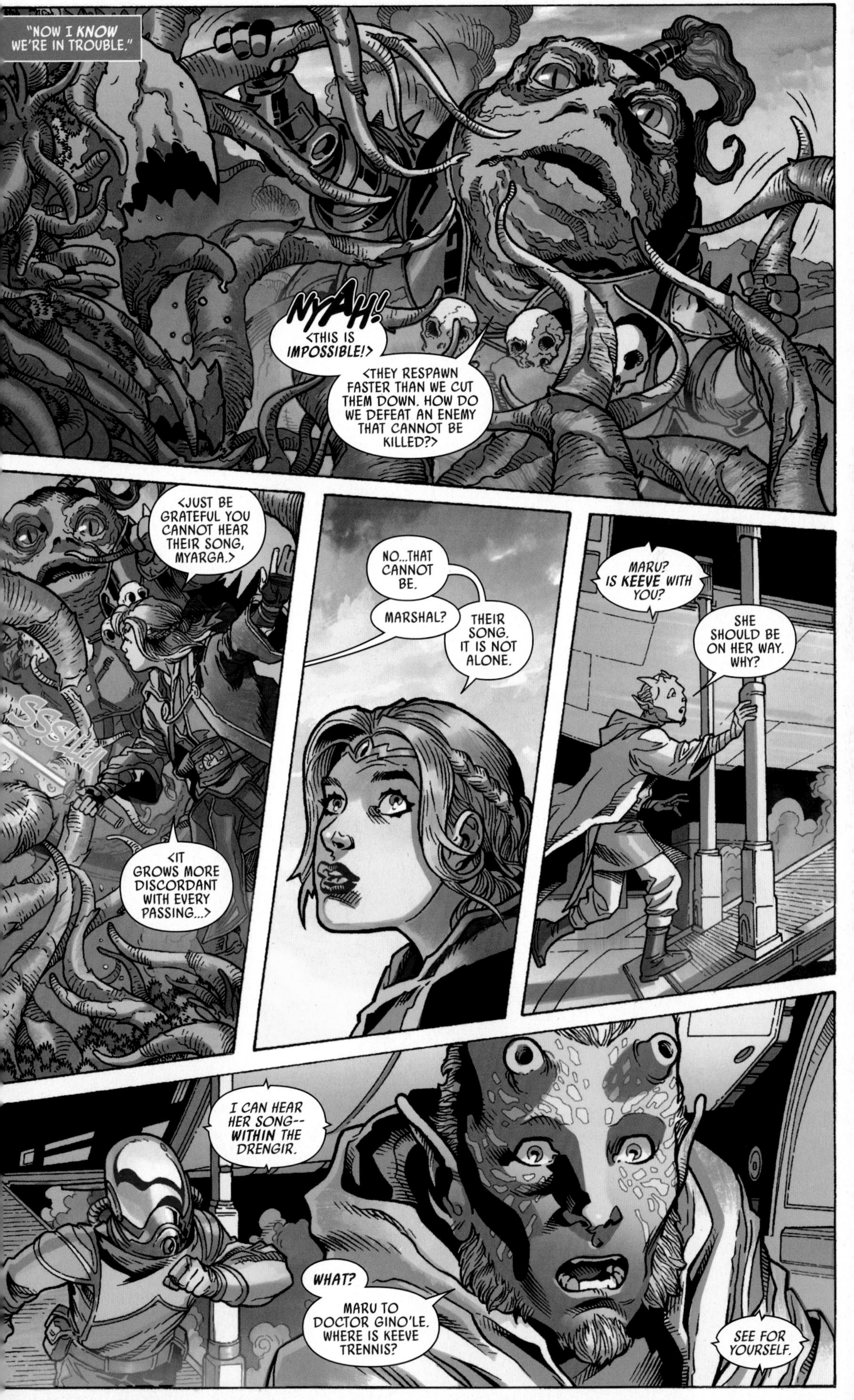
"NOW I KNOW WE'RE IN TROUBLE."
NYAH!
<THIS IS IMPOSSIBLE!>
<THEY RESPAWN FASTER THAN WE CUT THEM DOWN. HOW DO WE DEFEAT AN ENEMY THAT CANNOT BE KILLED?>
<JUST BE GRATEFUL YOU CANNOT HEAR THEIR SONG, MYARGA.>
SSSLLLL
<IT GROWS MORE DISCORDANT WITH EVERY PASSING...>
NO...THAT CANNOT BE.
THEIR SONG. IT IS NOT ALONE.
MARSHAL?
MARU? IS KEEVE WITH YOU?
SHE SHOULD BE ON HER WAY. WHY?
I CAN HEAR HER SONG-- WITHIN THE DRENGIR.
WHAT?
MARU TO DOCTOR GINO'LE. WHERE IS KEEVE TRENNIS?
SEE FOR YOURSELF.

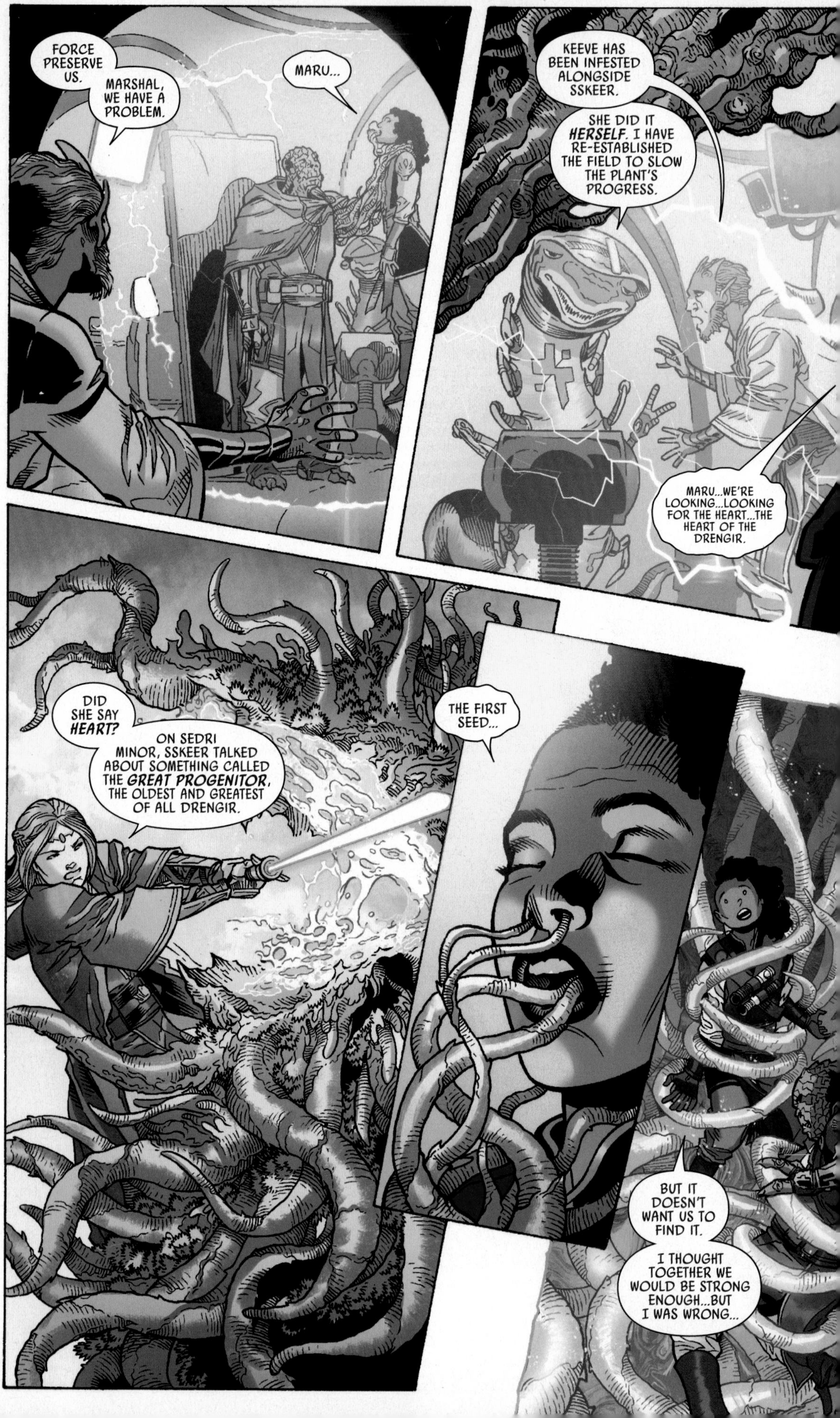
FORCE PRESERVE US.
MARSHAL, WE HAVE A PROBLEM.
MARU...
KEEVE HAS BEEN INFESTED ALONGSIDE SSKEER.
SHE DID IT **HERSELF**. I HAVE RE-ESTABLISHED THE FIELD TO SLOW THE PLANT'S PROGRESS.
MARU...WE'RE LOOKING...LOOKING FOR THE HEART...THE HEART OF THE DRENGIR.
DID SHE SAY **HEART?**
ON SEDRI MINOR, SSKEER TALKED ABOUT SOMETHING CALLED THE **GREAT PROGENITOR**, THE OLDEST AND GREATEST OF ALL DRENGIR.
THE FIRST SEED...
BUT IT DOESN'T WANT US TO FIND IT.
I THOUGHT TOGETHER WE WOULD BE STRONG ENOUGH...BUT I WAS WRONG...

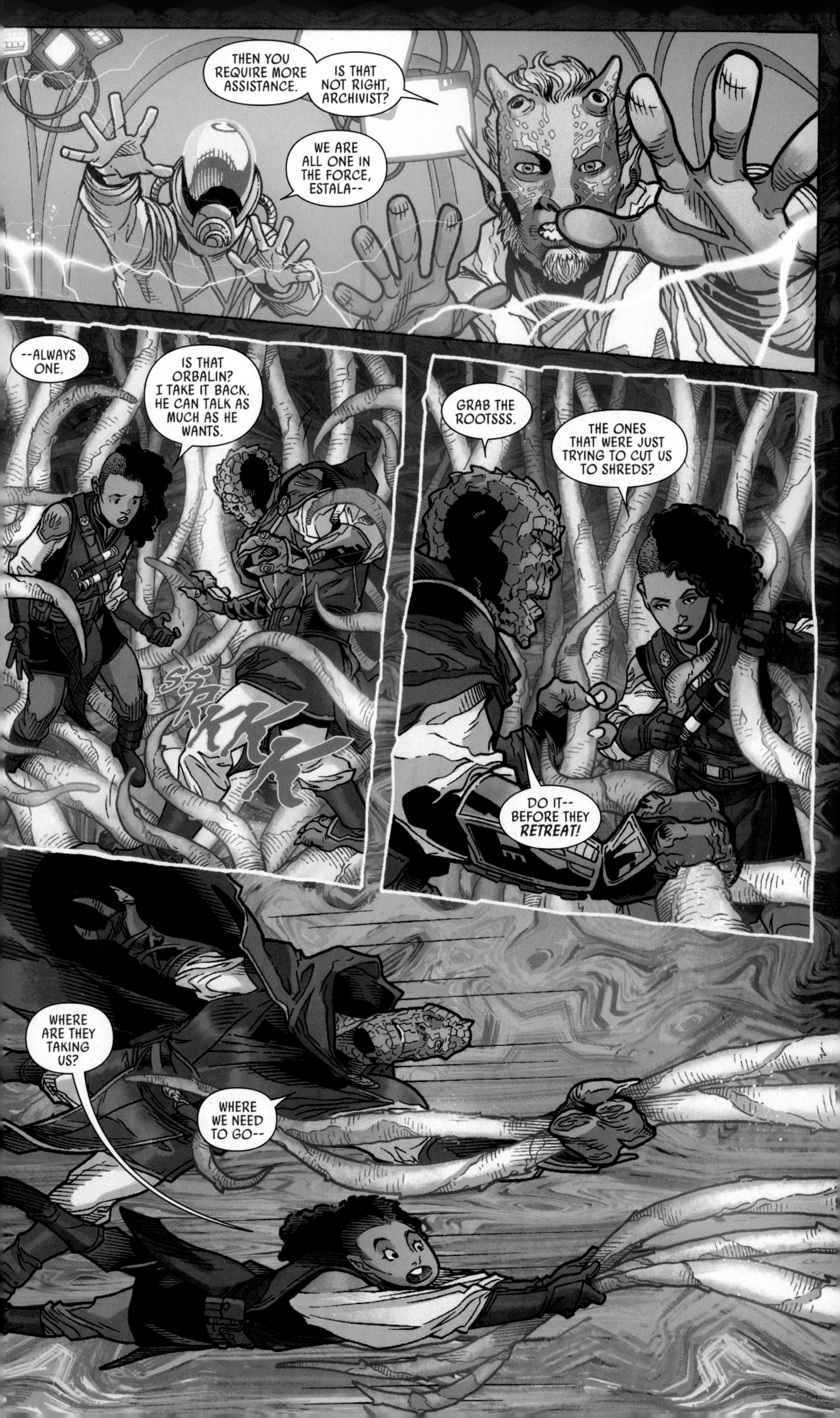
THEN YOU REQUIRE MORE ASSISTANCE.
IS THAT NOT RIGHT, ARCHIVIST?
WE ARE ALL ONE IN THE FORCE, ESTALA--
--ALWAYS ONE.
IS THAT ORBALIN? I TAKE IT BACK. HE CAN TALK AS MUCH AS HE WANTS.
SSRKKKK
GRAB THE ROOTSSS.
THE ONES THAT WERE JUST TRYING TO CUT US TO SHREDS?
DO IT-- BEFORE THEY RETREAT!
WHERE ARE THEY TAKING US?
WHERE WE NEED TO GO--

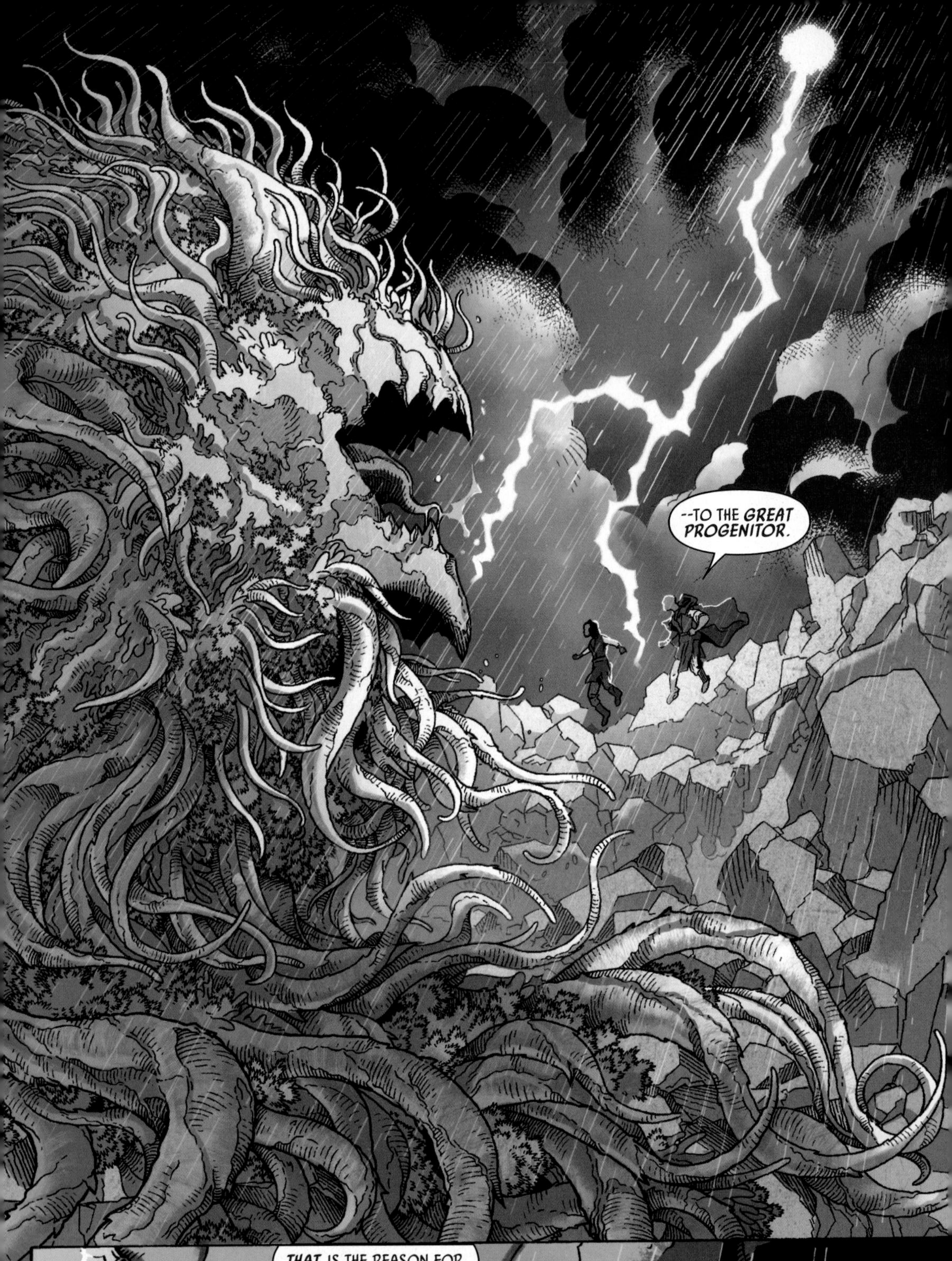
--TO THE GREAT PROGENITOR.

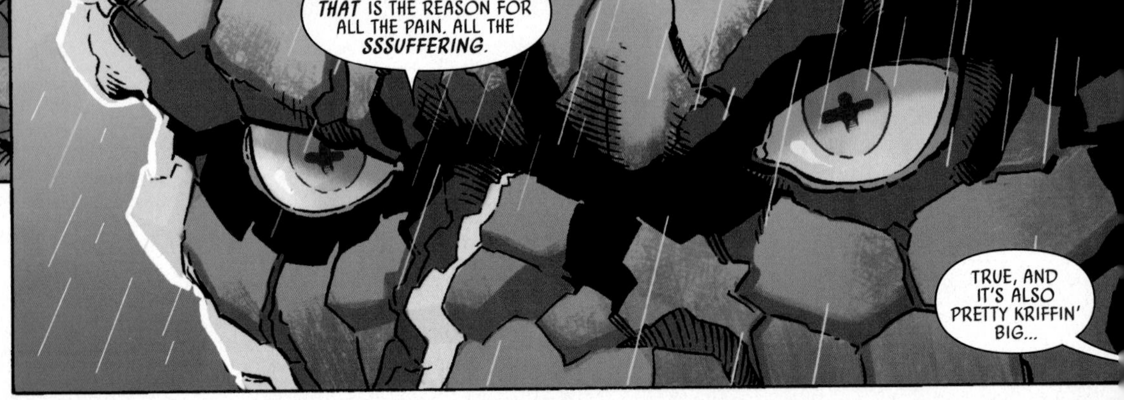
THAT IS THE REASON FOR ALL THE PAIN. ALL THE SSSUFFERING.
TRUE, AND IT'S ALSO PRETTY KRIFFIN' BIG...

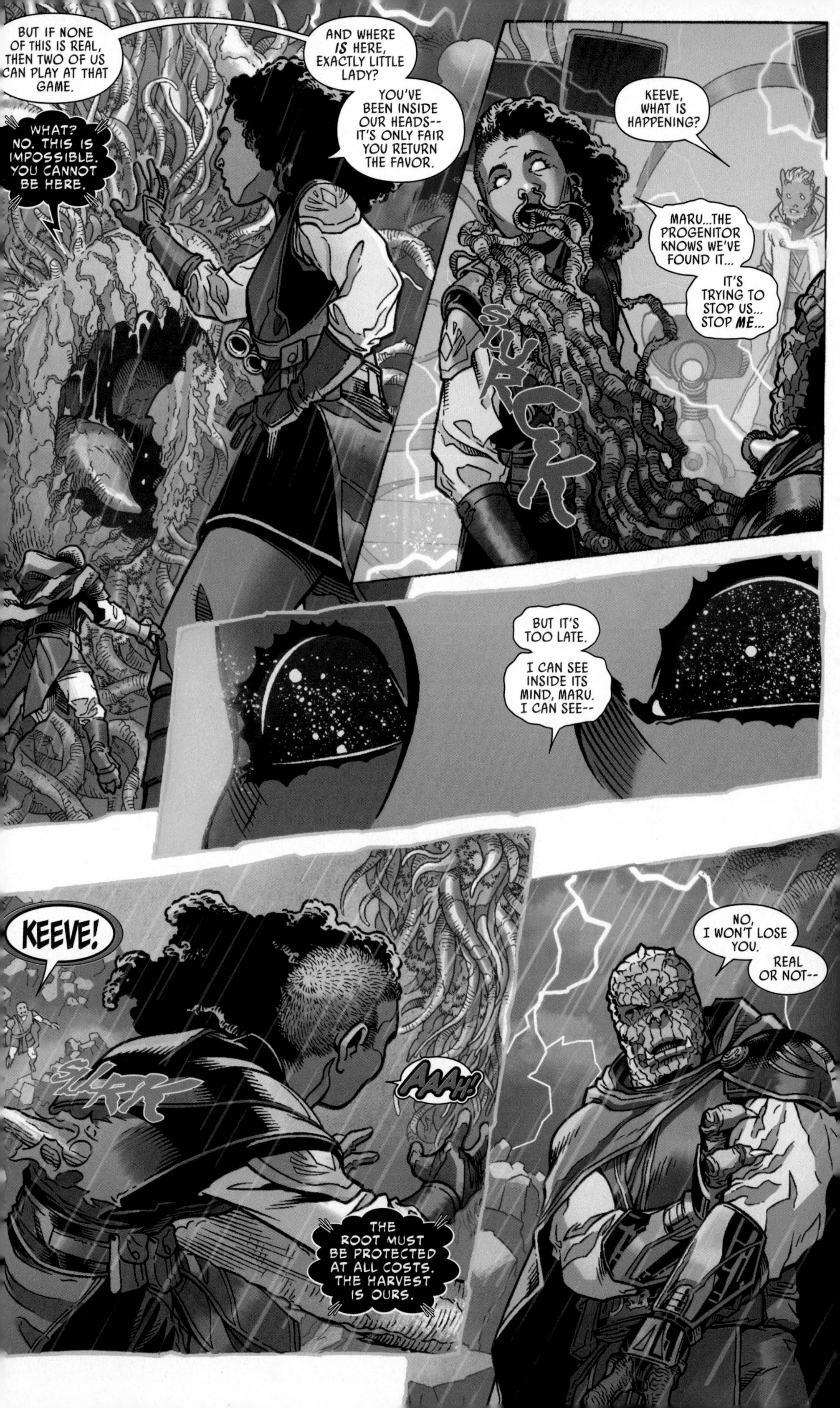

BUT IF NONE OF THIS IS REAL, THEN TWO OF US CAN PLAY AT THAT GAME.
AND WHERE IS HERE, EXACTLY LITTLE LADY?
YOU'VE BEEN INSIDE OUR HEADS-- IT'S ONLY FAIR YOU RETURN THE FAVOR.
WHAT? NO. THIS IS IMPOSSIBLE. YOU CANNOT BE HERE.
KEEVE, WHAT IS HAPPENING?
MARU...THE PROGENITOR KNOWS WE'VE FOUND IT...
IT'S TRYING TO STOP US... STOP ME...
SLURCK
BUT IT'S TOO LATE.
I CAN SEE INSIDE ITS MIND, MARU. I CAN SEE--
KEEVE!
SLURK
AAAH!
THE ROOT MUST BE PROTECTED AT ALL COSTS. THE HARVEST IS OURS.
NO, I WON'T LOSE YOU.
REAL OR NOT--

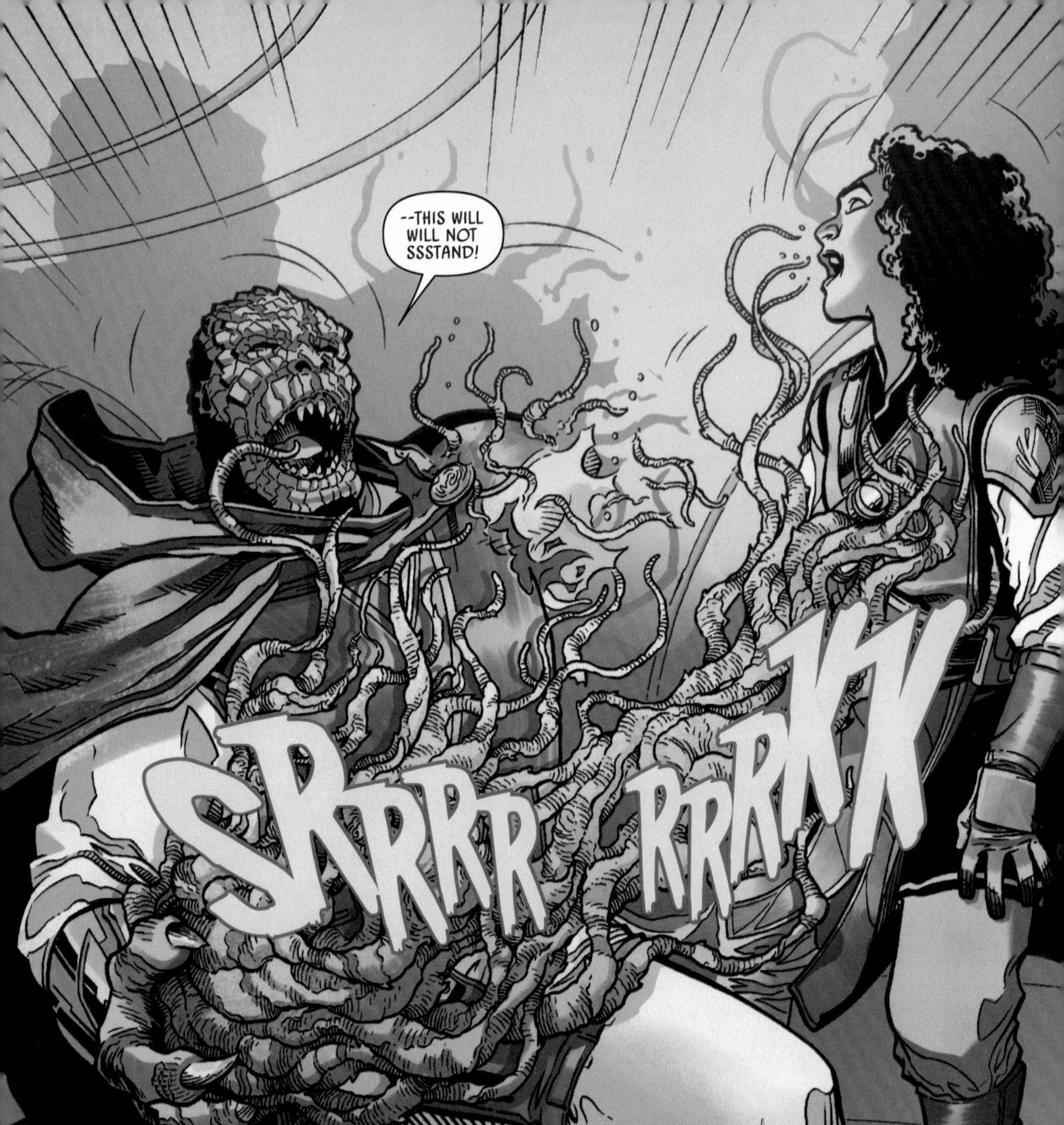
--THIS WILL
WILL NOT
SSSTAND!
SRRRR RRRKK

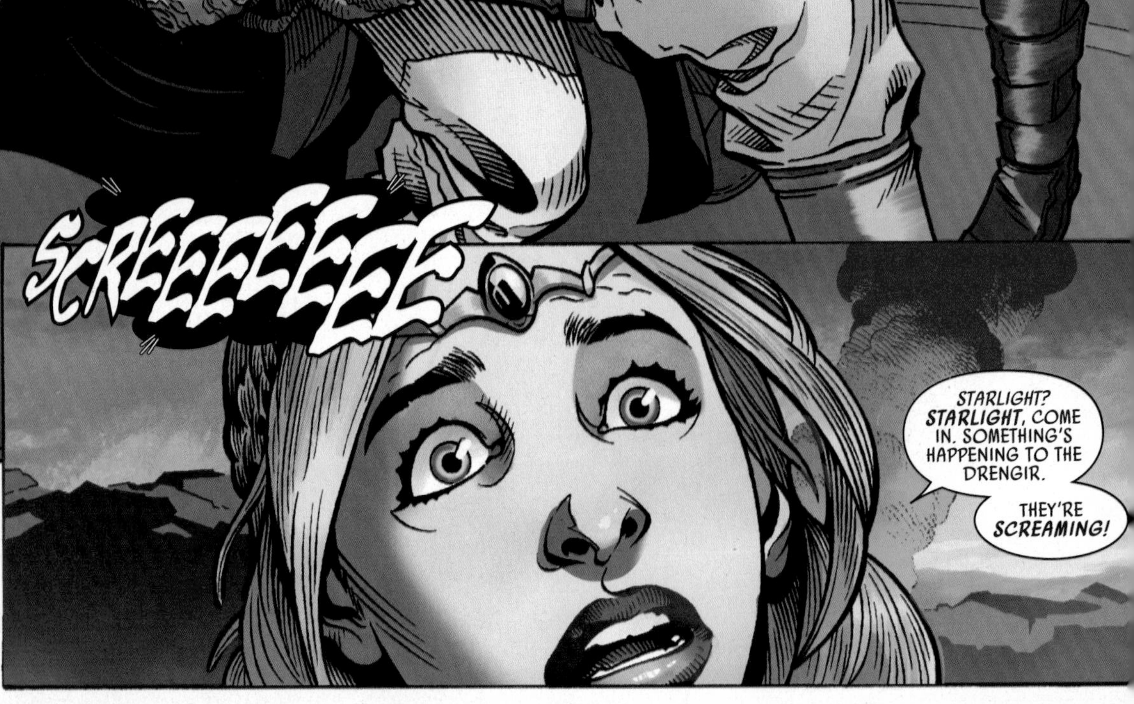
SCREEEEEEE
STARLIGHT? STARLIGHT, COME IN. SOMETHING'S HAPPENING TO THE DRENGIR.
THEY'RE SCREAMING!

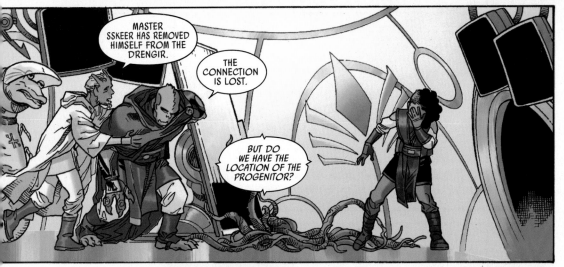

MASTER SSKEER HAS REMOVED HIMSELF FROM THE DRENGIR.

THE CONNECTION IS LOST.

BUT DO WE HAVE THE LOCATION OF THE PROGENITOR?

NO. WE HAVE FAILED.

SPEAK FOR YOURSELF.

WHAT DO YOU MAKE OF THIS?

SSSCRATCHES... FROM THE THORNS... THEY LOOK...

YES?

THEY LOOK LIKE A *NAME*-- MULITA!

AMAZING WHAT YOU CAN FIND WHEN YOU'RE RUMMAGING AROUND A DRENGIR'S BRAIN.

OR NUCLEUS.

OR *WHATEVER* THE KRIFF THEY HAVE.

THAT'S THE TROUBLE WITH TELEPATHY--

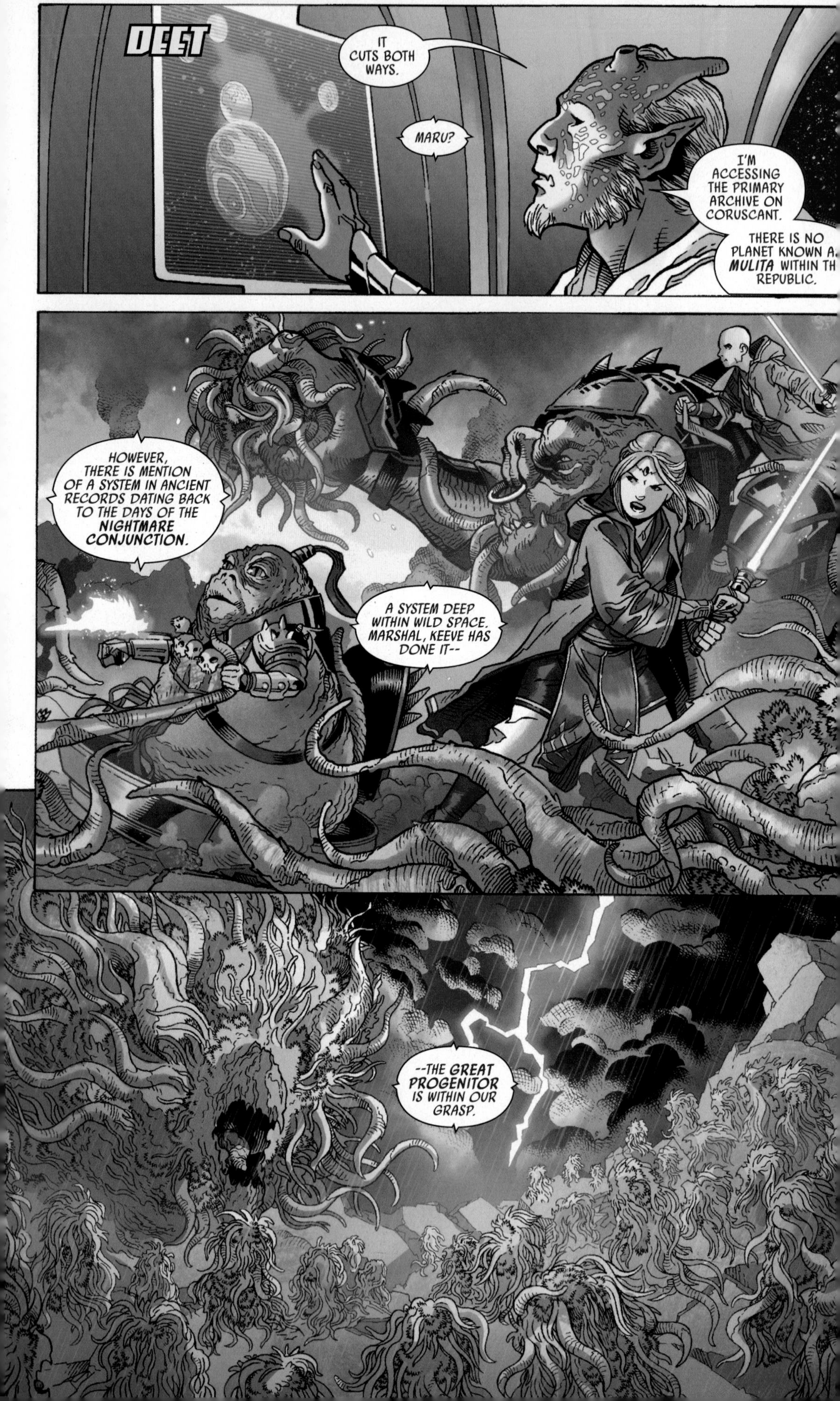
DEET
IT CUTS BOTH WAYS.
MARU?
I'M ACCESSING THE PRIMARY ARCHIVE ON CORUSCANT.
THERE IS NO PLANET KNOWN A MULITA WITHIN TH REPUBLIC.
HOWEVER, THERE IS MENTION OF A SYSTEM IN ANCIENT RECORDS DATING BACK TO THE DAYS OF THE NIGHTMARE CONJUNCTION.
A SYSTEM DEEP WITHIN WILD SPACE. MARSHAL, KEEVE HAS DONE IT--
--THE GREAT PROGENITOR IS WITHIN OUR GRASP.

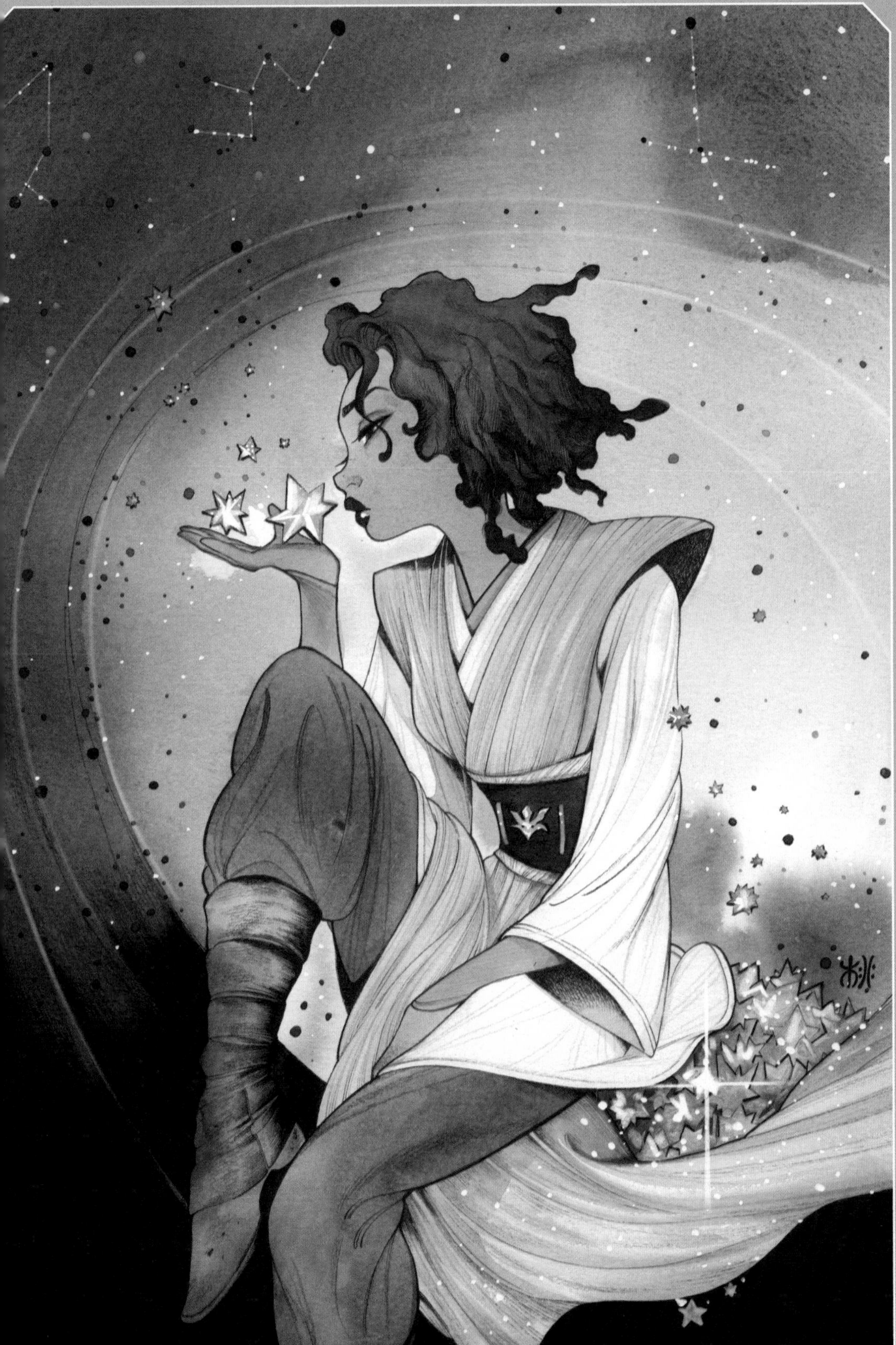

#6 Variant by
PEACH MOMOKO

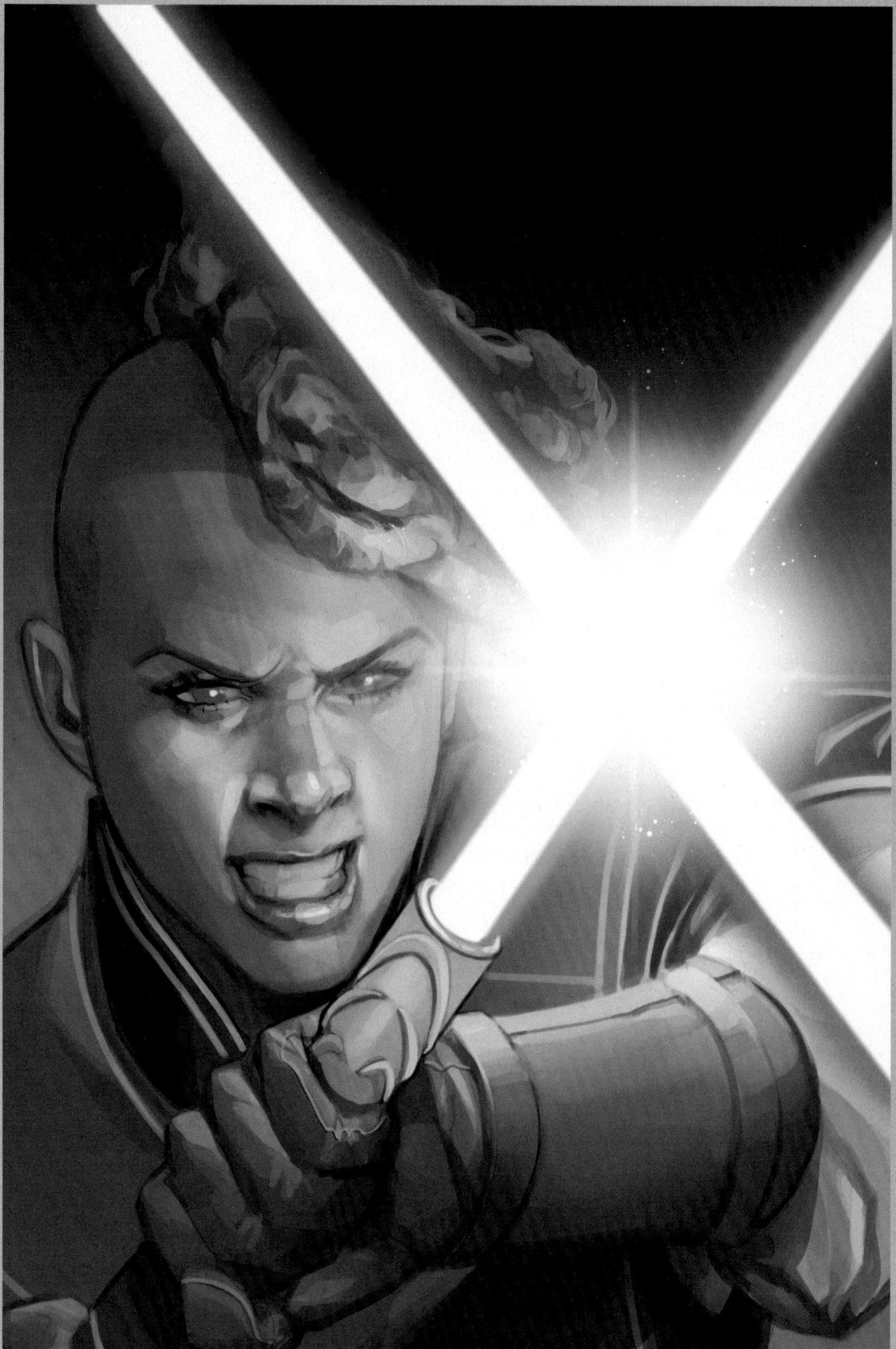
noto

7 | OF SITH AND SHADOWS

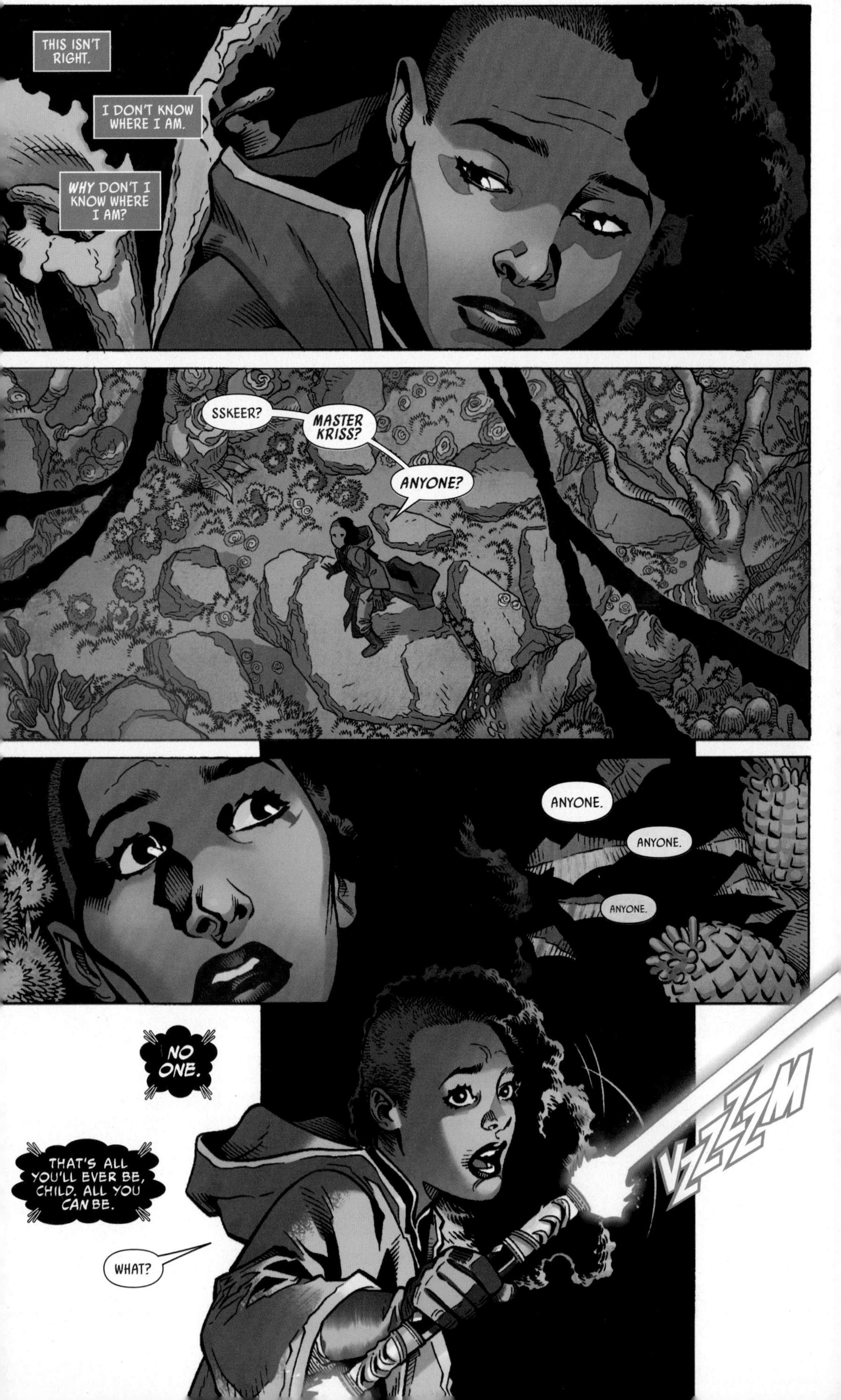

THIS ISN'T RIGHT.
I DON'T KNOW WHERE I AM.
WHY DON'T I KNOW WHERE I AM?
SSKEER?
MASTER KRISS?
ANYONE?
ANYONE.
ANYONE.
ANYONE.
NO ONE.
THAT'S ALL YOU'LL EVER BE, CHILD. ALL YOU CAN BE.
WHAT?
VZZZM

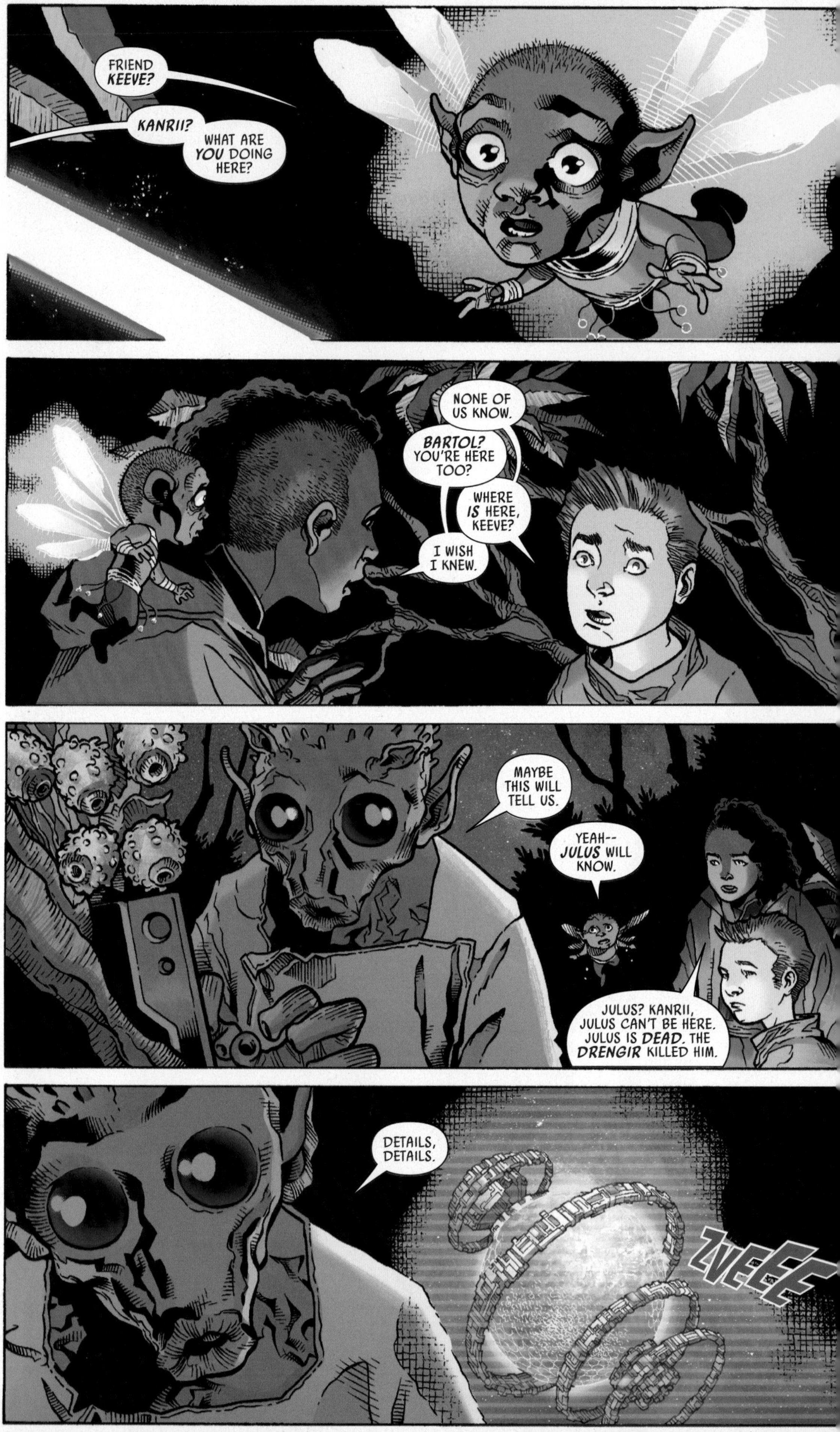
FRIEND KEEVE?
KANRII?
WHAT ARE YOU DOING HERE?
NONE OF US KNOW.
BARTOL? YOU'RE HERE TOO?
WHERE IS HERE, KEEVE?
I WISH I KNEW.
MAYBE THIS WILL TELL US.
YEAH-- JULUS WILL KNOW.
JULUS? KANRII, JULUS CAN'T BE HERE. JULUS IS DEAD. THE DRENGIR KILLED HIM.
DETAILS, DETAILS.
ZVEEE

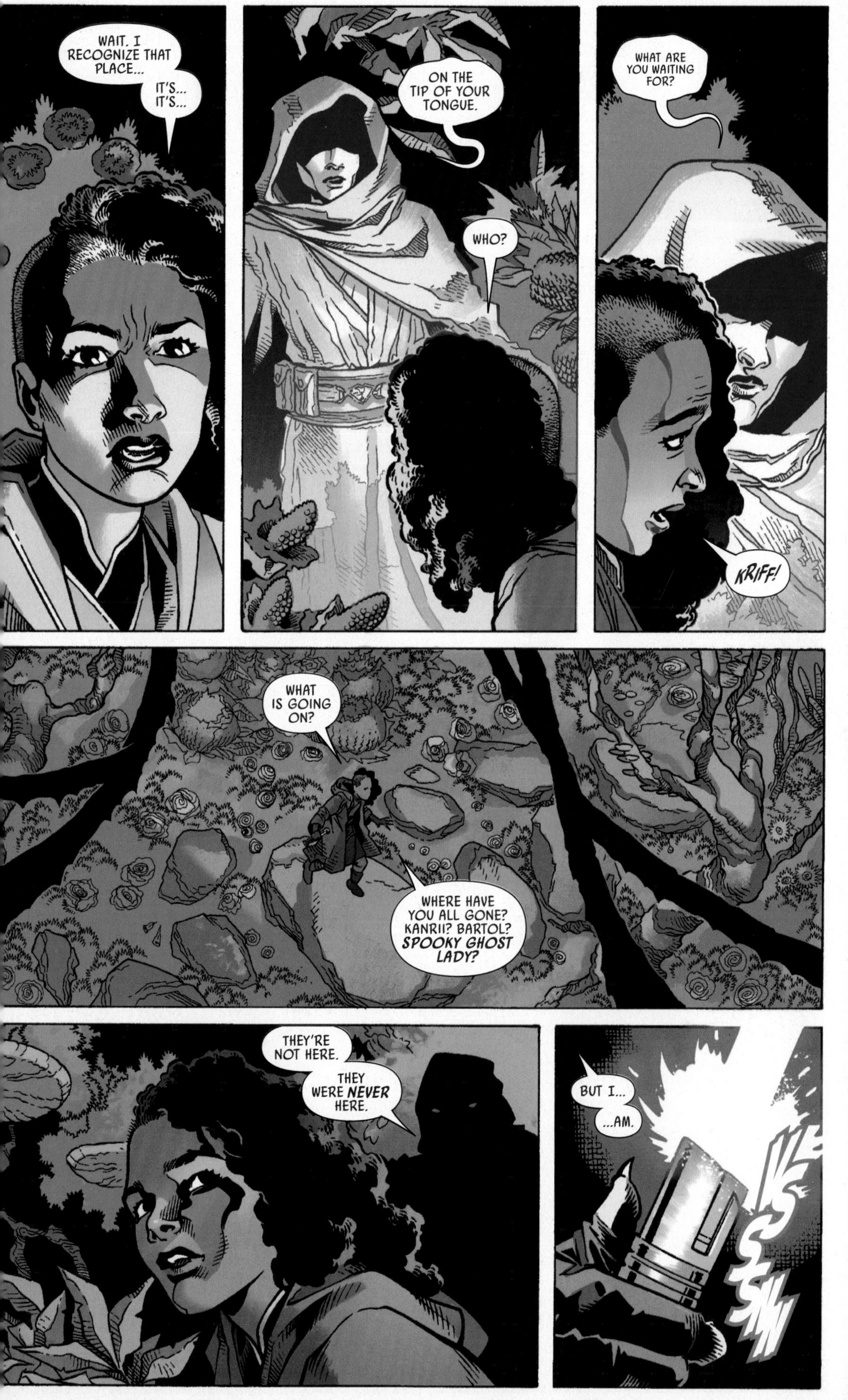
WAIT. I RECOGNIZE THAT PLACE...
IT'S... IT'S...
ON THE TIP OF YOUR TONGUE.
WHO?
WHAT ARE YOU WAITING FOR?
KRIFF!
WHAT IS GOING ON?
WHERE HAVE YOU ALL GONE? KANRII? BARTOL? *SPOOKY GHOST LADY?*
THEY'RE NOT HERE.
THEY WERE *NEVER* HERE.
BUT I...
...AM.
VSSSHH

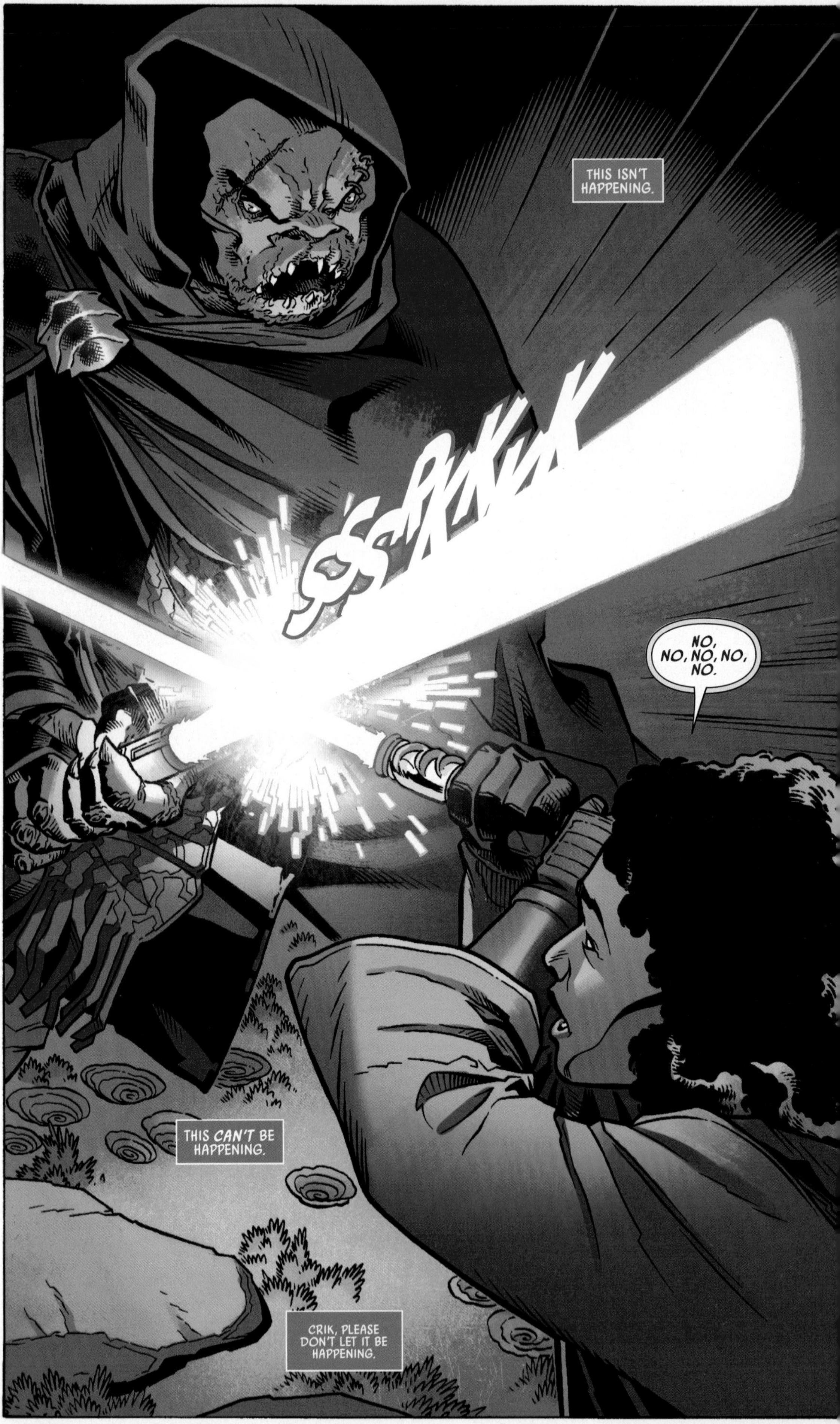
THIS ISN'T HAPPENING.
SSSRKKK
NO, NO, NO, NO, NO.
THIS *CAN'T* BE HAPPENING.
CRIK, PLEASE DON'T LET IT BE HAPPENING.

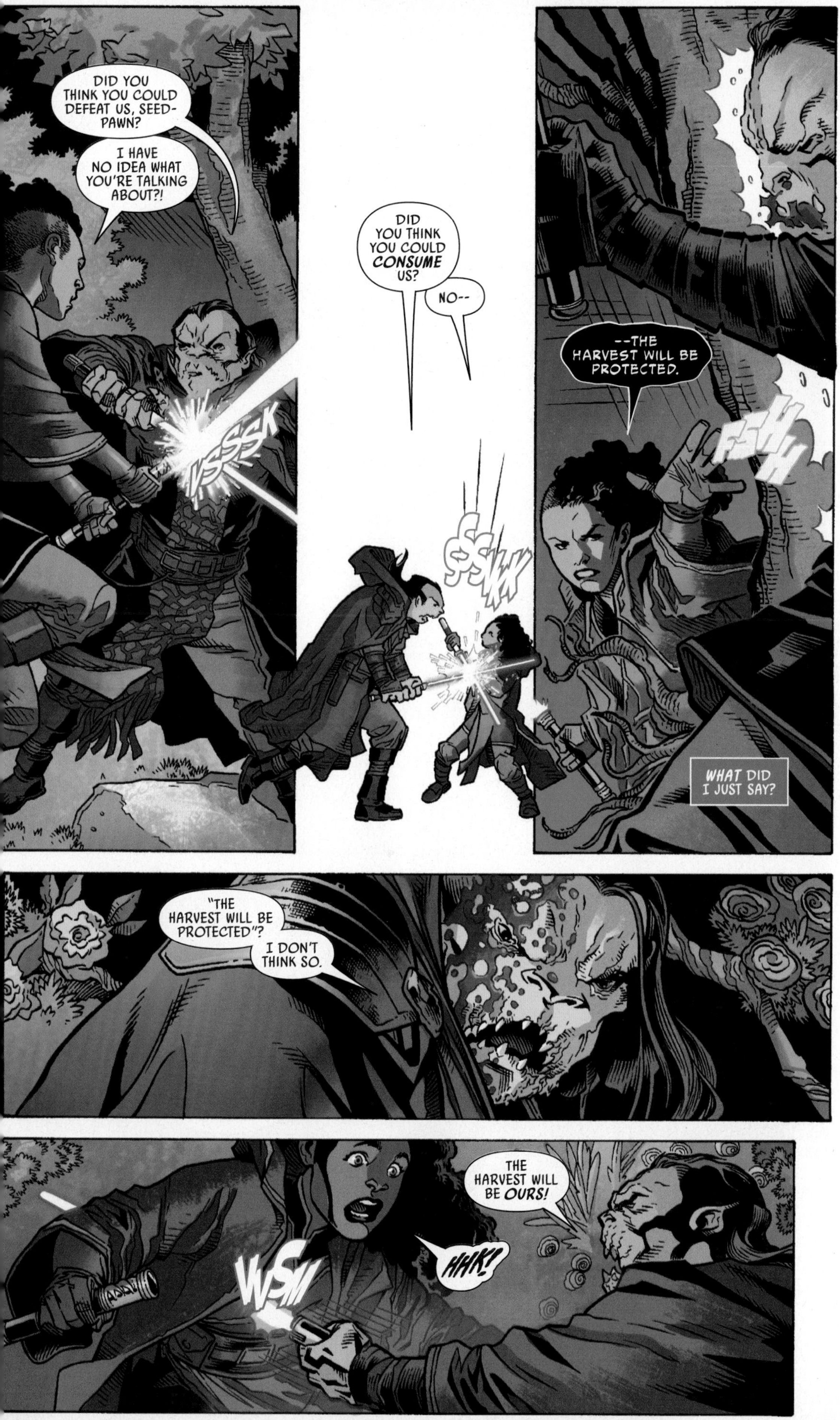
DID YOU THINK YOU COULD DEFEAT US, SEED-PAWN?
I HAVE NO IDEA WHAT YOU'RE TALKING ABOUT?!
VSSSK
DID YOU THINK YOU COULD CONSUME US?
NO--
SSNKK
--THE HARVEST WILL BE PROTECTED.
FSHH
WHAT DID I JUST SAY?
"THE HARVEST WILL BE PROTECTED"?
I DON'T THINK SO.
THE HARVEST WILL BE OURS!
HHK!
VVSM

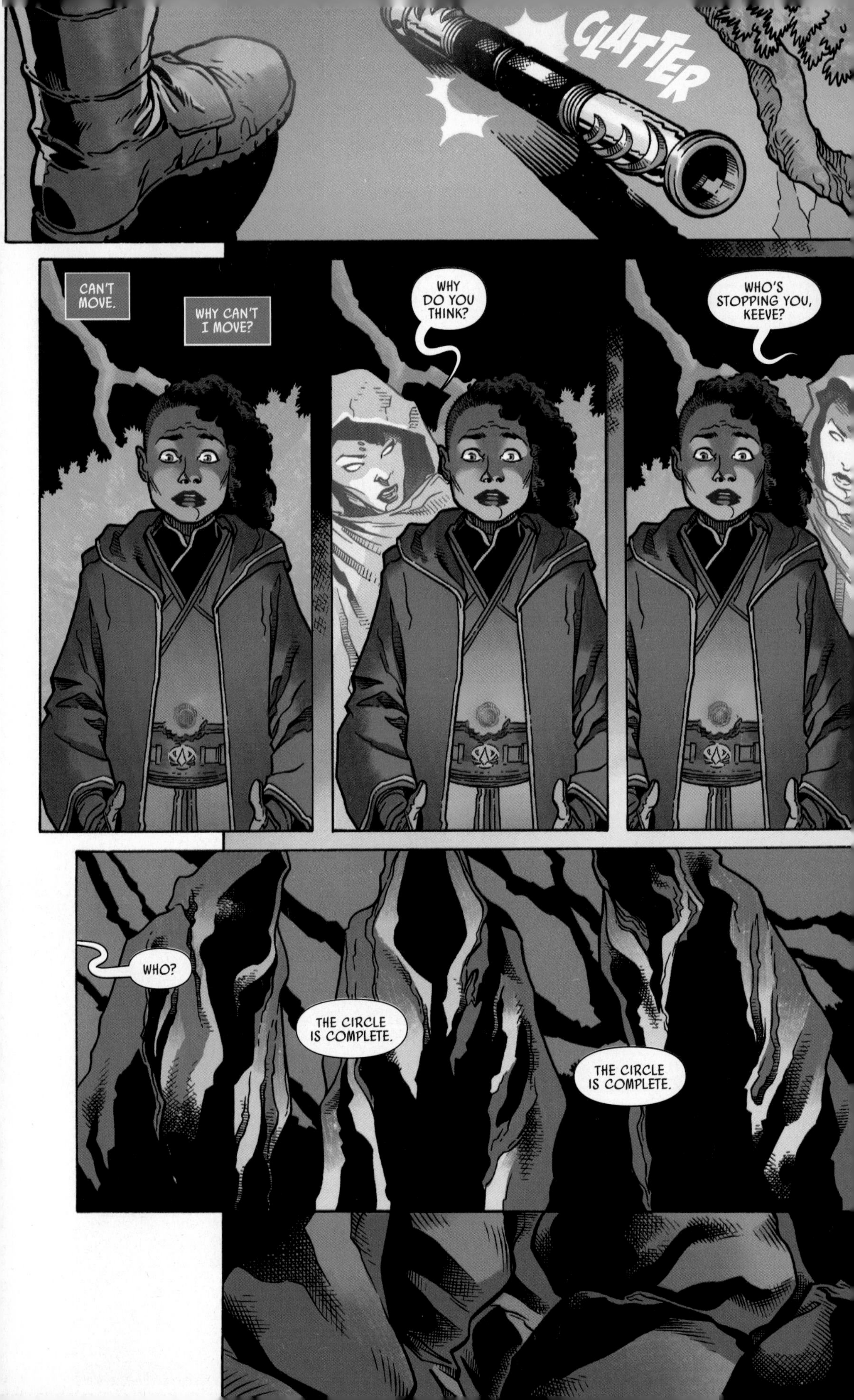
CLATTER
CAN'T MOVE.
WHY CAN'T I MOVE?
WHY DO YOU THINK?
WHO'S STOPPING YOU, KEEVE?
WHO?
THE CIRCLE IS COMPLETE.
THE CIRCLE IS COMPLETE.

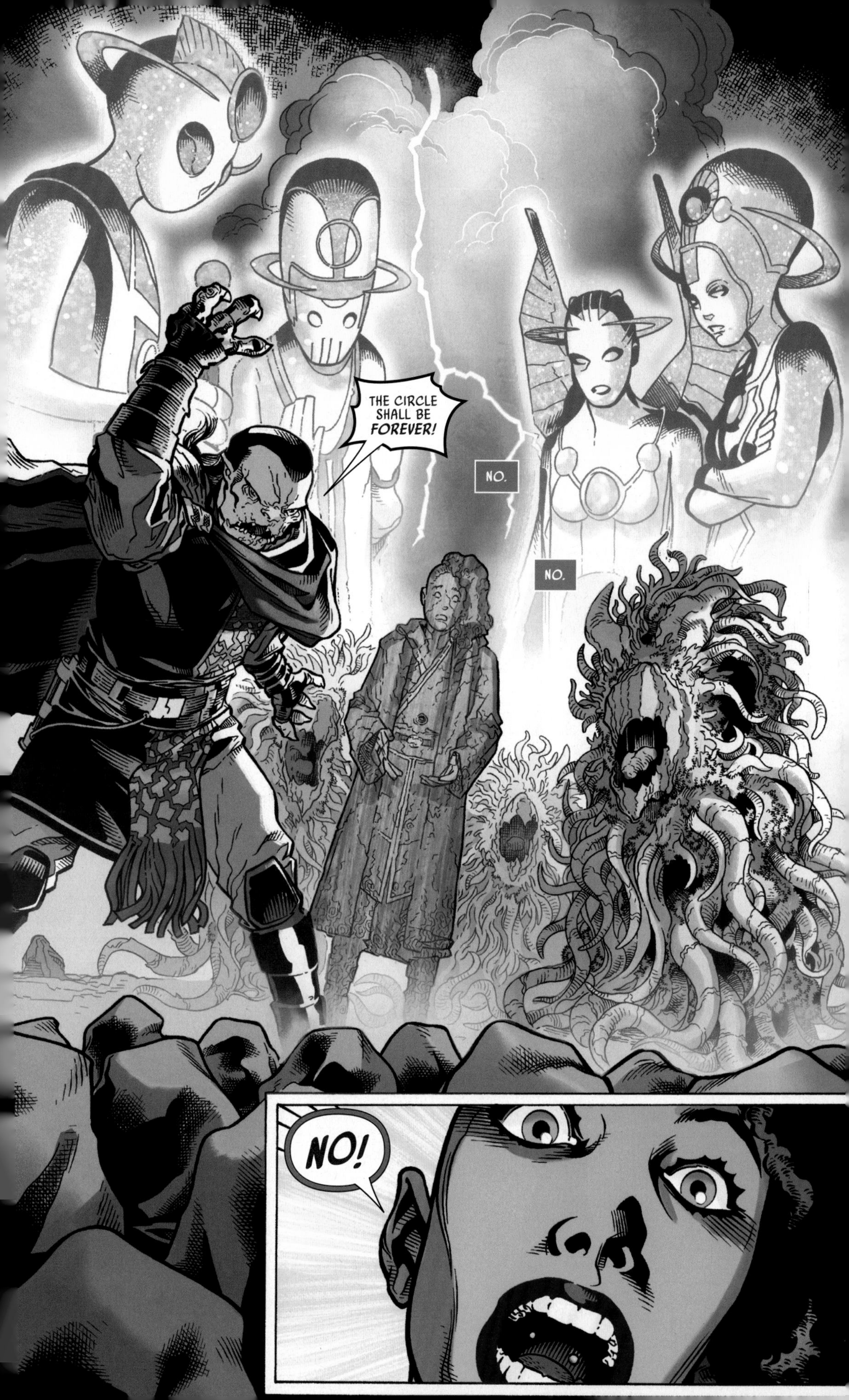
THE CIRCLE SHALL BE FOREVER!
NO.
NO.
NO!

MEDITATION CHAMBER.

STARLIGHT BEACON.

JEDI TRENNIS? JEDI TRENNIS, PLEASE COME IN.

WHAT THE VARP WAS *THAT?*

JEDI TRENNIS. THIS IS DR. GINO'LE.

YEAH. YEAH, I'M HERE, DOC.

I THINK.

YOU THINK?

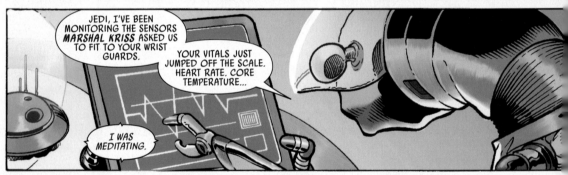

JEDI, I'VE BEEN MONITORING THE SENSORS *MARSHAL KRISS* ASKED US TO FIT TO YOUR WRIST GUARDS.

YOUR VITALS JUST JUMPED OFF THE SCALE. HEART RATE. CORE TEMPERATURE...

I WAS MEDITATING.

SHOULDN'T THAT HAVE THE *OPPOSITE* EFFECT?

LOOK, I APPRECIATE YOU CHECKING IN ON ME, BUT I'M FINE, REALLY I AM...

ARE YOU SURE?

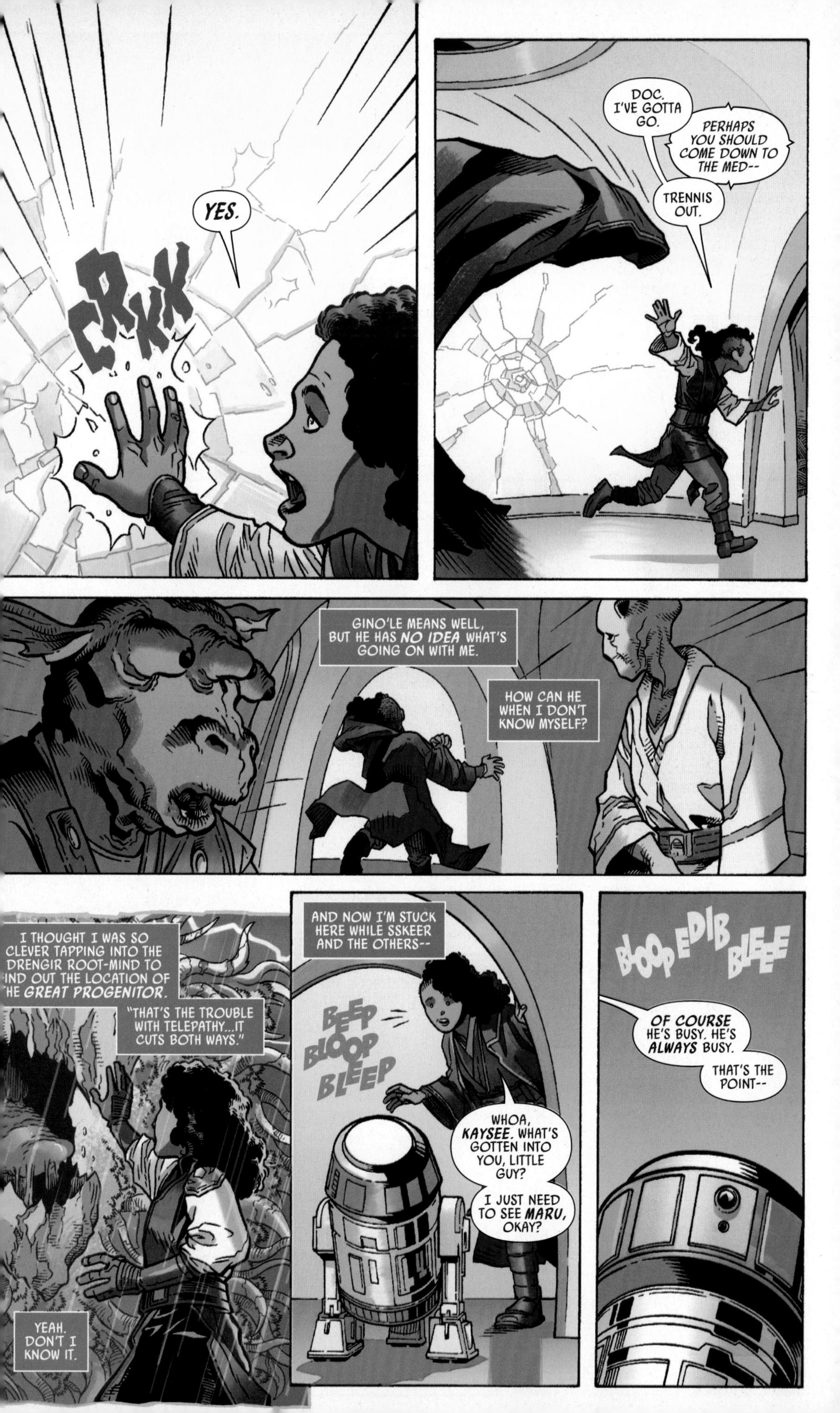
YES.
CRKK
DOC. I'VE GOTTA GO.
PERHAPS YOU SHOULD COME DOWN TO THE MED--
TRENNIS OUT.
GINO'LE MEANS WELL, BUT HE HAS NO IDEA WHAT'S GOING ON WITH ME.
HOW CAN HE WHEN I DON'T KNOW MYSELF?
I THOUGHT I WAS SO CLEVER TAPPING INTO THE DRENGIR ROOT-MIND TO FIND OUT THE LOCATION OF THE GREAT PROGENITOR.
"THAT'S THE TROUBLE WITH TELEPATHY...IT CUTS BOTH WAYS."
YEAH. DON'T I KNOW IT.
AND NOW I'M STUCK HERE WHILE SSKEER AND THE OTHERS--
BEEP BLOOP BLEEP
WHOA, KAYSEE. WHAT'S GOTTEN INTO YOU, LITTLE GUY?
I JUST NEED TO SEE MARU, OKAY?
BLOOP EDIB BLEEE
OF COURSE HE'S BUSY. HE'S ALWAYS BUSY.
THAT'S THE POINT--

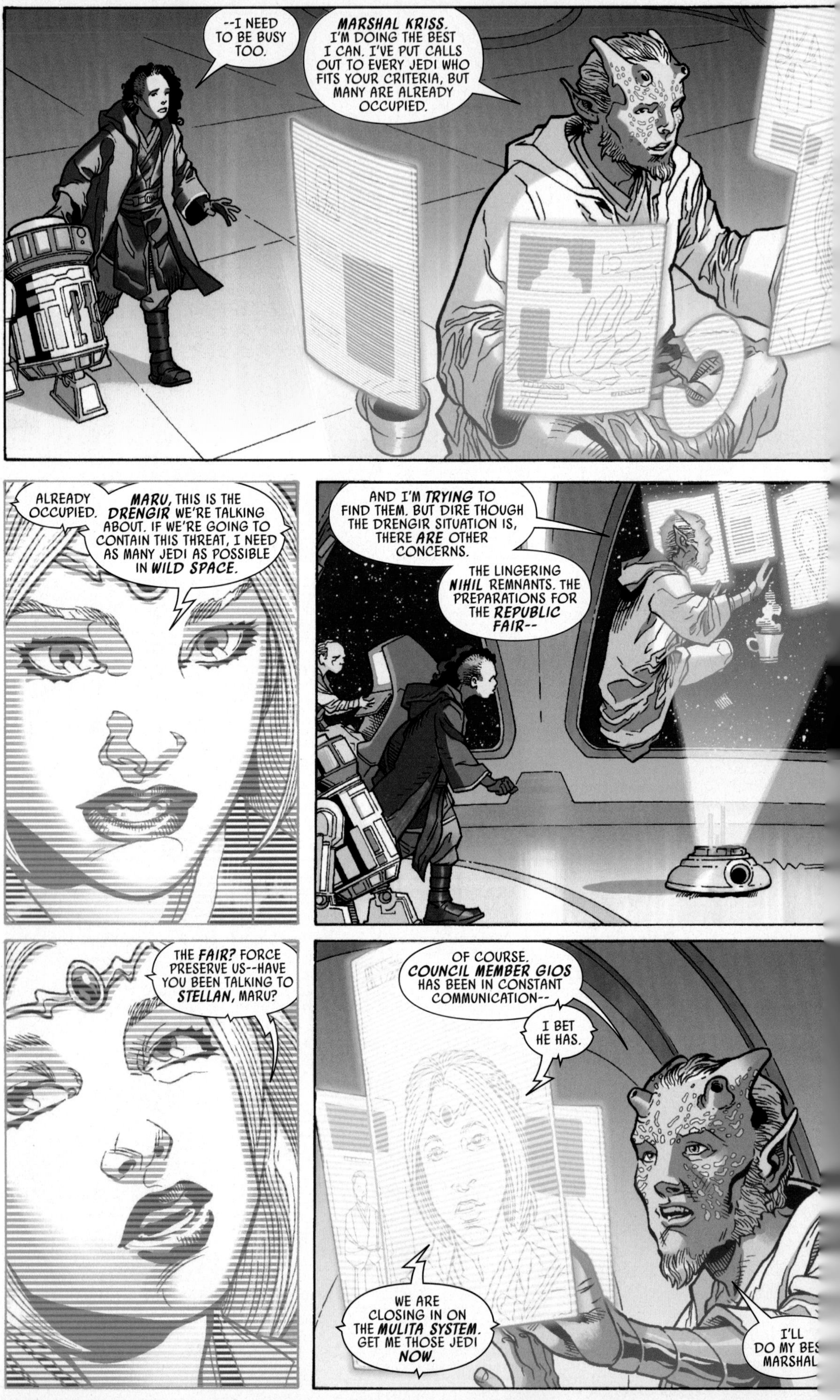
--I NEED TO BE BUSY TOO.
MARSHAL KRISS. I'M DOING THE BEST I CAN. I'VE PUT CALLS OUT TO EVERY JEDI WHO FITS YOUR CRITERIA, BUT MANY ARE ALREADY OCCUPIED.
ALREADY OCCUPIED.
MARU, THIS IS THE DRENGIR WE'RE TALKING ABOUT. IF WE'RE GOING TO CONTAIN THIS THREAT, I NEED AS MANY JEDI AS POSSIBLE IN WILD SPACE.
AND I'M TRYING TO FIND THEM. BUT DIRE THOUGH THE DRENGIR SITUATION IS, THERE ARE OTHER CONCERNS.
THE LINGERING NIHIL REMNANTS. THE PREPARATIONS FOR THE REPUBLIC FAIR--
THE FAIR? FORCE PRESERVE US--HAVE YOU BEEN TALKING TO STELLAN, MARU?
OF COURSE. COUNCIL MEMBER GIOS HAS BEEN IN CONSTANT COMMUNICATION--
I BET HE HAS.
WE ARE CLOSING IN ON THE MULITA SYSTEM. GET ME THOSE JEDI NOW.

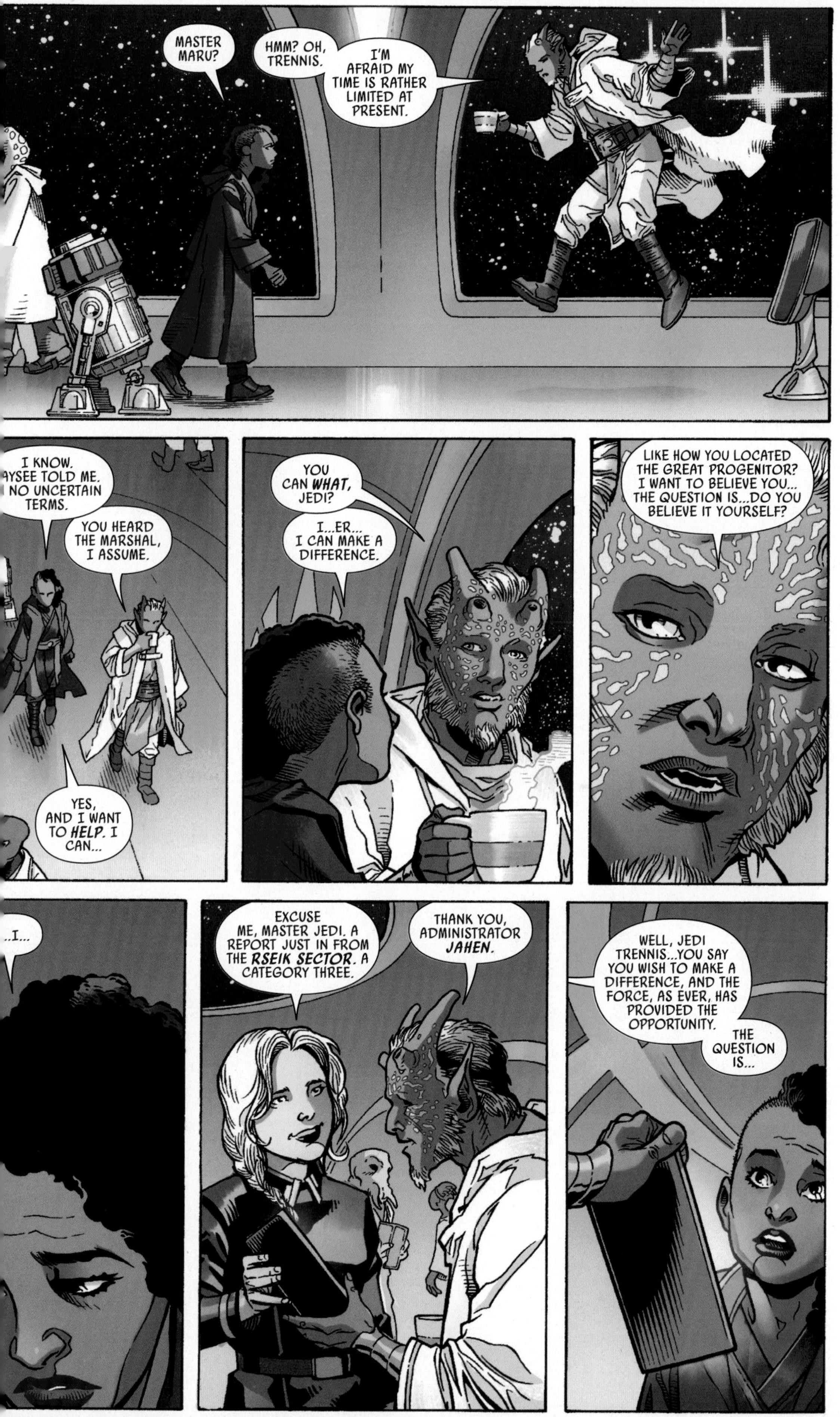
MASTER MARU?
HMM? OH, TRENNIS.
I'M AFRAID MY TIME IS RATHER LIMITED AT PRESENT.
I KNOW. AYSEE TOLD ME. NO UNCERTAIN TERMS.
YOU HEARD THE MARSHAL, I ASSUME.
YES, AND I WANT TO HELP. I CAN...
YOU CAN WHAT, JEDI?
I...ER... I CAN MAKE A DIFFERENCE.
LIKE HOW YOU LOCATED THE GREAT PROGENITOR? I WANT TO BELIEVE YOU... THE QUESTION IS...DO YOU BELIEVE IT YOURSELF?
...I...
EXCUSE ME, MASTER JEDI. A REPORT JUST IN FROM THE RSEIK SECTOR. A CATEGORY THREE.
THANK YOU, ADMINISTRATOR JAHEN.
WELL, JEDI TRENNIS...YOU SAY YOU WISH TO MAKE A DIFFERENCE, AND THE FORCE, AS EVER, HAS PROVIDED THE OPPORTUNITY.
THE QUESTION IS...

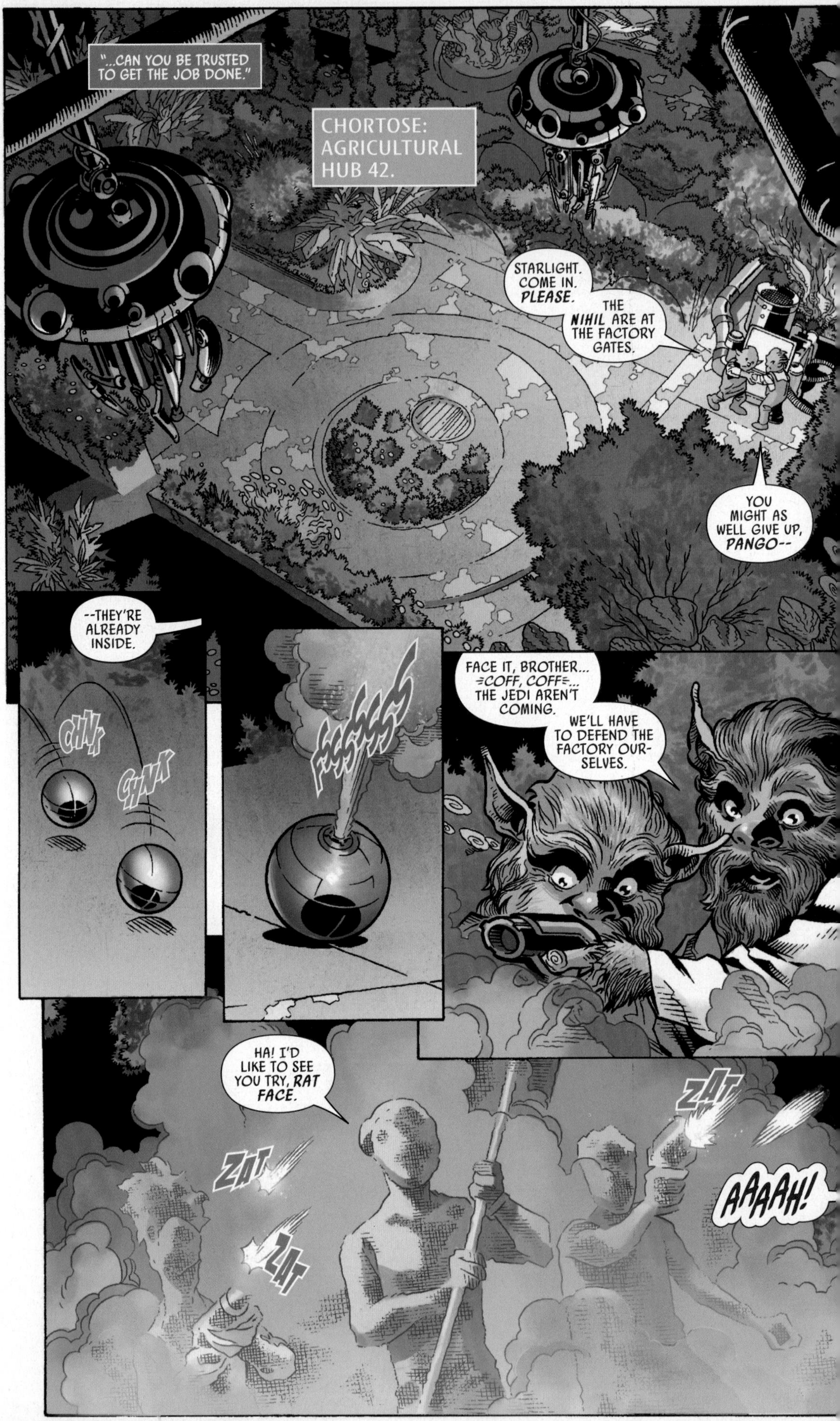
"...CAN YOU BE TRUSTED TO GET THE JOB DONE."
CHORTOSE: AGRICULTURAL HUB 42.
STARLIGHT. COME IN. PLEASE.
THE NIHIL ARE AT THE FACTORY GATES.
YOU MIGHT AS WELL GIVE UP, PANGO--
--THEY'RE ALREADY INSIDE.
CHNK
CHNK
FSSSSSS
FACE IT, BROTHER... =COFF, COFF=... THE JEDI AREN'T COMING.
WE'LL HAVE TO DEFEND THE FACTORY OUR-SELVES.
HA! I'D LIKE TO SEE YOU TRY, RAT FACE.
ZAT
ZAT
ZAT
AAAAH!

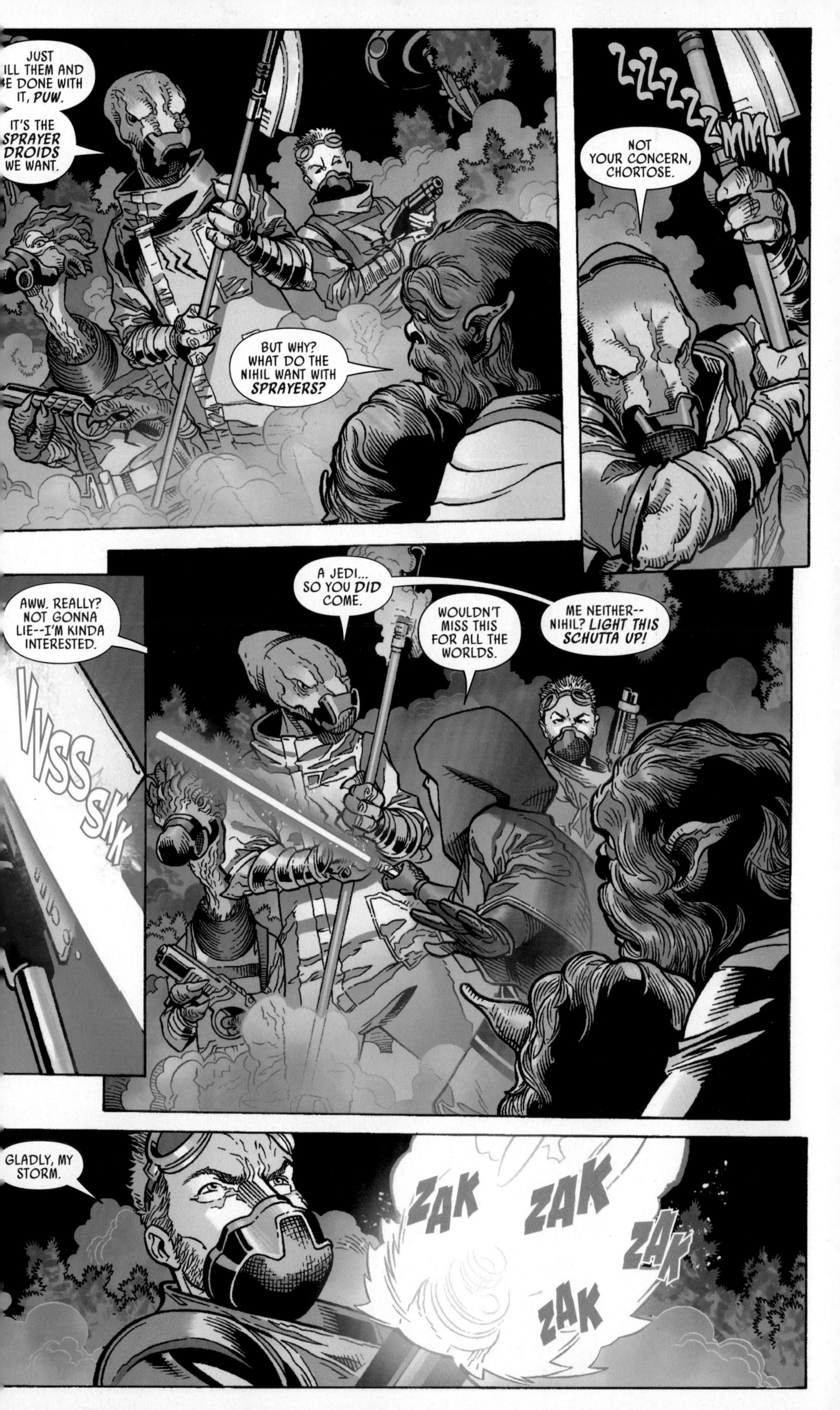
JUST
ILL THEM AND
E DONE WITH
IT, *PUW*.
IT'S THE
*SPRAYER
DROIDS*
WE WANT.
BUT WHY?
WHAT DO THE
NIHIL WANT WITH
SPRAYERS?
ZZZZZZMMM
NOT
YOUR CONCERN,
CHORTOSE.
AWW. REALLY?
NOT GONNA
LIE--I'M KINDA
INTERESTED.
VVSSSK
A JEDI...
SO YOU *DID*
COME.
WOULDN'T
MISS THIS
FOR ALL THE
WORLDS.
ME NEITHER--
NIHIL? *LIGHT THIS
SCHUTTA UP!*
GLADLY, MY
STORM.
ZAK
ZAK
ZAK
ZAK

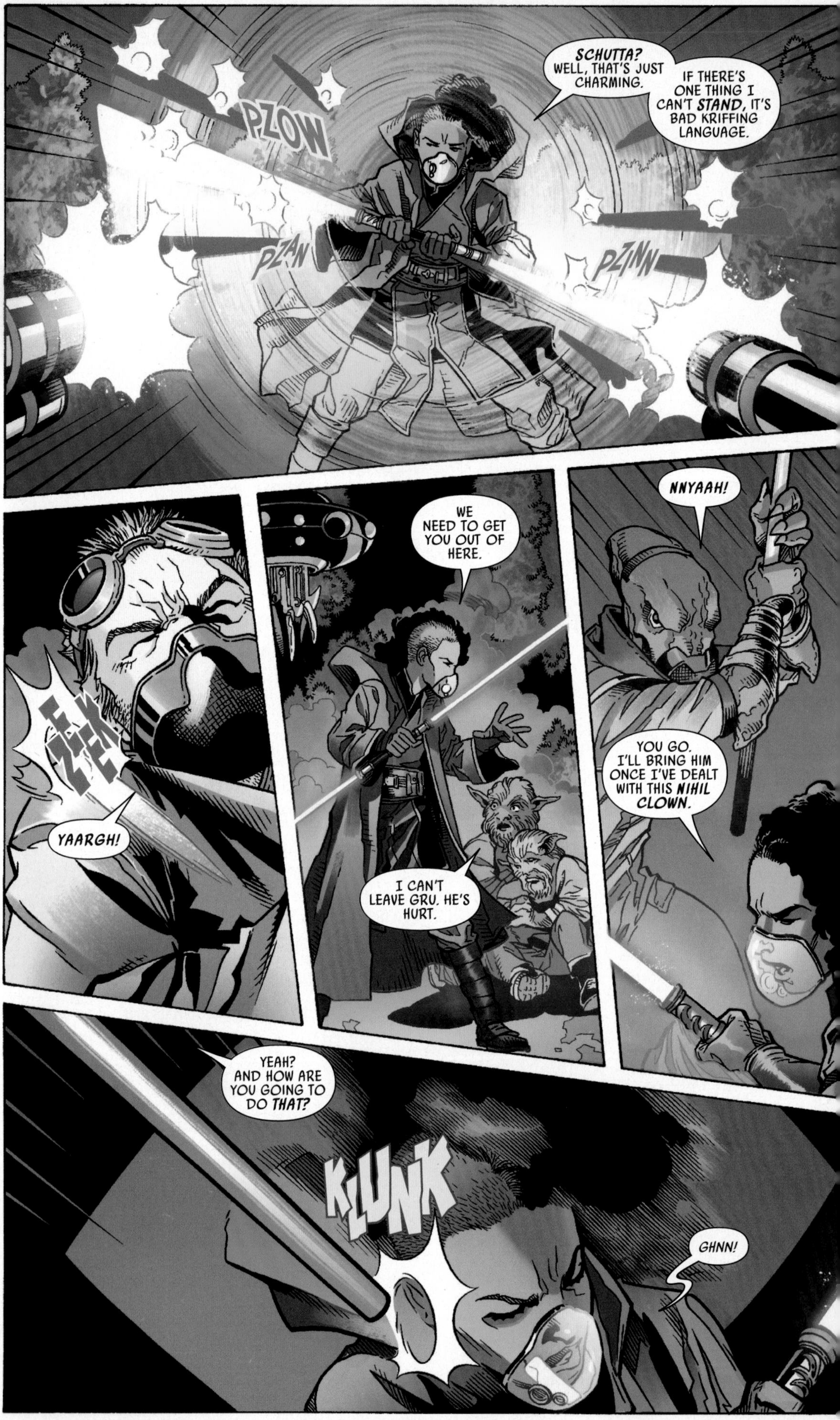

SCHUTTA? WELL, THAT'S JUST CHARMING.
IF THERE'S ONE THING I CAN'T STAND, IT'S BAD KRIFFING LANGUAGE.
PZOW
PZAN
PZINN
ZZEEK
YAARGH!
WE NEED TO GET YOU OUT OF HERE.
I CAN'T LEAVE GRU. HE'S HURT.
NNYAAH!
YOU GO. I'LL BRING HIM ONCE I'VE DEALT WITH THIS NIHIL CLOWN.
YEAH? AND HOW ARE YOU GOING TO DO THAT?
KLUNK
GHNN!

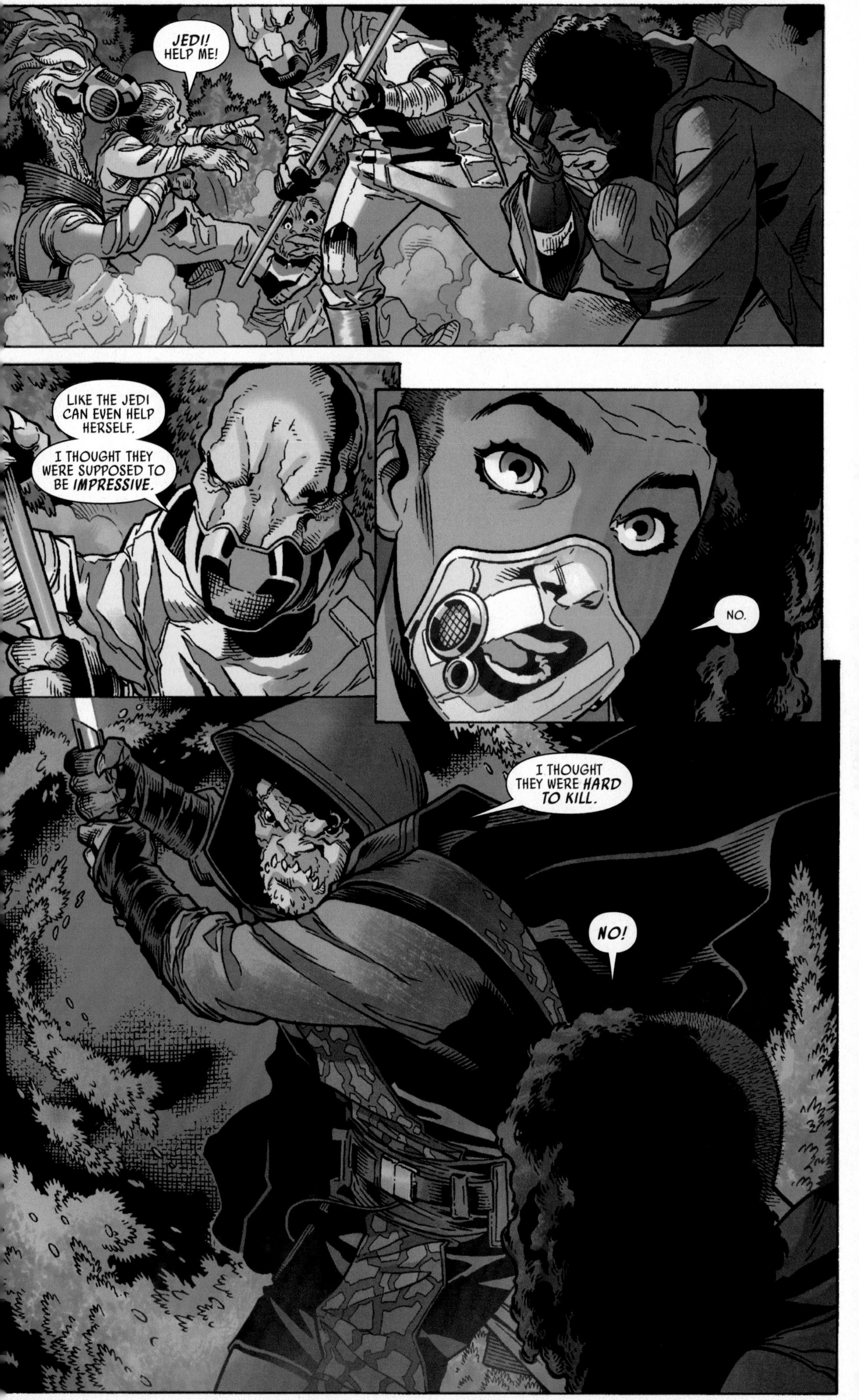
JEDI! HELP ME!
LIKE THE JEDI CAN EVEN HELP HERSELF.
I THOUGHT THEY WERE SUPPOSED TO BE IMPRESSIVE.
NO.
I THOUGHT THEY WERE HARD TO KILL.
NO!

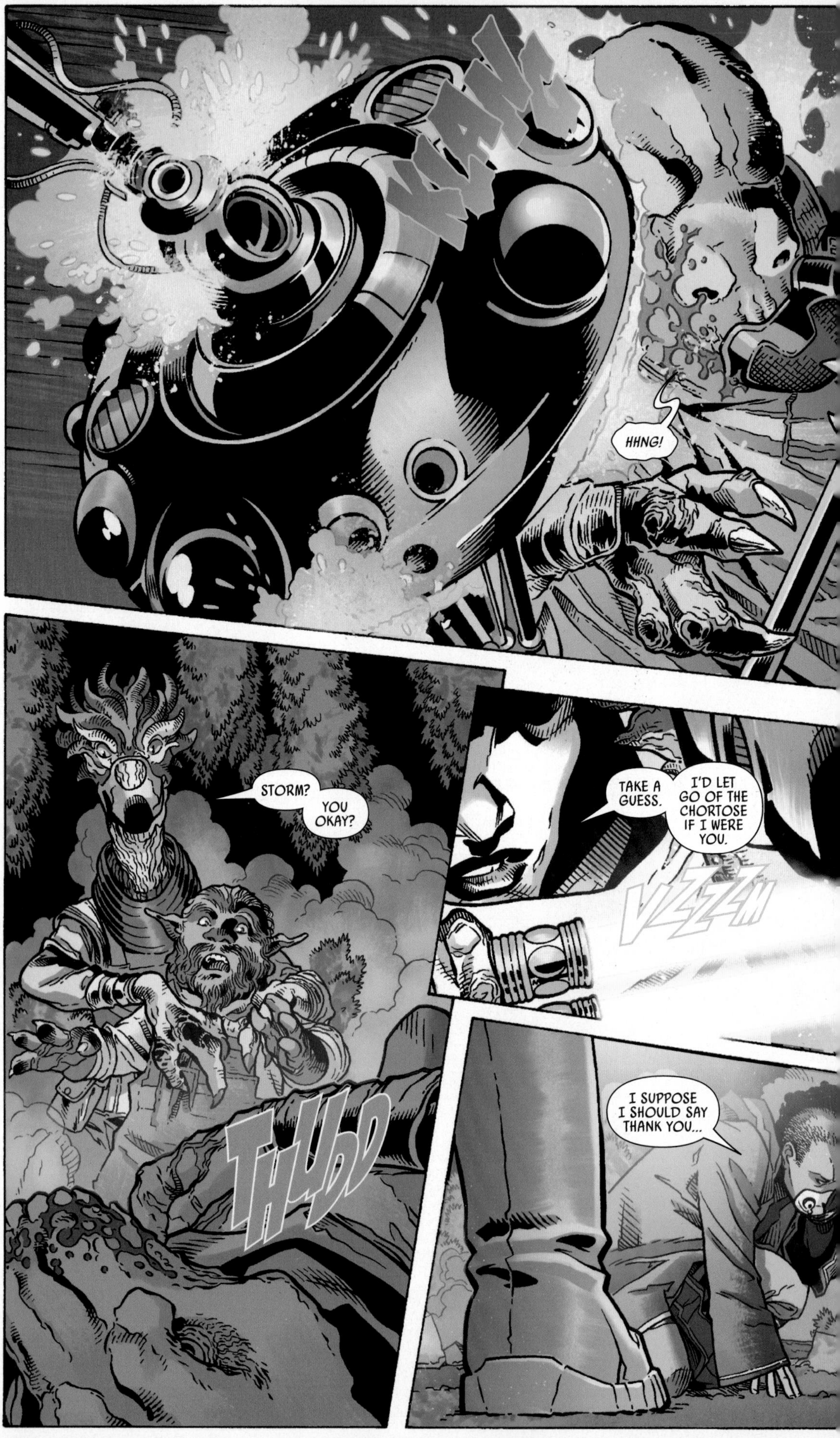
KRANG
HHNG!
STORM?
YOU OKAY?
TAKE A GUESS.
I'D LET GO OF THE CHORTOSE IF I WERE YOU.
VZZZM
THUDD
I SUPPOSE I SHOULD SAY THANK YOU...

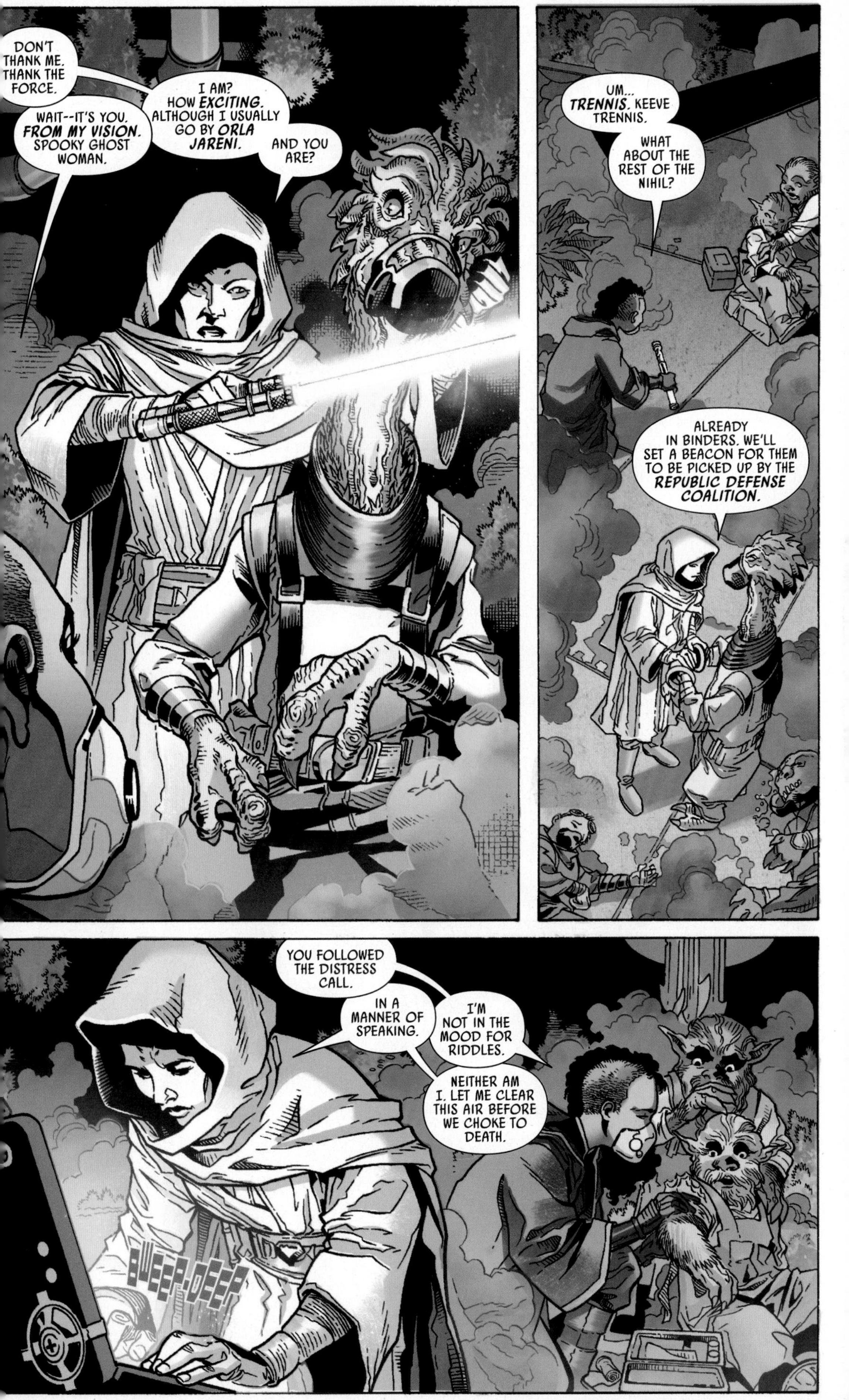
DON'T THANK ME. THANK THE FORCE.
WAIT--IT'S YOU. FROM MY VISION. SPOOKY GHOST WOMAN.
I AM? HOW EXCITING. ALTHOUGH I USUALLY GO BY ORLA JARENI.
AND YOU ARE?
UM... TRENNIS. KEEVE TRENNIS.
WHAT ABOUT THE REST OF THE NIHIL?
ALREADY IN BINDERS. WE'LL SET A BEACON FOR THEM TO BE PICKED UP BY THE REPUBLIC DEFENSE COALITION.
YOU FOLLOWED THE DISTRESS CALL.
IN A MANNER OF SPEAKING.
I'M NOT IN THE MOOD FOR RIDDLES.
NEITHER AM I. LET ME CLEAR THIS AIR BEFORE WE CHOKE TO DEATH.
BLEEP-DEEP

WHICH TEMPLE DO YOU BELONG TO?

NONE. THAT'S THE THING ABOUT *WAYSEEKERS*. WE GO WHERE THE FORCE LEADS US--AND THE FORCE LED ME TO COME HERE.

TO STOP THE NIHIL?

NO--TO FIND A JEDI IN DANGER OF LOSING HERSELF.

I DON'T KNOW WHAT YOU'RE TALKING ABOUT.

I THINK YOU DO.

DEET

ALL AVAILABLE JEDI ARE TO REPORT TO THE FOLLOWING COORDINATES IN WILD SPACE. REPEAT: ALL AVAILABLE JEDI--

STARLIGHT'S MARSHAL ISSUES A *DIRECT ORDER*, AND YOU HEAD IN THE OPPOSITE DIRECTION.

BUT THE DIFFERENCE IS THAT YOU BELONG WITH *THEM*. I CAN SENSE IT IN YOU. I CAN SENSE IT IN THE FORCE.

I COULD SAY THE SAME ABOUT YOU.

THEY DON'T NEED ME.

AND THEY TOLD YOU THAT?

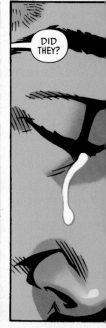

DID THEY?

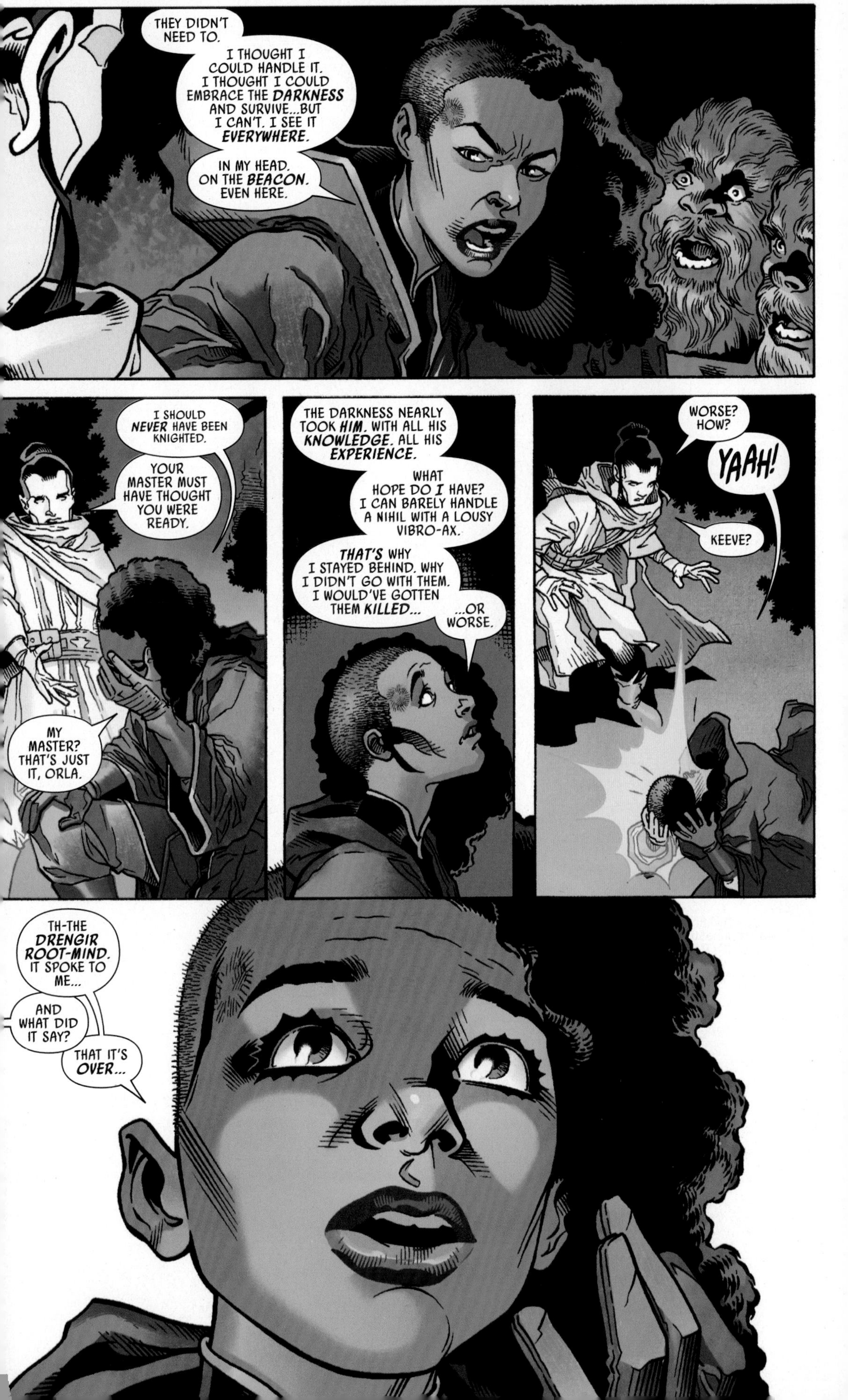
THEY DIDN'T NEED TO.
I THOUGHT I COULD HANDLE IT. I THOUGHT I COULD EMBRACE THE DARKNESS AND SURVIVE...BUT I CAN'T. I SEE IT EVERYWHERE.
IN MY HEAD. ON THE BEACON. EVEN HERE.
I SHOULD NEVER HAVE BEEN KNIGHTED.
YOUR MASTER MUST HAVE THOUGHT YOU WERE READY.
MY MASTER? THAT'S JUST IT, ORLA.
THE DARKNESS NEARLY TOOK HIM. WITH ALL HIS KNOWLEDGE. ALL HIS EXPERIENCE.
WHAT HOPE DO I HAVE? I CAN BARELY HANDLE A NIHIL WITH A LOUSY VIBRO-AX.
THAT'S WHY I STAYED BEHIND. WHY I DIDN'T GO WITH THEM. I WOULD'VE GOTTEN THEM KILLED...
...OR WORSE.
WORSE? HOW?
YAAH!
KEEVE?
TH-THE DRENGIR ROOT-MIND. IT SPOKE TO ME...
AND WHAT DID IT SAY?
THAT IT'S OVER...

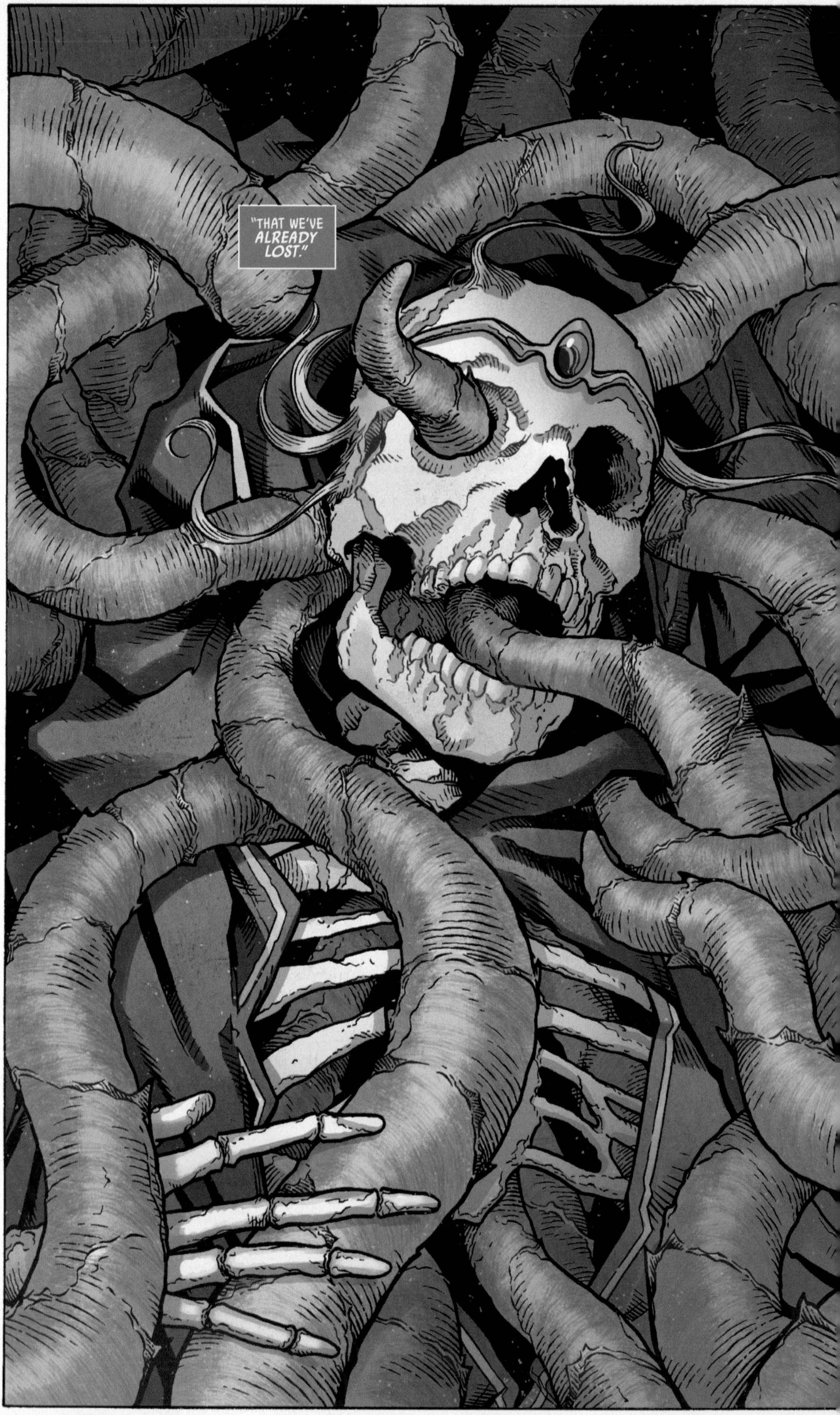
"THAT WE'VE *ALREADY* LOST."

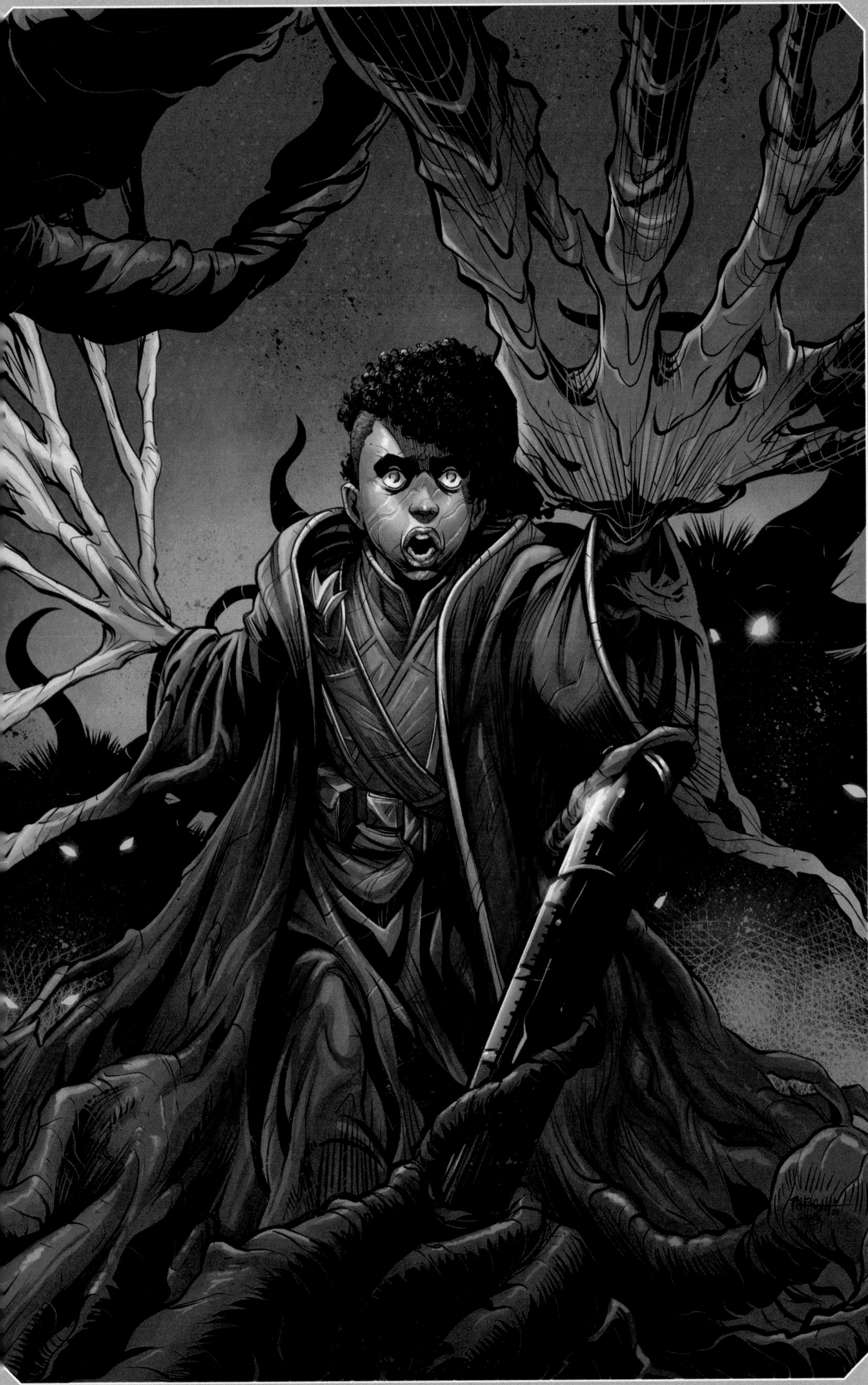

#7 Variant by
RAY-ANTHONY HEIGHT & RACHELLE ROSENBERG

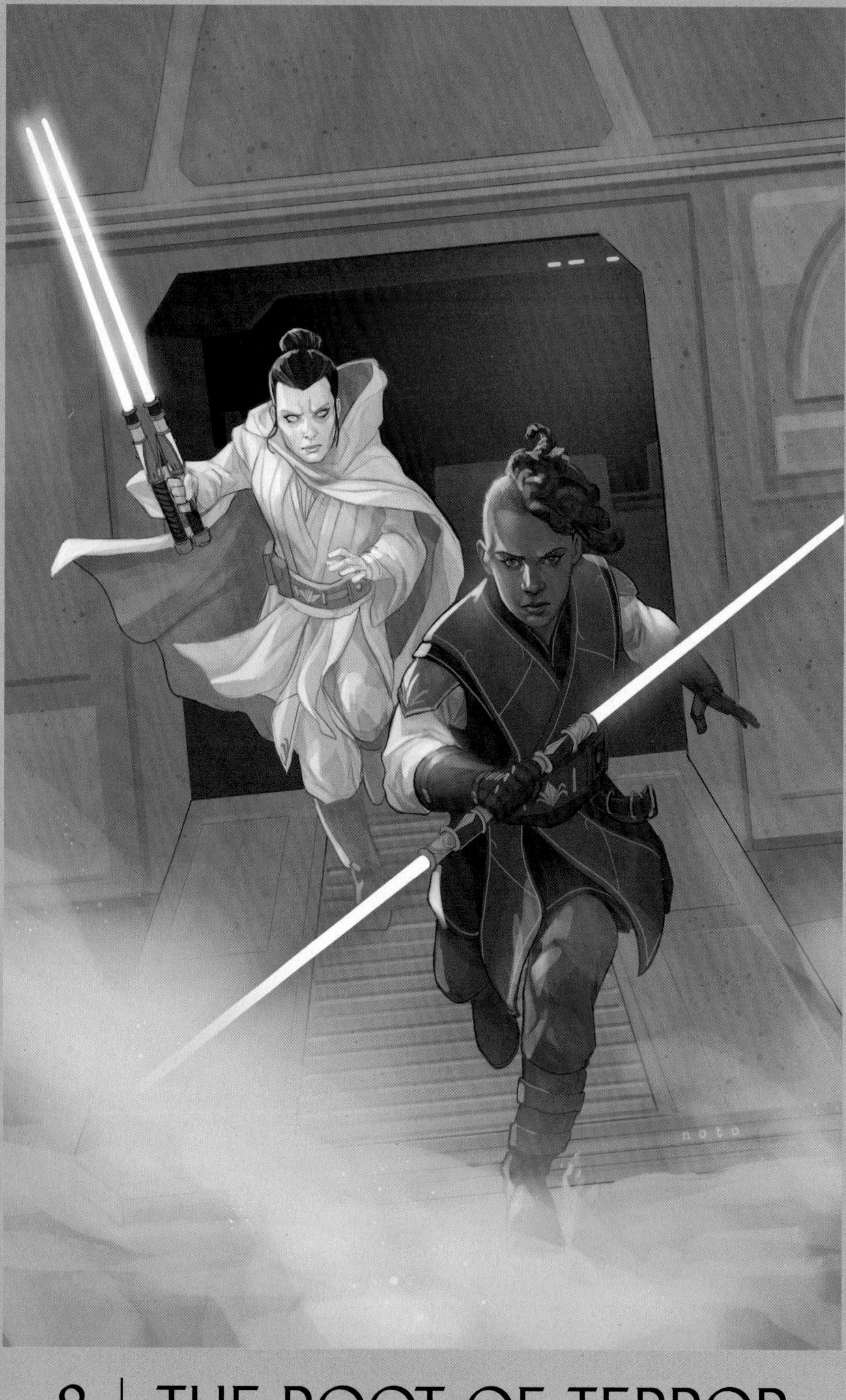
noto

8 | THE ROOT OF TERROR

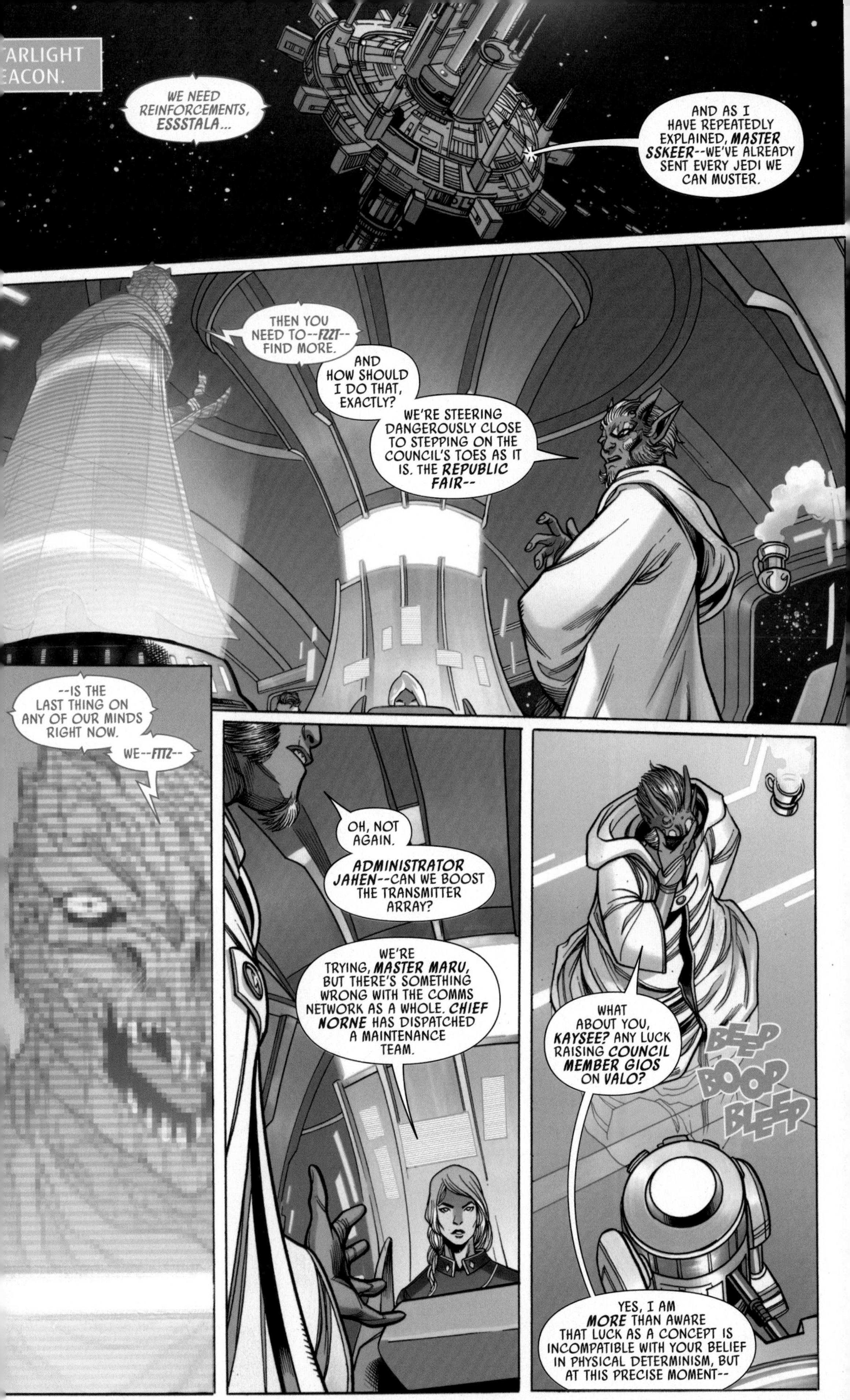

TARLIGHT
EACON.
WE NEED REINFORCEMENTS, ESSSTALA...
AND AS I HAVE REPEATEDLY EXPLAINED, MASTER SSKEER--WE'VE ALREADY SENT EVERY JEDI WE CAN MUSTER.
THEN YOU NEED TO--FZZT--FIND MORE.
AND HOW SHOULD I DO THAT, EXACTLY?
WE'RE STEERING DANGEROUSLY CLOSE TO STEPPING ON THE COUNCIL'S TOES AS IT IS. THE REPUBLIC FAIR--
--IS THE LAST THING ON ANY OF OUR MINDS RIGHT NOW.
WE--FTTZ--
OH, NOT AGAIN.
ADMINISTRATOR JAHEN--CAN WE BOOST THE TRANSMITTER ARRAY?
WE'RE TRYING, MASTER MARU, BUT THERE'S SOMETHING WRONG WITH THE COMMS NETWORK AS A WHOLE. CHIEF NORNE HAS DISPATCHED A MAINTENANCE TEAM.
WHAT ABOUT YOU, KAYSEE? ANY LUCK RAISING COUNCIL MEMBER GIOS ON VALO?
BEEP BOOP BLEEP
YES, I AM MORE THAN AWARE THAT LUCK AS A CONCEPT IS INCOMPATIBLE WITH YOUR BELIEF IN PHYSICAL DETERMINISM, BUT AT THIS PRECISE MOMENT--

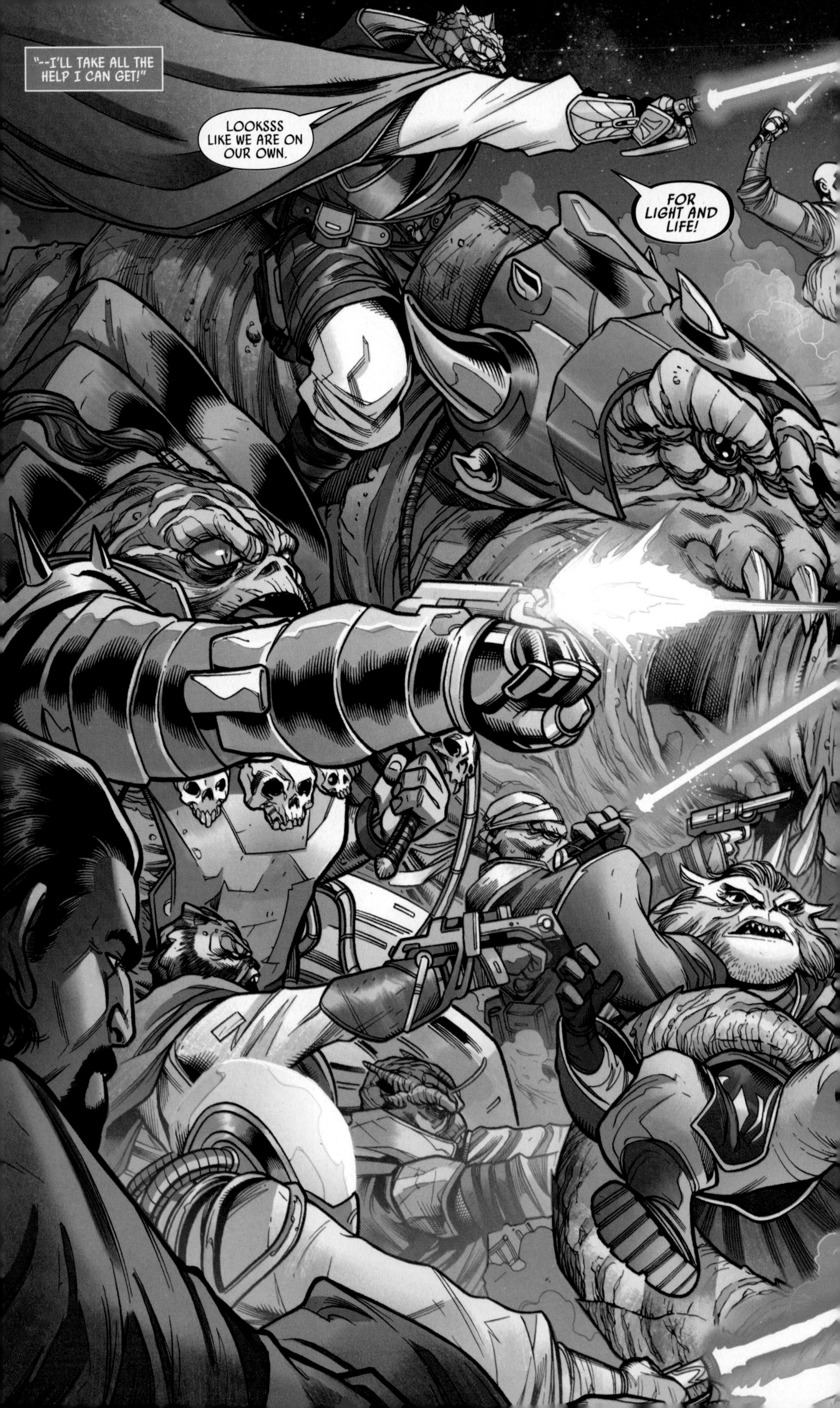
"--I'LL TAKE ALL THE HELP I CAN GET!"
LOOKSSS LIKE WE ARE ON OUR OWN.
FOR LIGHT AND LIFE!

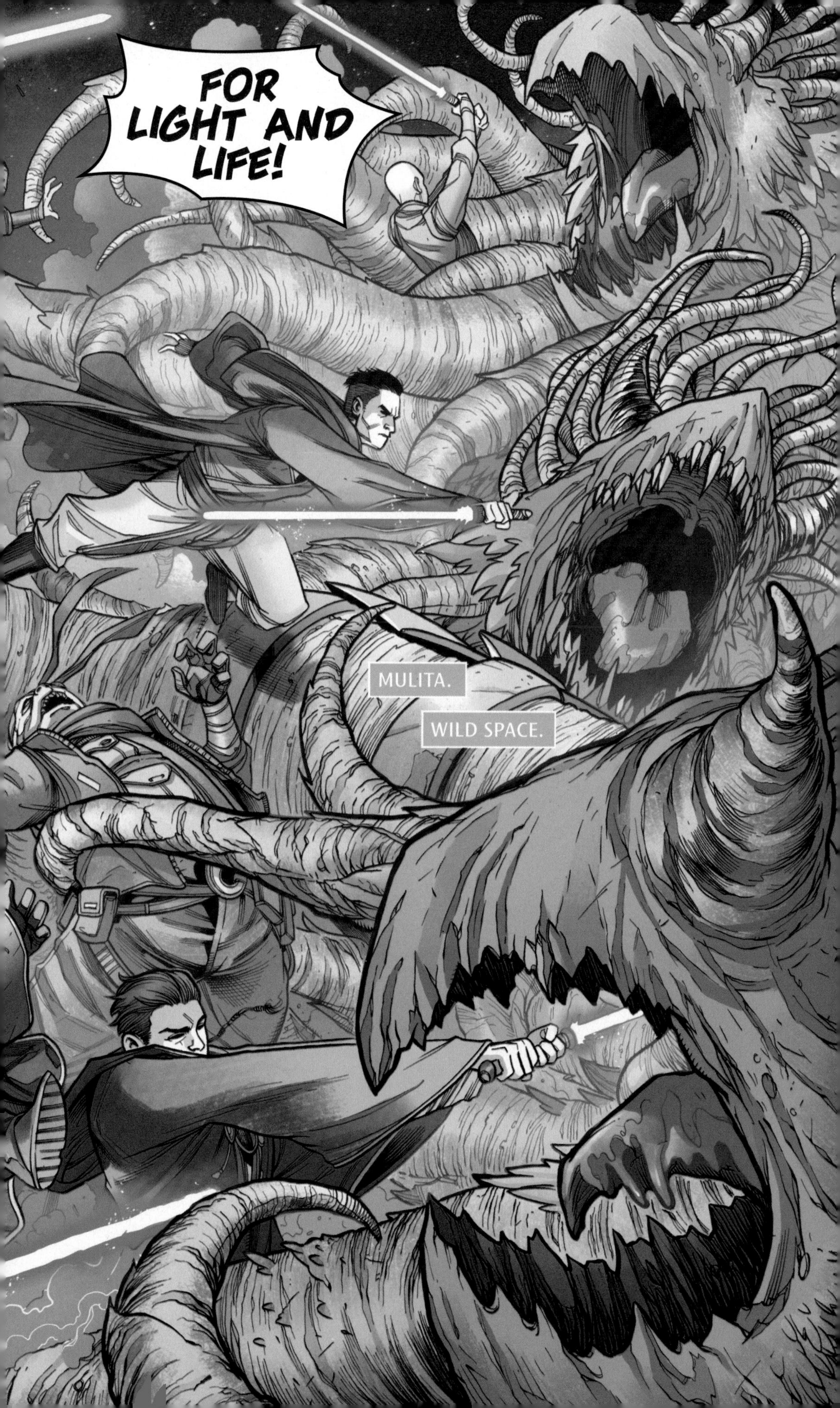
FOR LIGHT AND LIFE!
MULITA.
WILD SPACE.

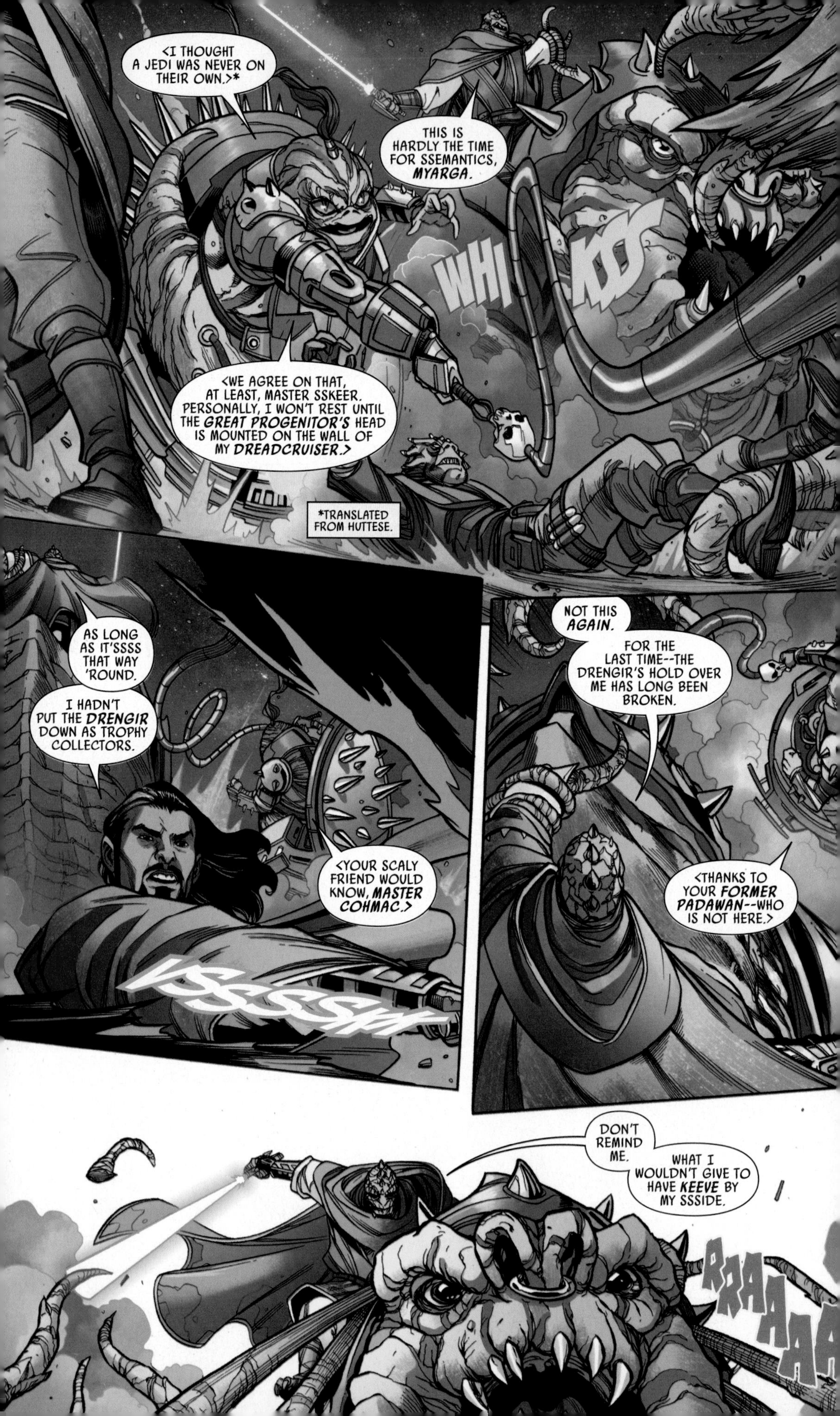

<I THOUGHT A JEDI WAS NEVER ON THEIR OWN.>*
THIS IS HARDLY THE TIME FOR SSEMANTICS, MYARGA.
WHI KSS
<WE AGREE ON THAT, AT LEAST, MASTER SSKEER. PERSONALLY, I WON'T REST UNTIL THE GREAT PROGENITOR'S HEAD IS MOUNTED ON THE WALL OF MY DREADCRUISER.>
*TRANSLATED FROM HUTTESE.
AS LONG AS IT'SSSS THAT WAY 'ROUND.
I HADN'T PUT THE DRENGIR DOWN AS TROPHY COLLECTORS.
<YOUR SCALY FRIEND WOULD KNOW, MASTER COHMAC.>
VSSSSH
NOT THIS AGAIN.
FOR THE LAST TIME--THE DRENGIR'S HOLD OVER ME HAS LONG BEEN BROKEN.
<THANKS TO YOUR FORMER PADAWAN--WHO IS NOT HERE.>
DON'T REMIND ME.
WHAT I WOULDN'T GIVE TO HAVE KEEVE BY MY SSSIDE.
RRAAAA

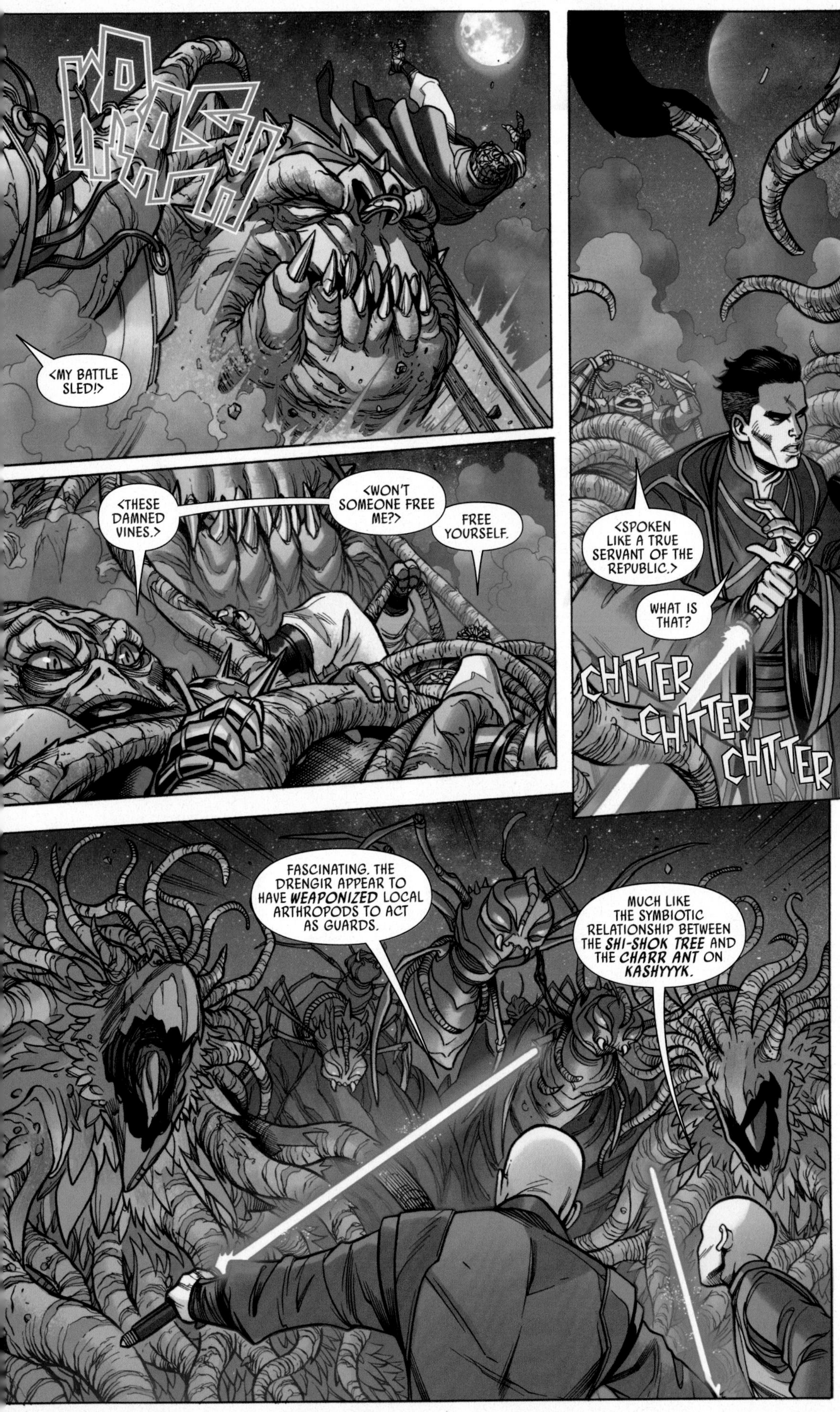
<MY BATTLE SLED!>
<THESE DAMNED VINES.>
<WON'T SOMEONE FREE ME?>
FREE YOURSELF.
<SPOKEN LIKE A TRUE SERVANT OF THE REPUBLIC.>
WHAT IS THAT?
CHITTER
CHITTER
CHITTER
FASCINATING. THE DRENGIR APPEAR TO HAVE *WEAPONIZED* LOCAL ARTHROPODS TO ACT AS GUARDS.
MUCH LIKE THE SYMBIOTIC RELATIONSHIP BETWEEN THE *SHI-SHOK TREE* AND THE *CHARR ANT* ON *KASHYYYK*.

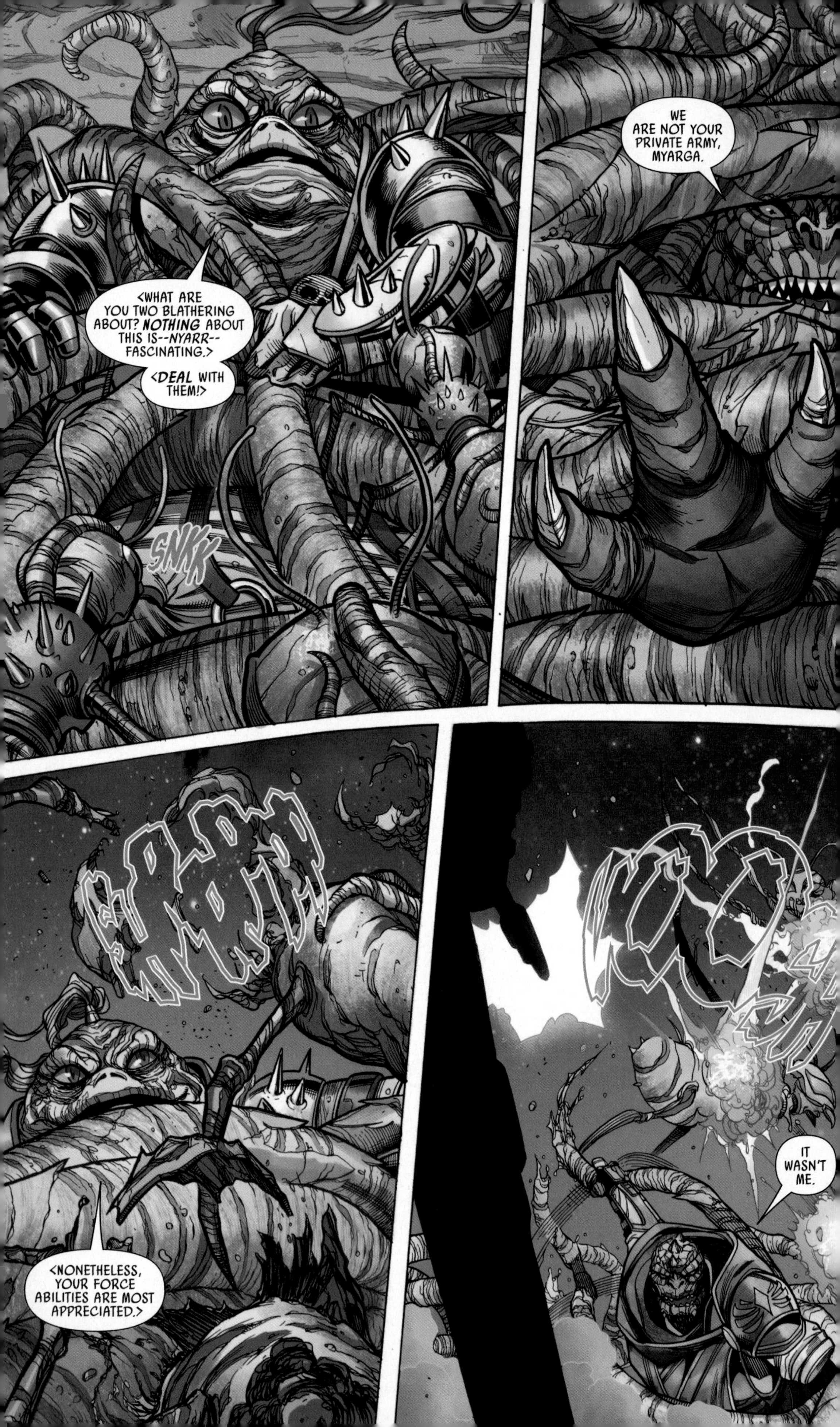

<WHAT ARE YOU TWO BLATHERING ABOUT? **NOTHING** ABOUT THIS IS--*NYARR*--FASCINATING.>
<**DEAL** WITH THEM!>
SNKK
WE ARE NOT YOUR PRIVATE ARMY, MYARGA.
<NONETHELESS, YOUR FORCE ABILITIES ARE MOST APPRECIATED.>
IT WASN'T ME.

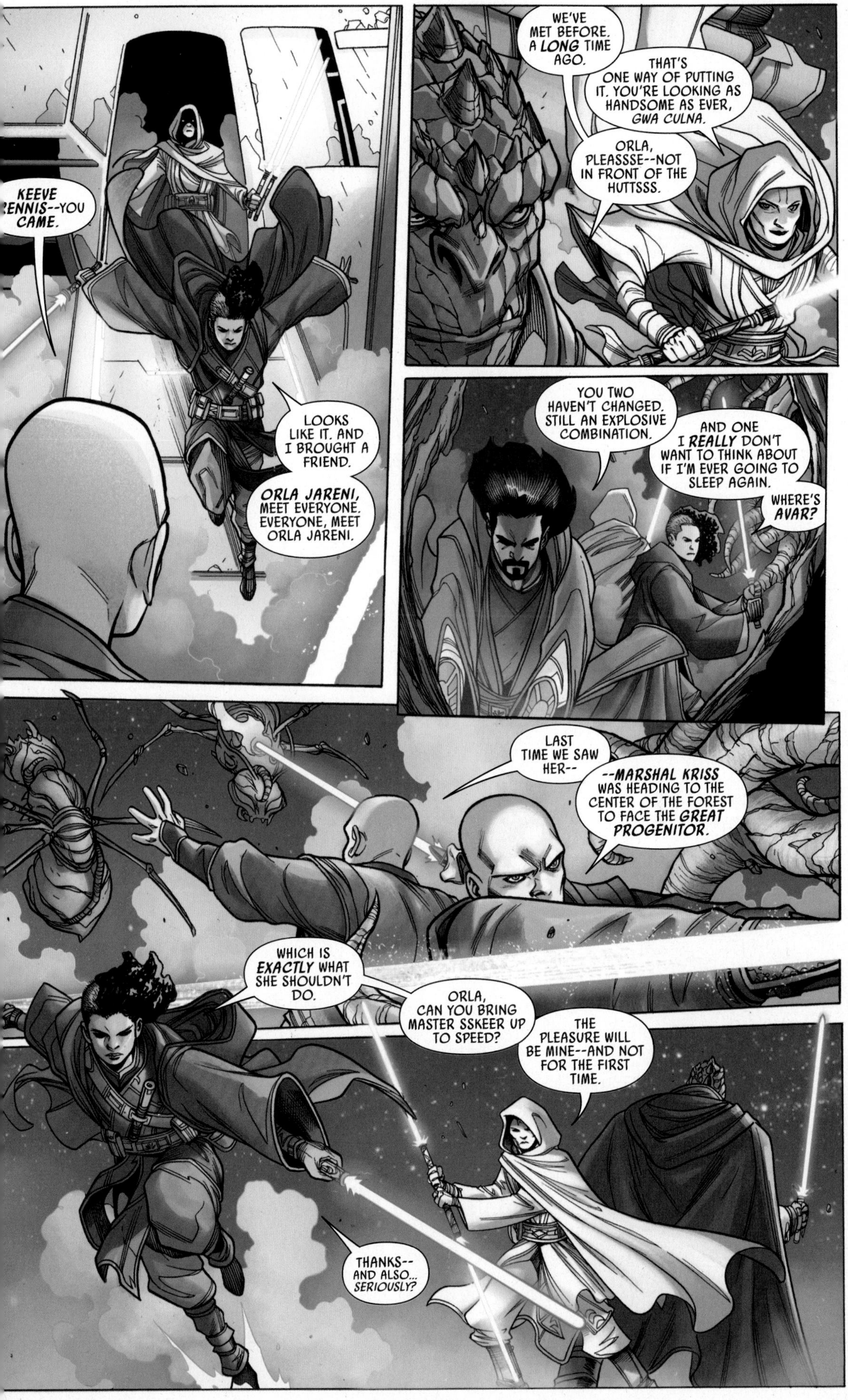
KEEVE
RENNIS--YOU
CAME.
LOOKS
LIKE IT. AND
I BROUGHT A
FRIEND.
ORLA JARENI,
MEET EVERYONE.
EVERYONE, MEET
ORLA JARENI.
WE'VE
MET BEFORE.
A LONG TIME
AGO.
THAT'S
ONE WAY OF PUTTING
IT. YOU'RE LOOKING AS
HANDSOME AS EVER,
GWA CULNA.
ORLA,
PLEASSSE--NOT
IN FRONT OF THE
HUTTSSS.
YOU TWO
HAVEN'T CHANGED.
STILL AN EXPLOSIVE
COMBINATION.
AND ONE
I REALLY DON'T
WANT TO THINK ABOUT
IF I'M EVER GOING TO
SLEEP AGAIN.
WHERE'S
AVAR?
LAST
TIME WE SAW
HER--
--MARSHAL KRISS
WAS HEADING TO THE
CENTER OF THE FOREST
TO FACE THE GREAT
PROGENITOR.
WHICH IS
EXACTLY WHAT
SHE SHOULDN'T
DO.
ORLA,
CAN YOU BRING
MASTER SSKEER UP
TO SPEED?
THE
PLEASURE WILL
BE MINE--AND NOT
FOR THE FIRST
TIME.
THANKS--
AND ALSO...
SERIOUSLY?

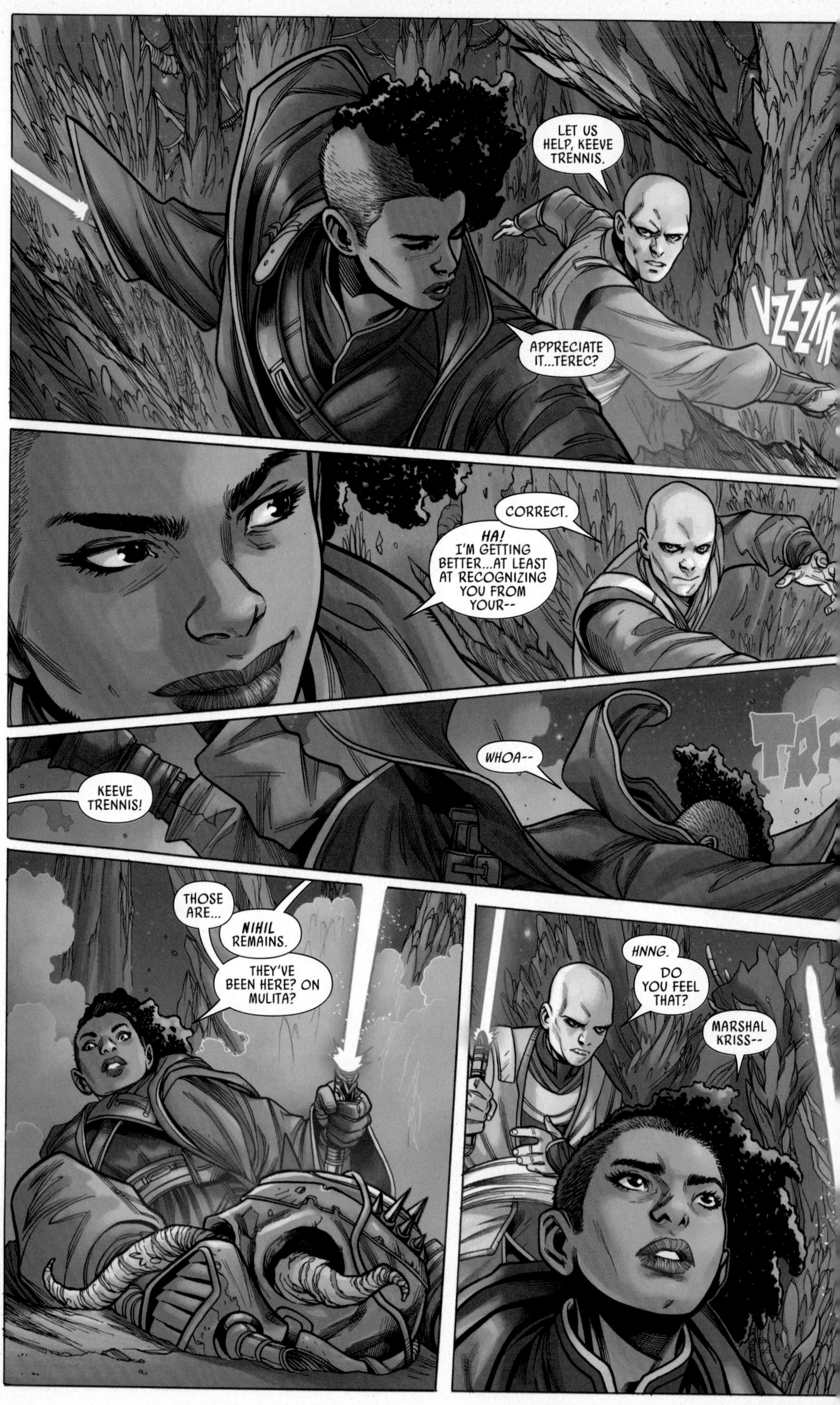
LET US HELP, KEEVE TRENNIS.
APPRECIATE IT...TEREC?
CORRECT.
HA! I'M GETTING BETTER...AT LEAST AT RECOGNIZING YOU FROM YOUR--
WHOA--
KEEVE TRENNIS!
THOSE ARE...
NIHIL REMAINS.
THEY'VE BEEN HERE? ON MULITA?
HNNG.
DO YOU FEEL THAT?
MARSHAL KRISS--

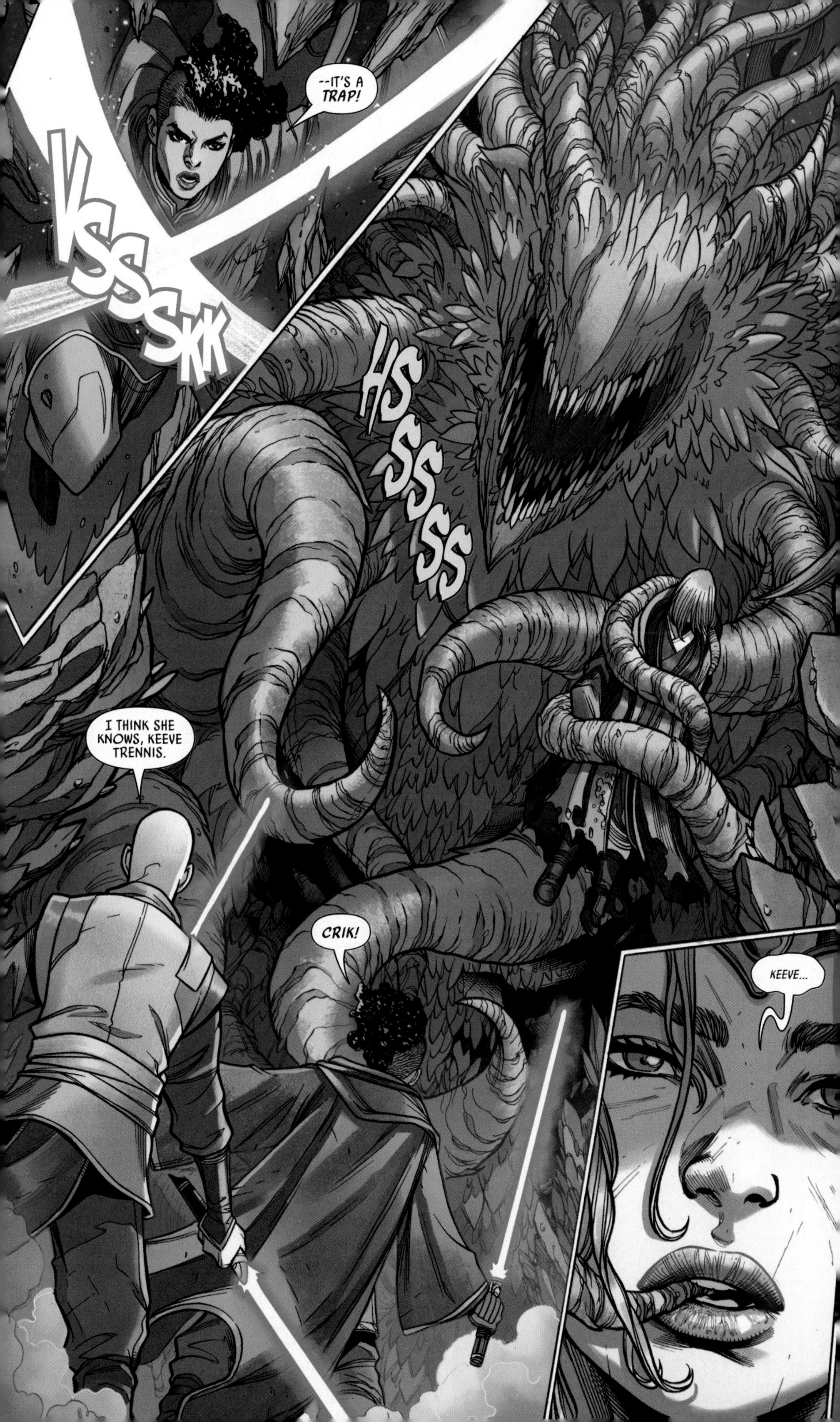
--IT'S A TRAP!
VSSSKK
HSSSSSS
I THINK SHE KNOWS, KEEVE TRENNIS.
CRIK!
KEEVE...

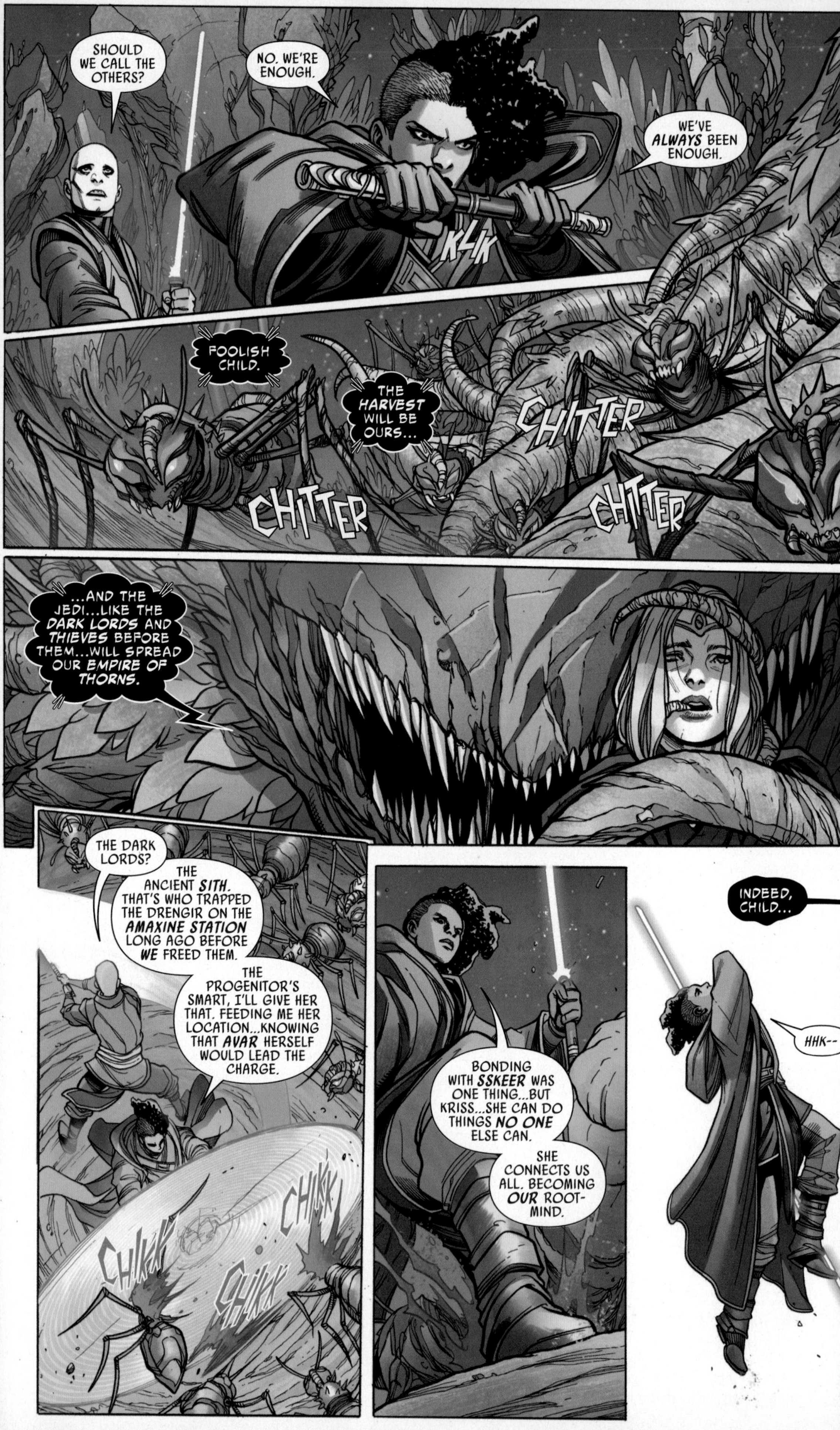

SHOULD WE CALL THE OTHERS?
NO. WE'RE ENOUGH.
WE'VE ALWAYS BEEN ENOUGH.
KLIK
FOOLISH CHILD.
THE HARVEST WILL BE OURS...
CHITTER
CHITTER
CHITTER
...AND THE JEDI...LIKE THE DARK LORDS AND THIEVES BEFORE THEM...WILL SPREAD OUR EMPIRE OF THORNS.
THE DARK LORDS?
THE ANCIENT SITH. THAT'S WHO TRAPPED THE DRENGIR ON THE AMAXINE STATION LONG AGO BEFORE WE FREED THEM.
THE PROGENITOR'S SMART, I'LL GIVE HER THAT. FEEDING ME HER LOCATION...KNOWING THAT AVAR HERSELF WOULD LEAD THE CHARGE.
CHIKK
CHIKK
CHIKK
BONDING WITH SSKEER WAS ONE THING...BUT KRISS...SHE CAN DO THINGS NO ONE ELSE CAN.
SHE CONNECTS US ALL. BECOMING OUR ROOT-MIND.
INDEED, CHILD...
HHK--

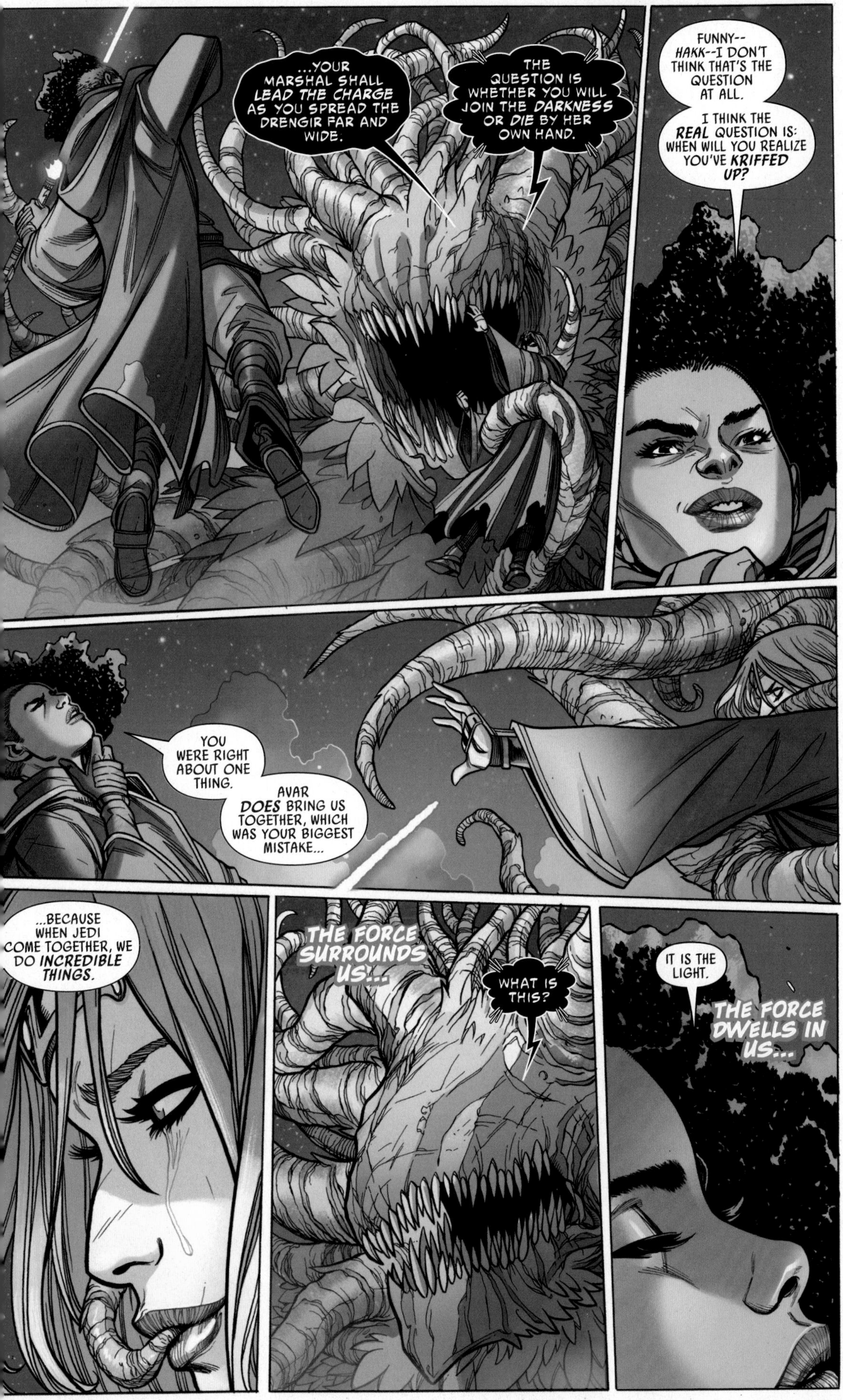
...YOUR MARSHAL SHALL LEAD THE CHARGE AS YOU SPREAD THE DRENGIR FAR AND WIDE.
THE QUESTION IS WHETHER YOU WILL JOIN THE DARKNESS OR DIE BY HER OWN HAND.
FUNNY-- HAKK--I DON'T THINK THAT'S THE QUESTION AT ALL.
I THINK THE REAL QUESTION IS: WHEN WILL YOU REALIZE YOU'VE KRIFFED UP?
YOU WERE RIGHT ABOUT ONE THING.
AVAR DOES BRING US TOGETHER, WHICH WAS YOUR BIGGEST MISTAKE...
...BECAUSE WHEN JEDI COME TOGETHER, WE DO INCREDIBLE THINGS.
THE FORCE SURROUNDS US...
WHAT IS THIS?
IT IS THE LIGHT.
THE FORCE DWELLS IN US...

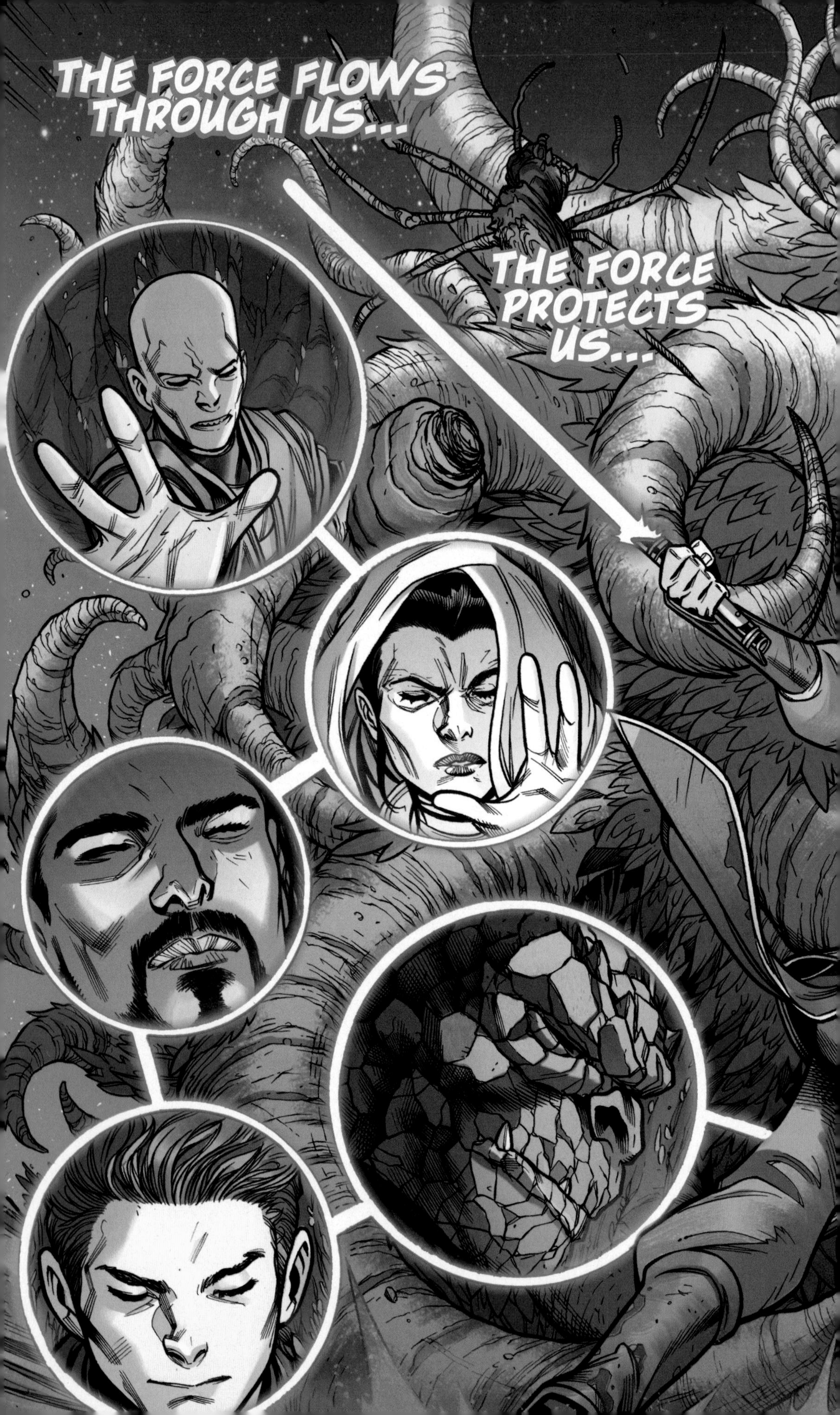
THE FORCE FLOWS THROUGH US...
THE FORCE PROTECTS US...

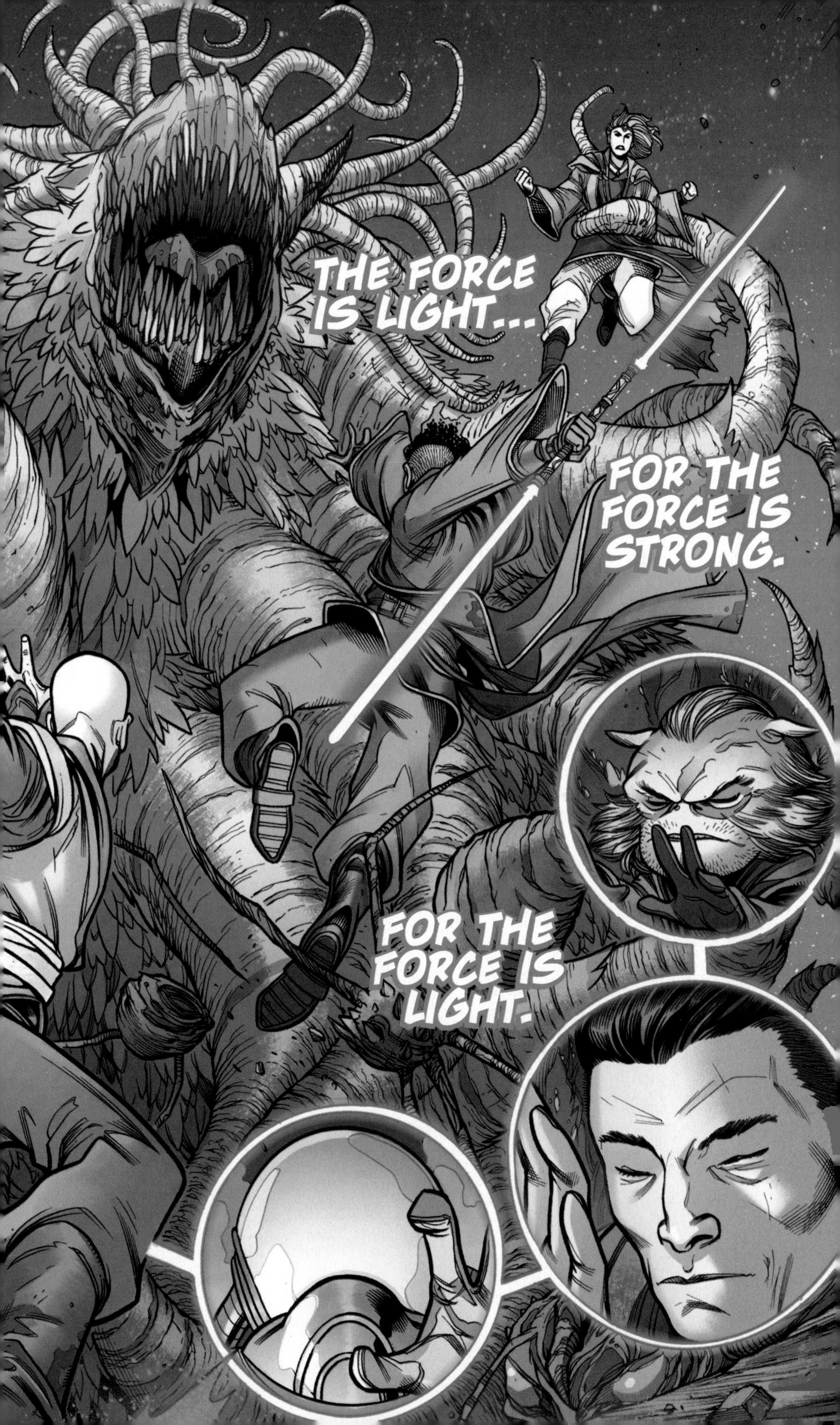
THE FORCE IS LIGHT...
FOR THE FORCE IS STRONG.
FOR THE FORCE IS LIGHT.

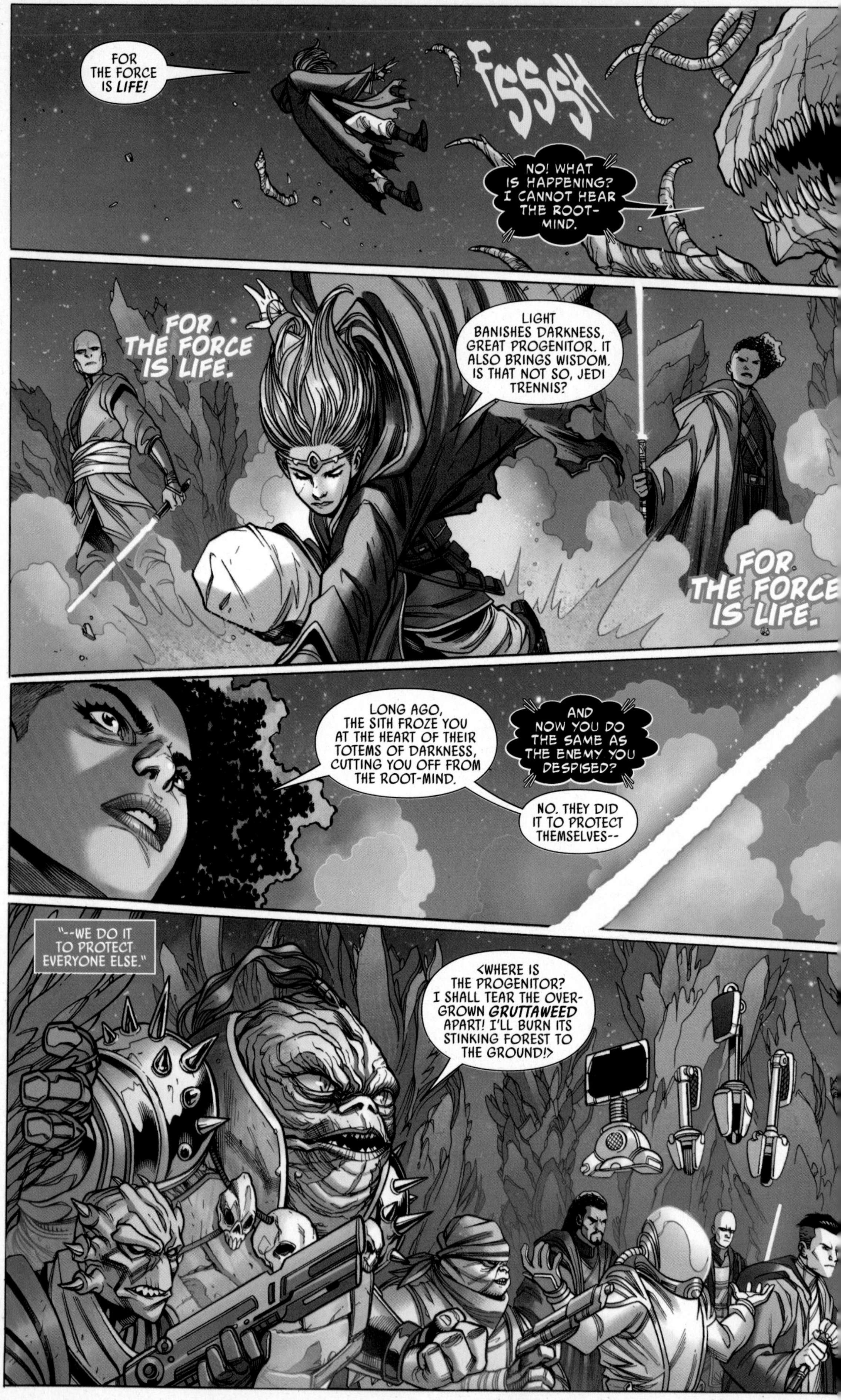
FOR THE FORCE IS LIFE!
fsssh
NO! WHAT IS HAPPENING? I CANNOT HEAR THE ROOT-MIND.
FOR THE FORCE IS LIFE.
LIGHT BANISHES DARKNESS, GREAT PROGENITOR. IT ALSO BRINGS WISDOM. IS THAT NOT SO, JEDI TRENNIS?
FOR THE FORCE IS LIFE.
LONG AGO, THE SITH FROZE YOU AT THE HEART OF THEIR TOTEMS OF DARKNESS, CUTTING YOU OFF FROM THE ROOT-MIND.
AND NOW YOU DO THE SAME AS THE ENEMY YOU DESPISED?
NO. THEY DID IT TO PROTECT THEMSELVES--
"--WE DO IT TO PROTECT EVERYONE ELSE."
<WHERE IS THE PROGENITOR? I SHALL TEAR THE OVER-GROWN *GRUTTAWEED* APART! I'LL BURN ITS STINKING FOREST TO THE GROUND!>

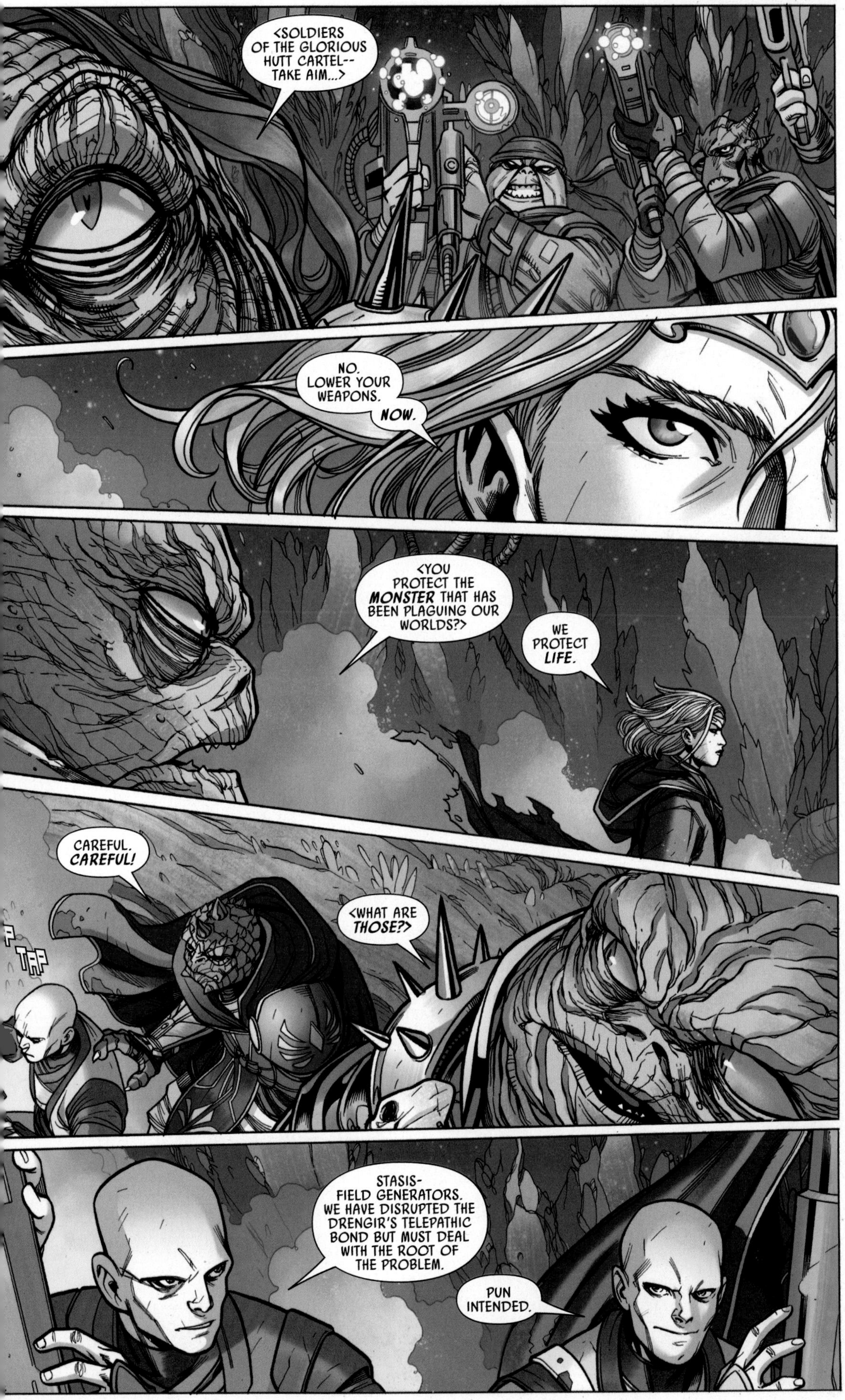
<SOLDIERS OF THE GLORIOUS HUTT CARTEL-- TAKE AIM...>
NO. LOWER YOUR WEAPONS.
NOW.
<YOU PROTECT THE MONSTER THAT HAS BEEN PLAGUING OUR WORLDS?>
WE PROTECT LIFE.
CAREFUL. CAREFUL!
TAP
<WHAT ARE THOSE?>
STASIS-FIELD GENERATORS. WE HAVE DISRUPTED THE DRENGIR'S TELEPATHIC BOND BUT MUST DEAL WITH THE ROOT OF THE PROBLEM.
PUN INTENDED.

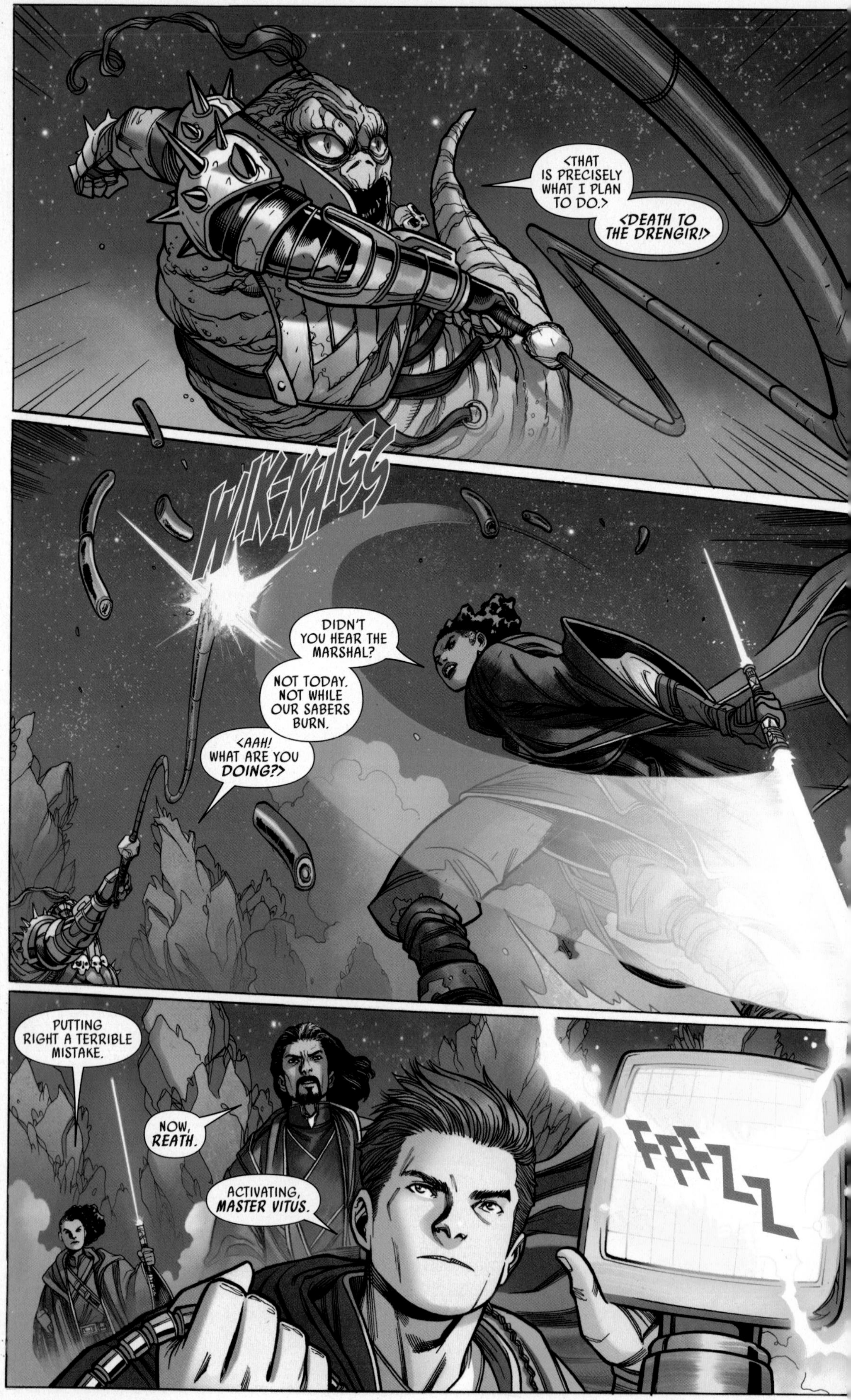
<THAT IS PRECISELY WHAT I PLAN TO DO.>
<DEATH TO THE DRENGIR!>
WHK-KHISS
DIDN'T YOU HEAR THE MARSHAL?
NOT TODAY. NOT WHILE OUR SABERS BURN.
<AAH! WHAT ARE YOU DOING?>
PUTTING RIGHT A TERRIBLE MISTAKE.
NOW, REATH.
ACTIVATING, MASTER VITUS.
FFFZZZ

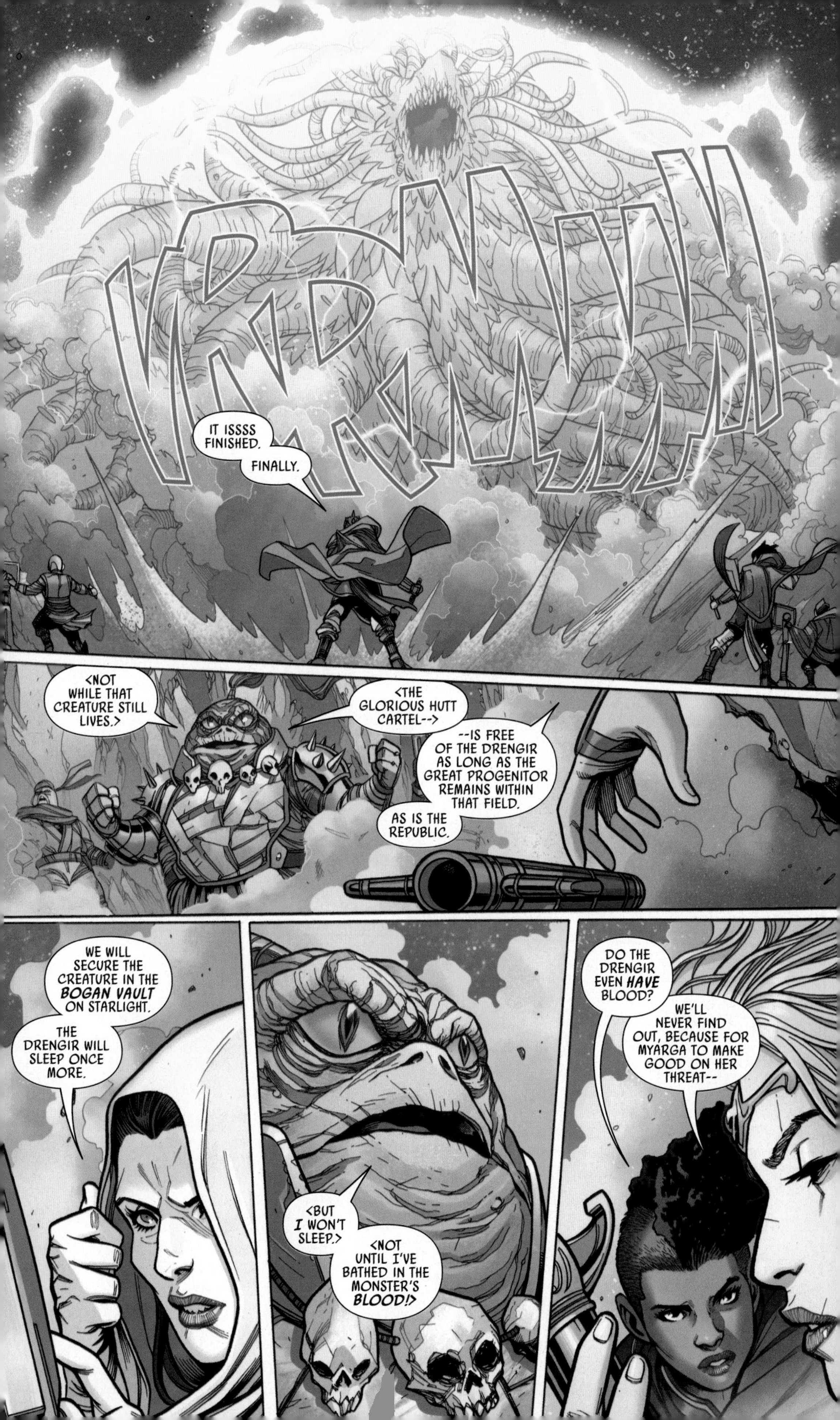
VRRMMMM
IT ISSSS FINISHED.
FINALLY.
<NOT WHILE THAT CREATURE STILL LIVES.>
<THE GLORIOUS HUTT CARTEL-->
--IS FREE OF THE DRENGIR AS LONG AS THE GREAT PROGENITOR REMAINS WITHIN THAT FIELD.
AS IS THE REPUBLIC.
WE WILL SECURE THE CREATURE IN THE BOGAN VAULT ON STARLIGHT.
THE DRENGIR WILL SLEEP ONCE MORE.
<BUT I WON'T SLEEP.>
<NOT UNTIL I'VE BATHED IN THE MONSTER'S BLOOD!>
DO THE DRENGIR EVEN HAVE BLOOD?
WE'LL NEVER FIND OUT, BECAUSE FOR MYARGA TO MAKE GOOD ON HER THREAT--

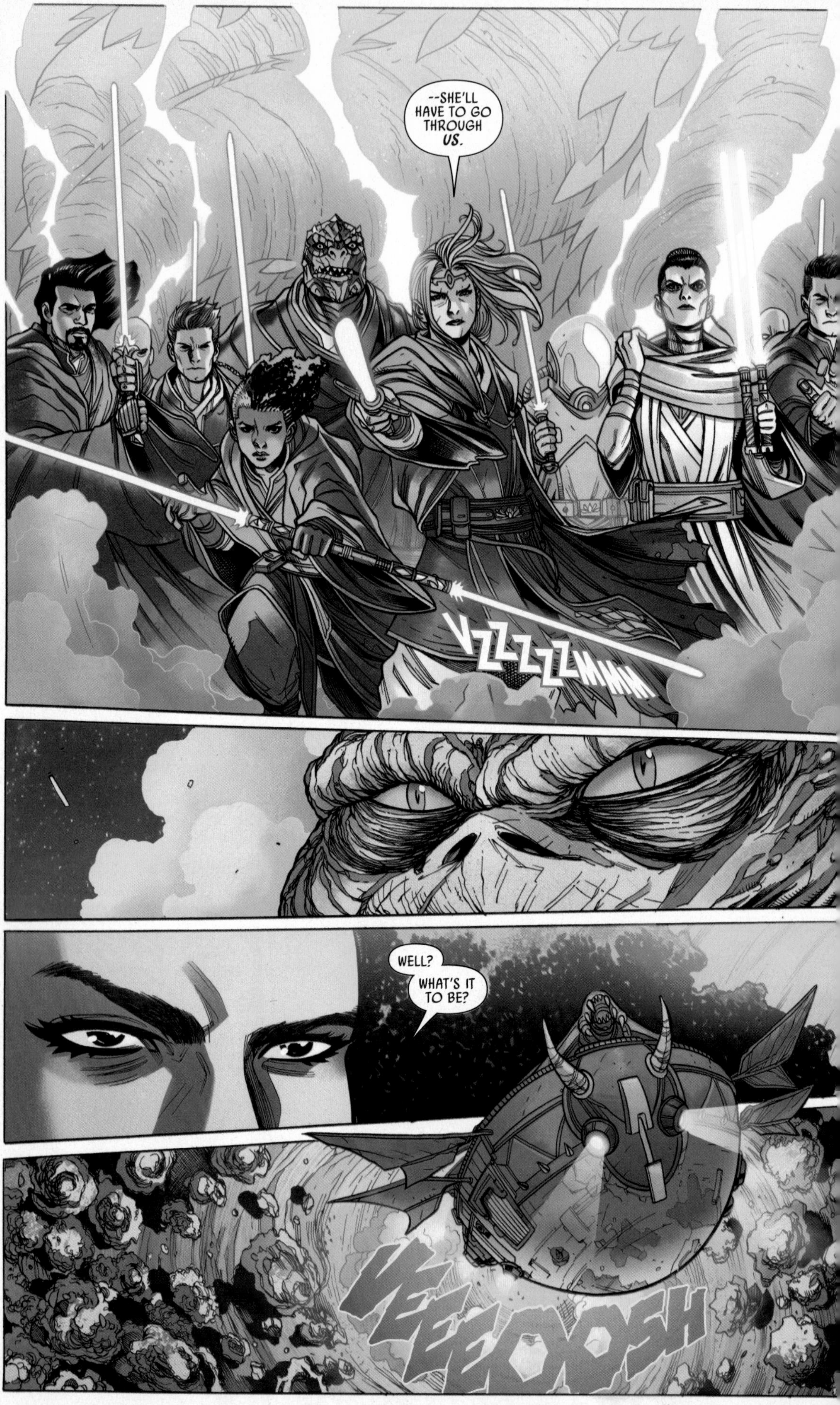
--SHE'LL HAVE TO GO THROUGH US.
VZZZZZZMMM
WELL?
WHAT'S IT TO BE?
VEEEOOSH

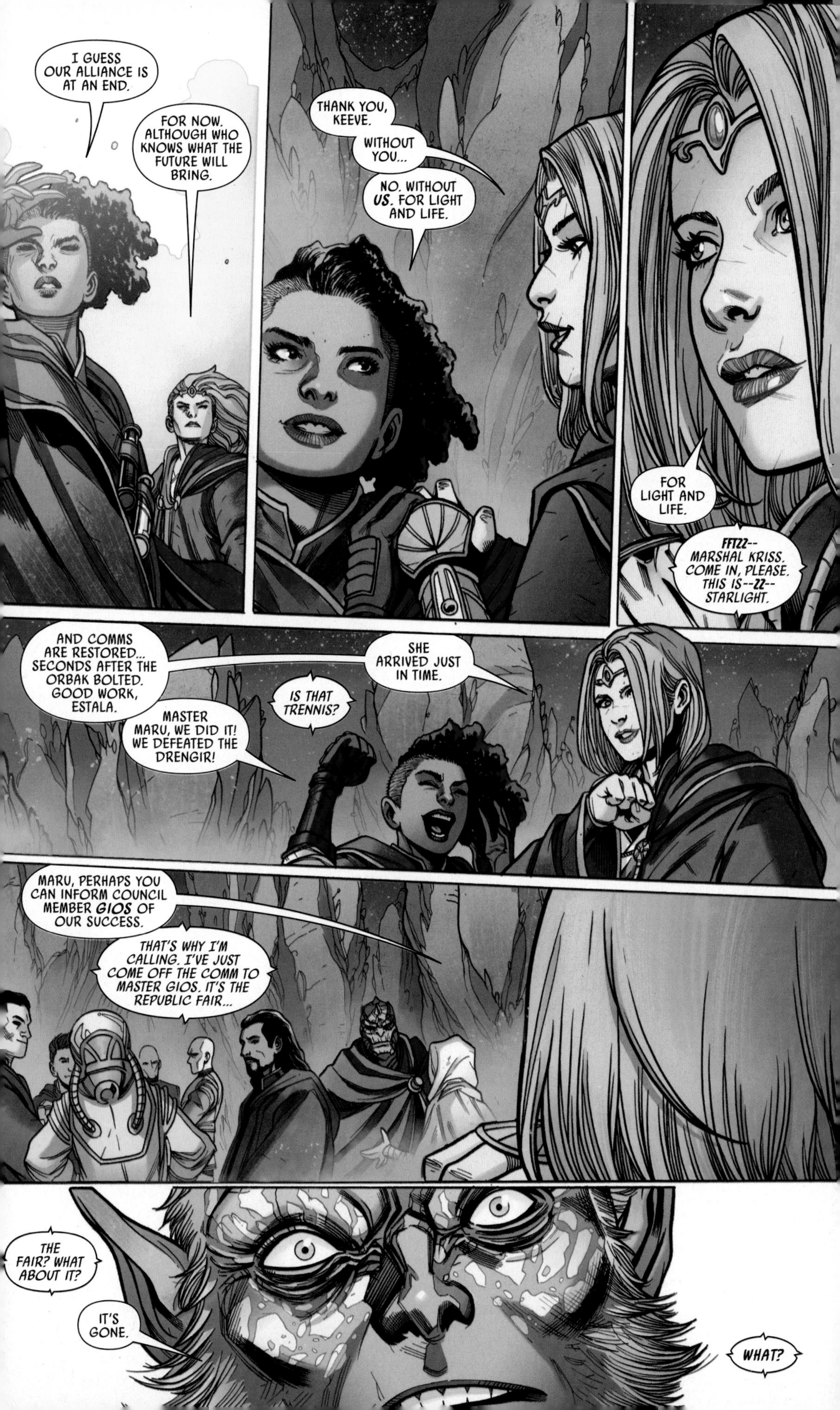
I GUESS OUR ALLIANCE IS AT AN END.
FOR NOW. ALTHOUGH WHO KNOWS WHAT THE FUTURE WILL BRING.
THANK YOU, KEEVE.
WITHOUT YOU...
NO. WITHOUT US. FOR LIGHT AND LIFE.
FOR LIGHT AND LIFE.
FFTZZ-- MARSHAL KRISS. COME IN, PLEASE. THIS IS--ZZ-- STARLIGHT.
AND COMMS ARE RESTORED... SECONDS AFTER THE ORBAK BOLTED. GOOD WORK, ESTALA.
MASTER MARU, WE DID IT! WE DEFEATED THE DRENGIR!
IS THAT TRENNIS?
SHE ARRIVED JUST IN TIME.
MARU, PERHAPS YOU CAN INFORM COUNCIL MEMBER GIOS OF OUR SUCCESS.
THAT'S WHY I'M CALLING. I'VE JUST COME OFF THE COMM TO MASTER GIOS. IT'S THE REPUBLIC FAIR...
THE FAIR? WHAT ABOUT IT?
IT'S GONE.
WHAT?

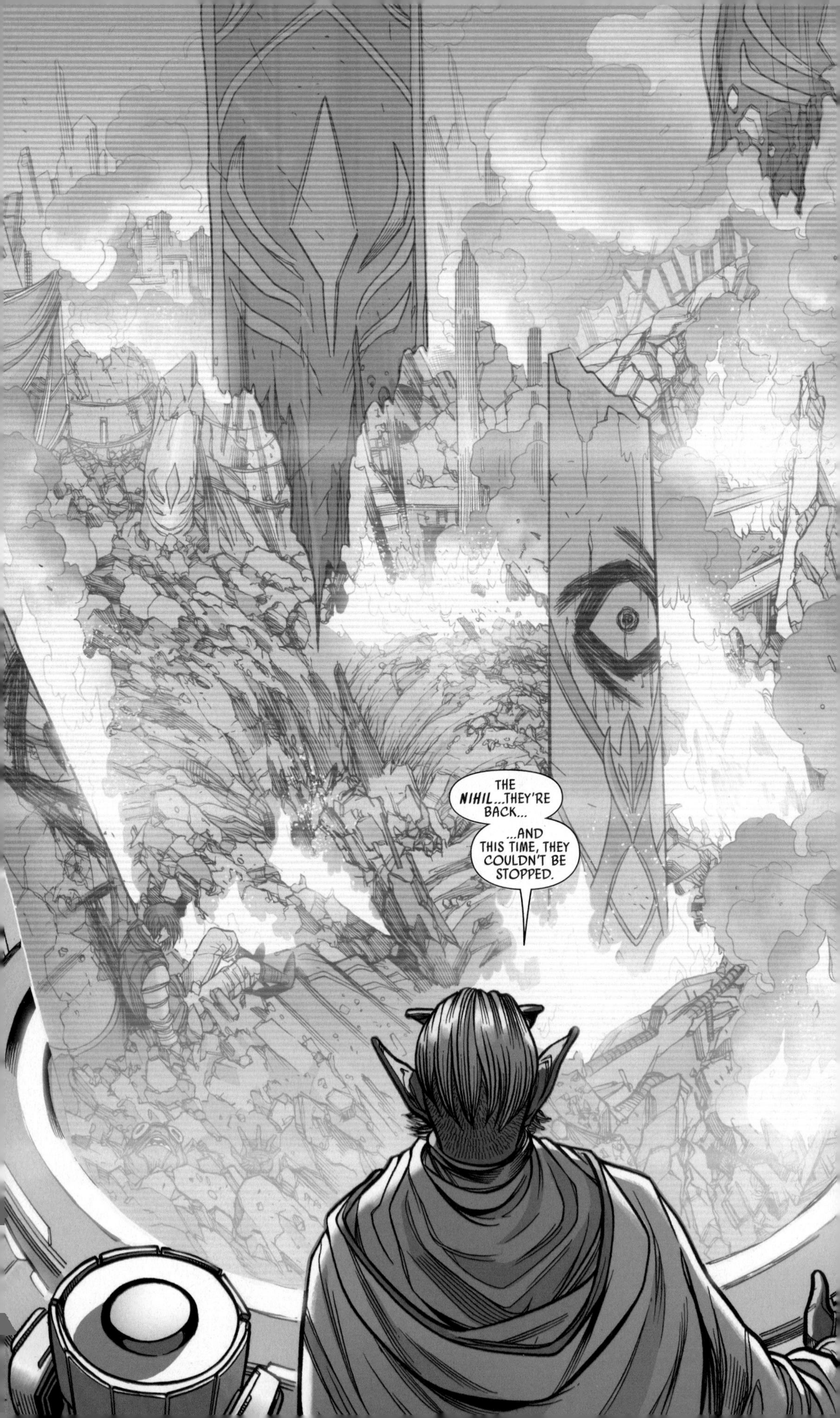
THE NIHIL...THEY'RE BACK...
...AND THIS TIME, THEY COULDN'T BE STOPPED.

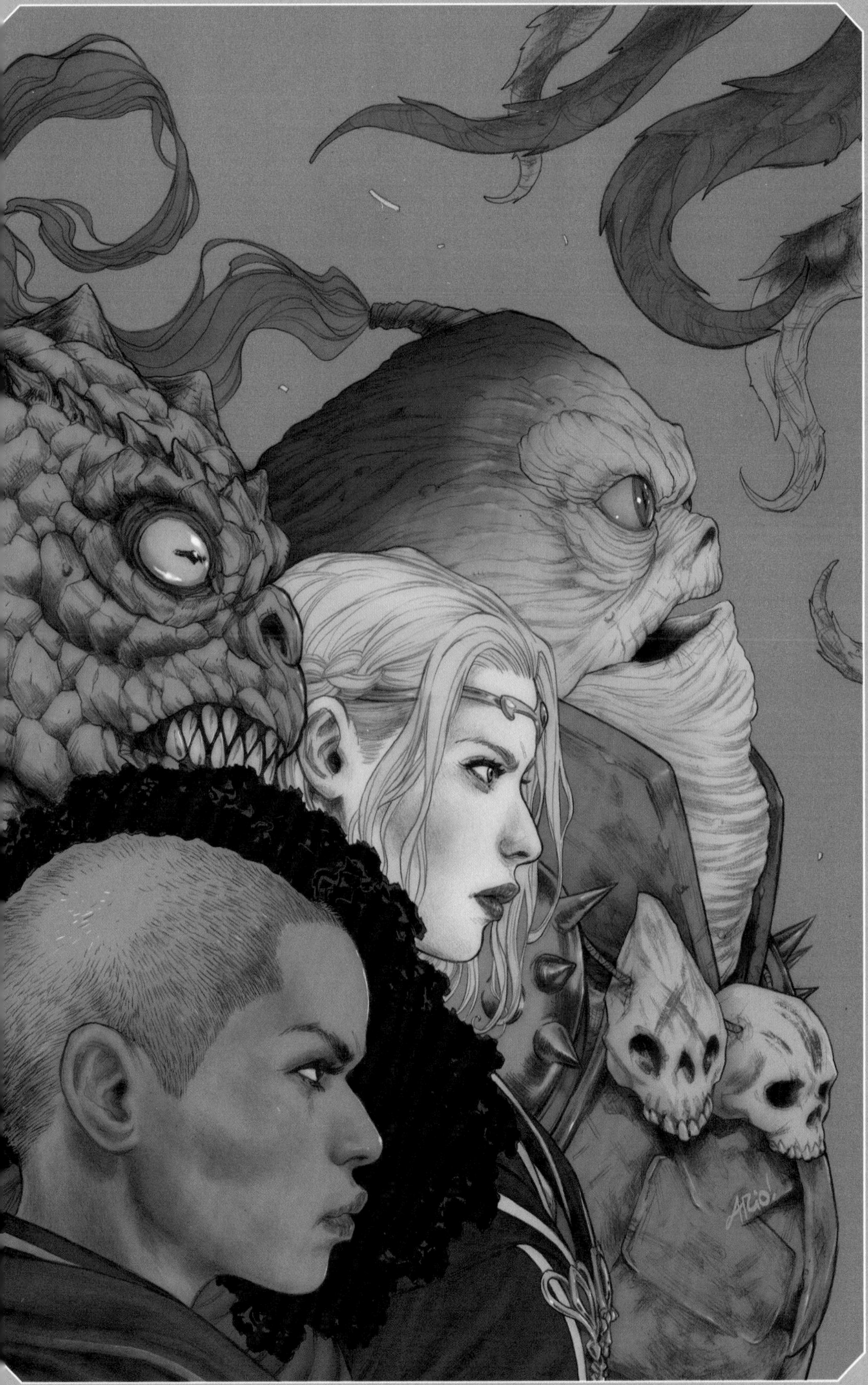

#8 Variant by
ARIO ANINDITO

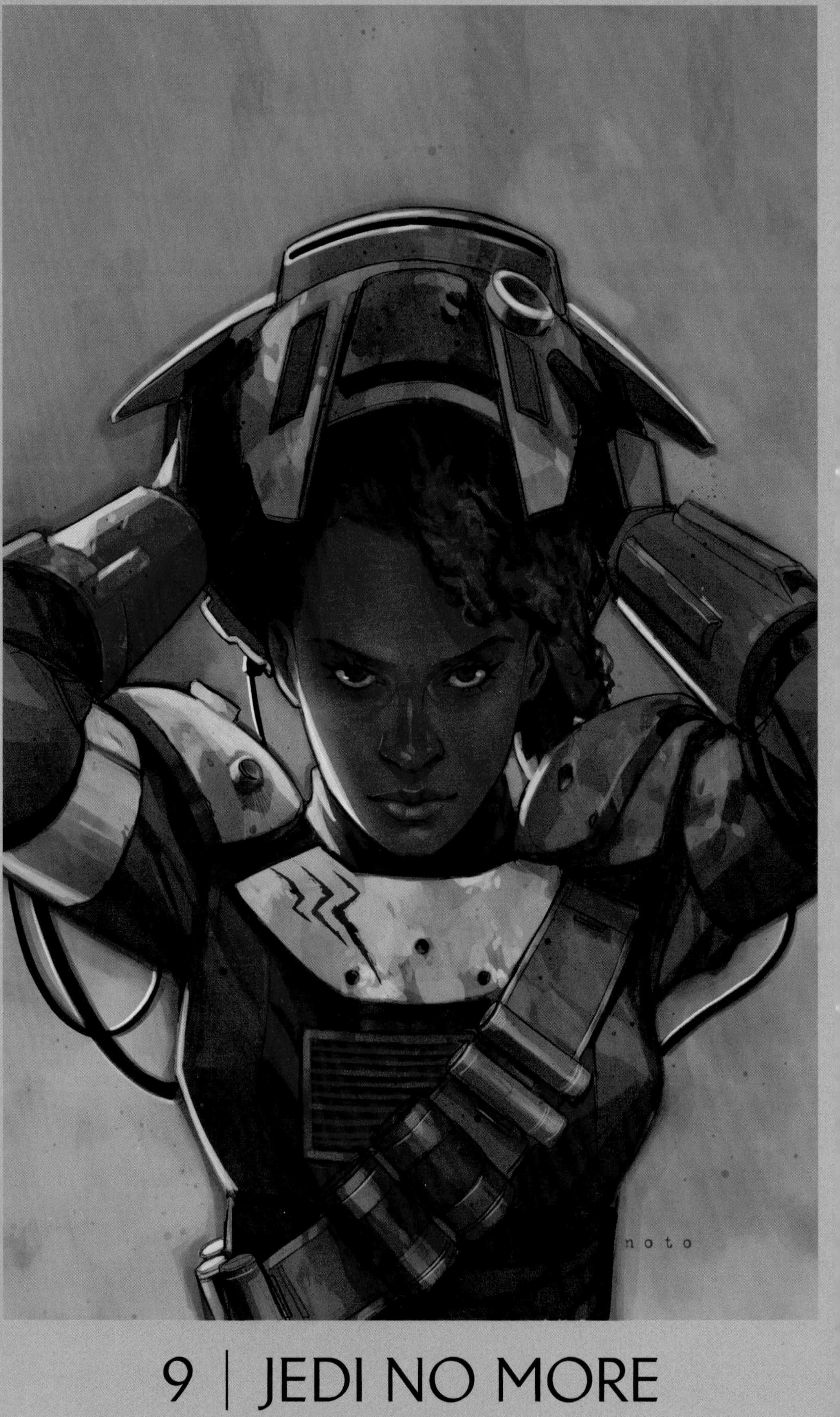
noto

9 | JEDI NO MORE

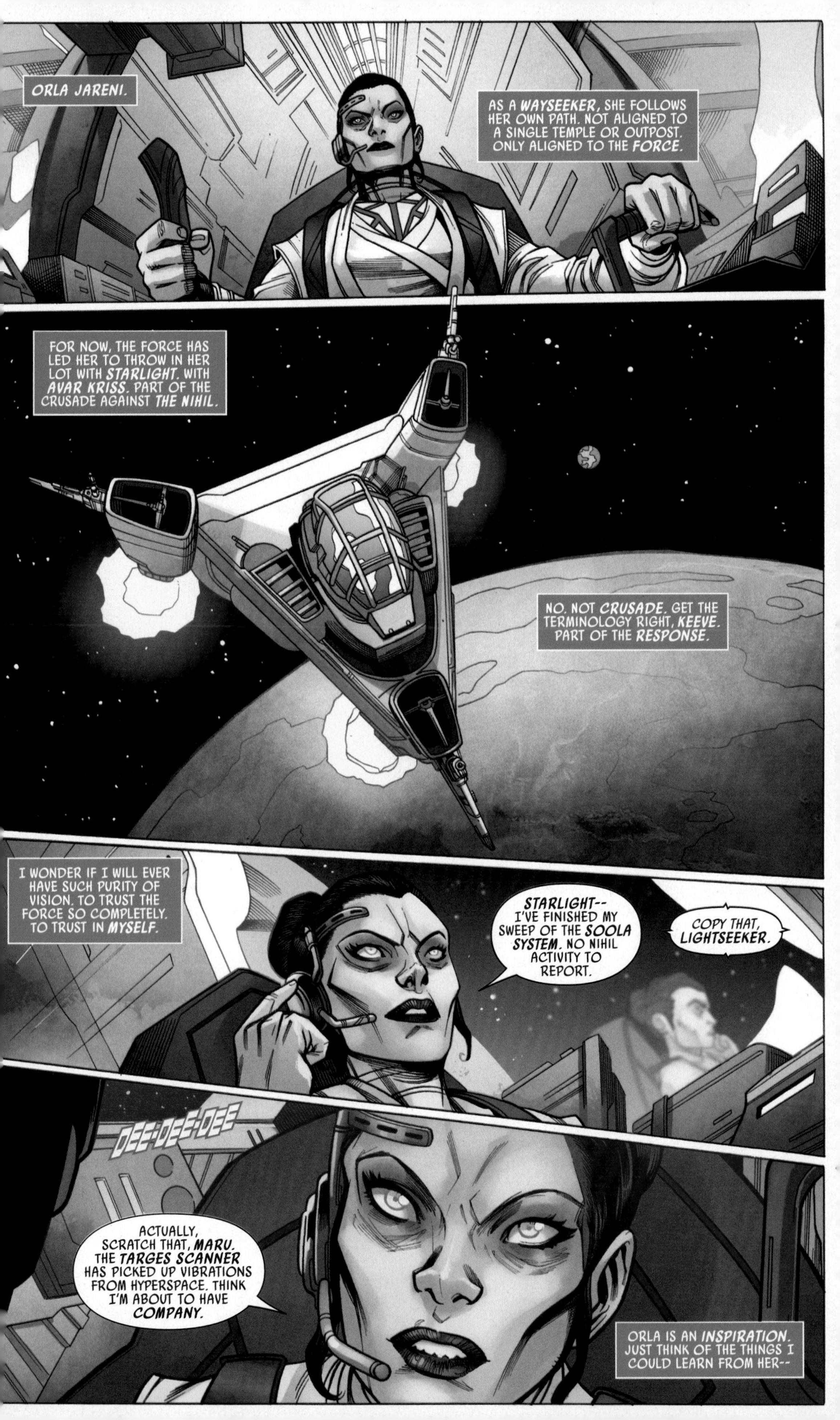
ORLA JARENI.
AS A WAYSEEKER, SHE FOLLOWS HER OWN PATH. NOT ALIGNED TO A SINGLE TEMPLE OR OUTPOST. ONLY ALIGNED TO THE FORCE.
FOR NOW, THE FORCE HAS LED HER TO THROW IN HER LOT WITH STARLIGHT. WITH AVAR KRISS. PART OF THE CRUSADE AGAINST THE NIHIL.
NO. NOT CRUSADE. GET THE TERMINOLOGY RIGHT, KEEVE. PART OF THE RESPONSE.
I WONDER IF I WILL EVER HAVE SUCH PURITY OF VISION. TO TRUST THE FORCE SO COMPLETELY. TO TRUST IN MYSELF.
STARLIGHT-- I'VE FINISHED MY SWEEP OF THE SOOLA SYSTEM. NO NIHIL ACTIVITY TO REPORT.
COPY THAT, LIGHTSEEKER.
DEE-DEE-DEE
ACTUALLY, SCRATCH THAT, MARU. THE TARGES SCANNER HAS PICKED UP VIBRATIONS FROM HYPERSPACE. THINK I'M ABOUT TO HAVE COMPANY.
ORLA IS AN INSPIRATION. JUST THINK OF THE THINGS I COULD LEARN FROM HER--

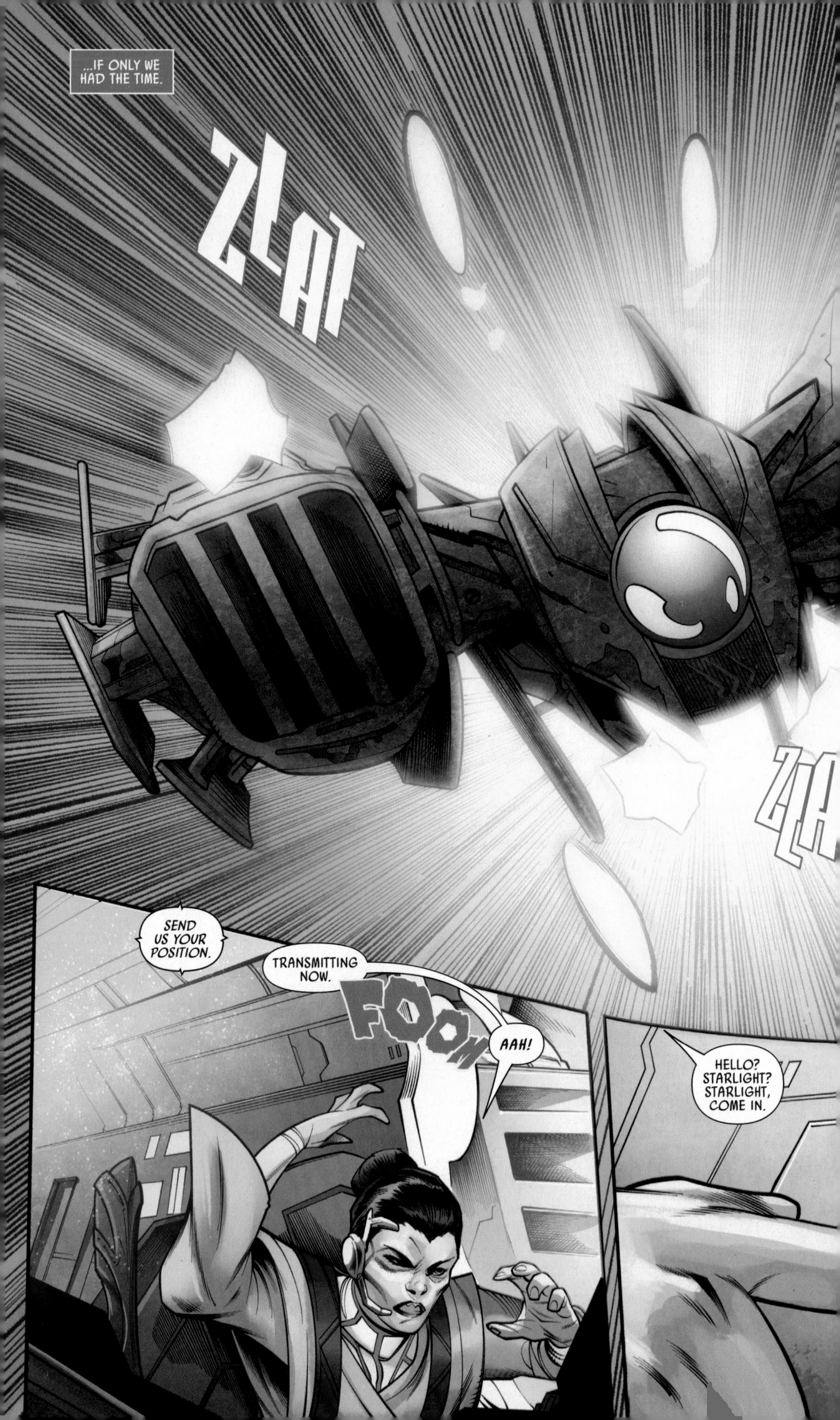

...IF ONLY WE HAD THE TIME.
ZZAT
ZZAT
SEND US YOUR POSITION.
TRANSMITTING NOW.
FOOM
AAH!
HELLO? STARLIGHT? STARLIGHT, COME IN.

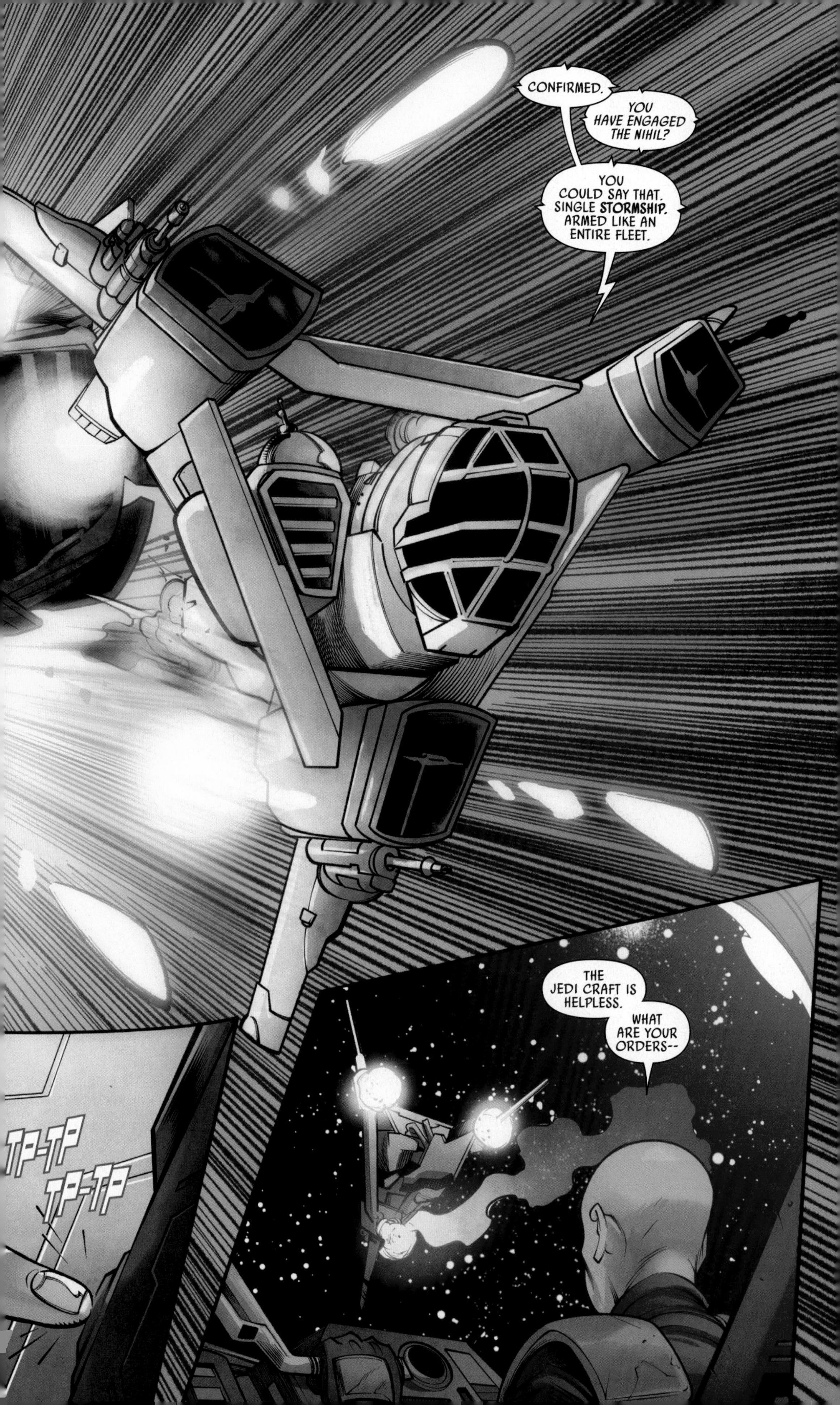
CONFIRMED.
YOU HAVE ENGAGED THE NIHIL?
YOU COULD SAY THAT. SINGLE STORMSHIP. ARMED LIKE AN ENTIRE FLEET.
THE JEDI CRAFT IS HELPLESS.
WHAT ARE YOUR ORDERS--
TP-TP
TP-TP

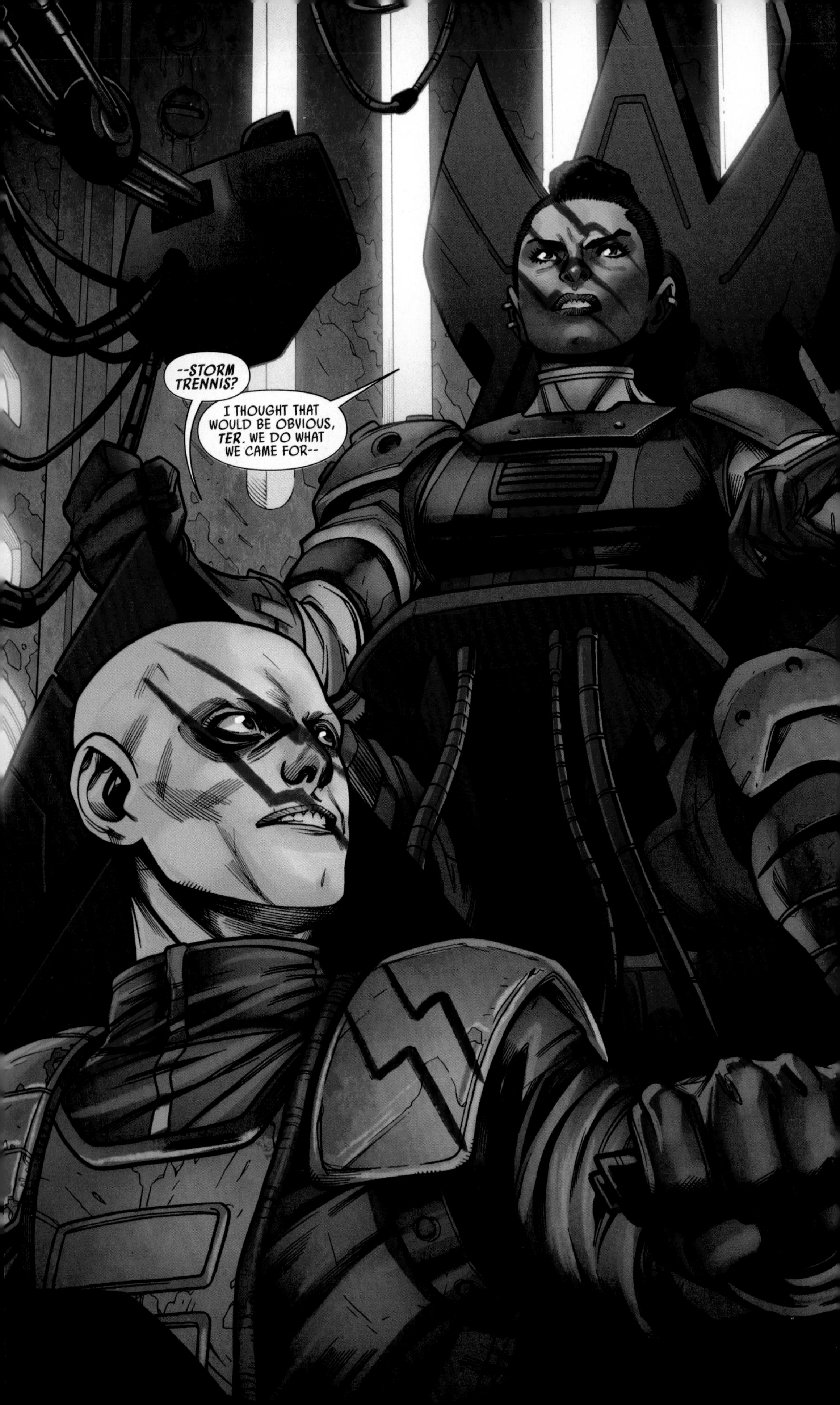
--STORM TRENNIS?
I THOUGHT THAT WOULD BE OBVIOUS, TER. WE DO WHAT WE CAME FOR--

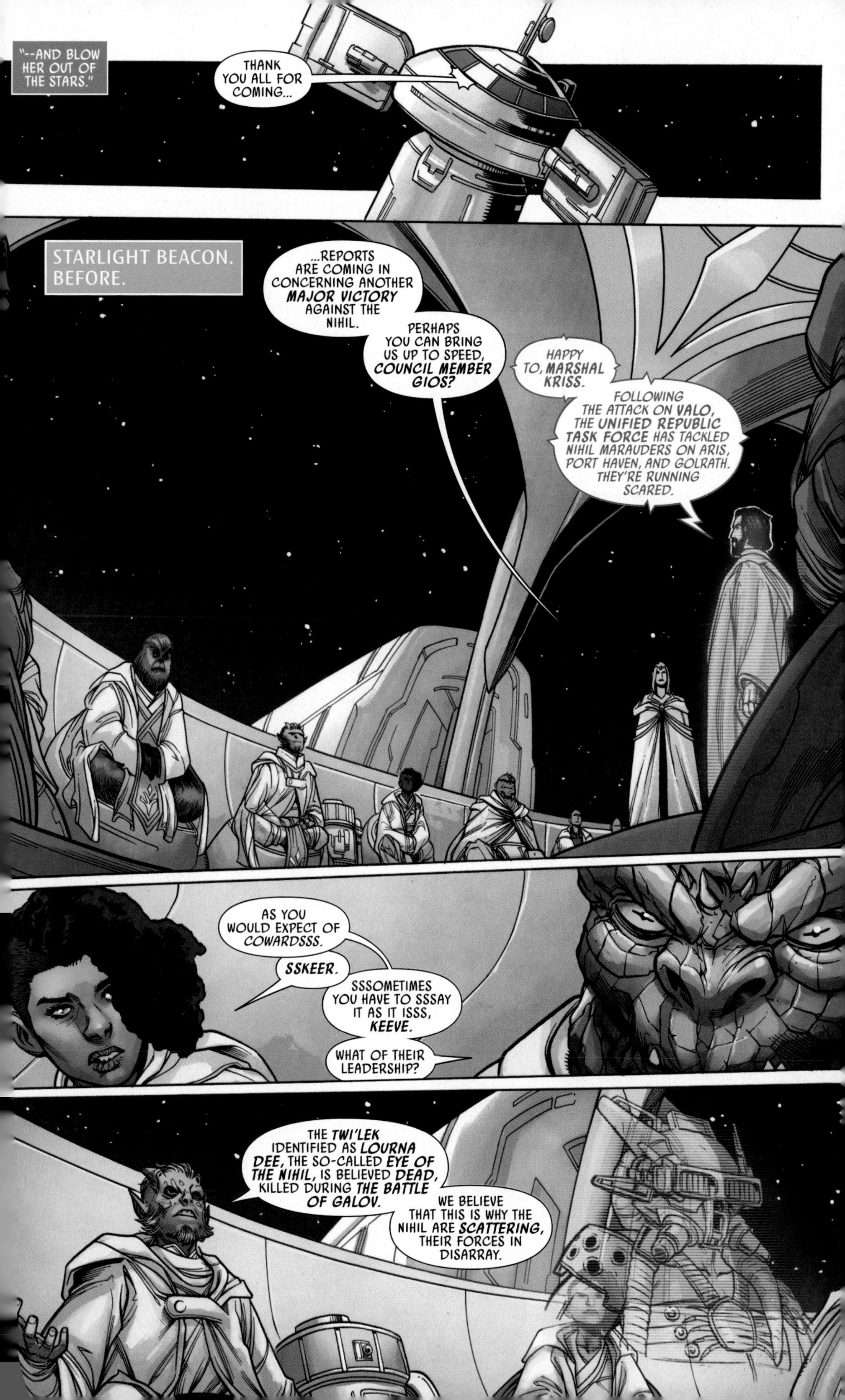
"--AND BLOW HER OUT OF THE STARS."
THANK YOU ALL FOR COMING...
STARLIGHT BEACON. BEFORE.
...REPORTS ARE COMING IN CONCERNING ANOTHER MAJOR VICTORY AGAINST THE NIHIL.
PERHAPS YOU CAN BRING US UP TO SPEED, COUNCIL MEMBER GIOS?
HAPPY TO, MARSHAL KRISS.
FOLLOWING THE ATTACK ON VALO, THE UNIFIED REPUBLIC TASK FORCE HAS TACKLED NIHIL MARAUDERS ON ARIS, PORT HAVEN, AND GOLRATH. THEY'RE RUNNING SCARED.
AS YOU WOULD EXPECT OF COWARDSSS.
SSKEER.
SSSOMETIMES YOU HAVE TO SSSAY IT AS IT ISSS, KEEVE.
WHAT OF THEIR LEADERSHIP?
THE TWI'LEK IDENTIFIED AS LOURNA DEE, THE SO-CALLED EYE OF THE NIHIL, IS BELIEVED DEAD, KILLED DURING THE BATTLE OF GALOV.
WE BELIEVE THAT THIS IS WHY THE NIHIL ARE SCATTERING, THEIR FORCES IN DISARRAY.

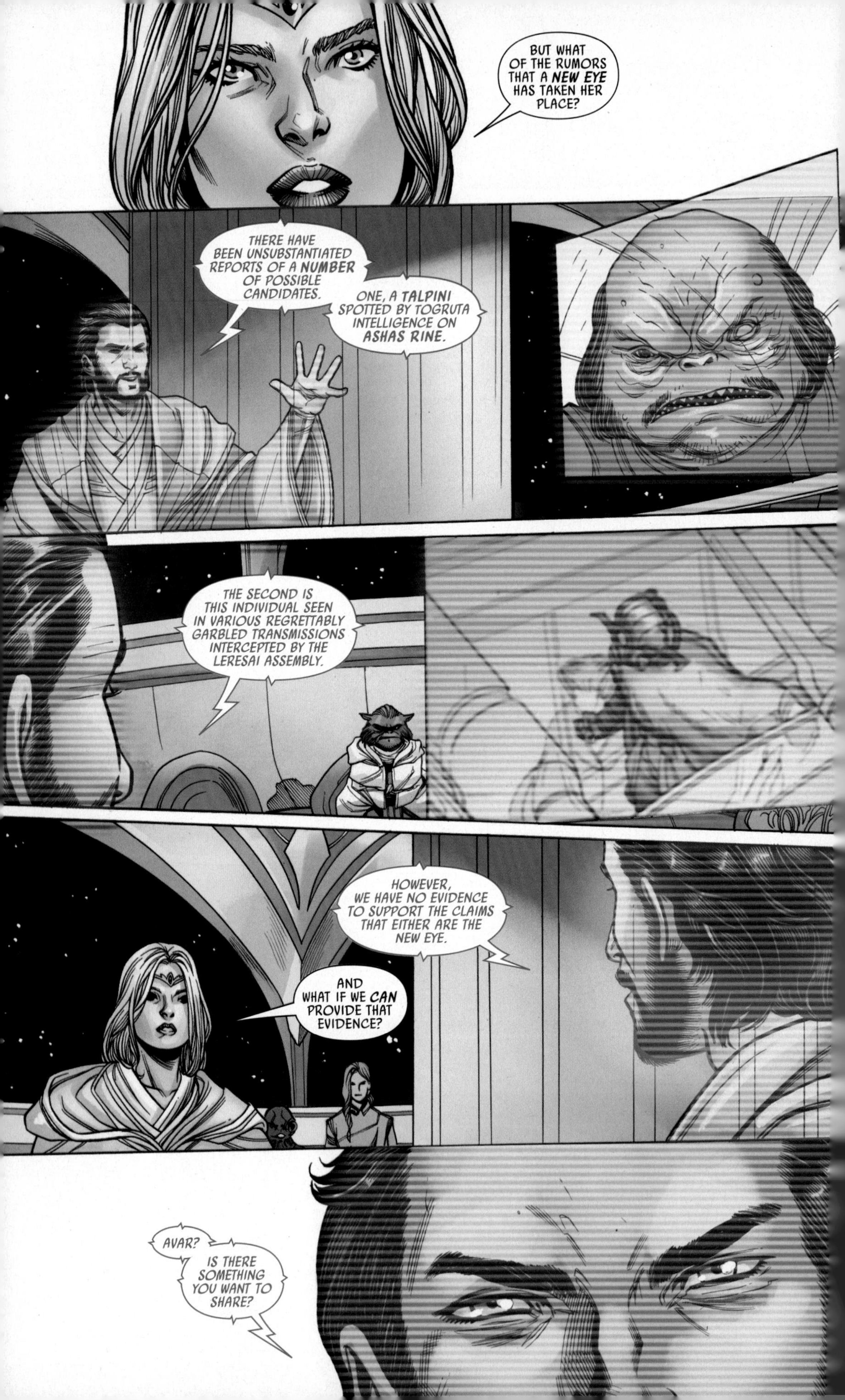
BUT WHAT OF THE RUMORS THAT A NEW EYE HAS TAKEN HER PLACE?
THERE HAVE BEEN UNSUBSTANTIATED REPORTS OF A NUMBER OF POSSIBLE CANDIDATES.
ONE, A TALPINI SPOTTED BY TOGRUTA INTELLIGENCE ON ASHAS RINE.
THE SECOND IS THIS INDIVIDUAL SEEN IN VARIOUS REGRETTABLY GARBLED TRANSMISSIONS INTERCEPTED BY THE LERESAI ASSEMBLY.
HOWEVER, WE HAVE NO EVIDENCE TO SUPPORT THE CLAIMS THAT EITHER ARE THE NEW EYE.
AND WHAT IF WE CAN PROVIDE THAT EVIDENCE?
AVAR?
IS THERE SOMETHING YOU WANT TO SHARE?

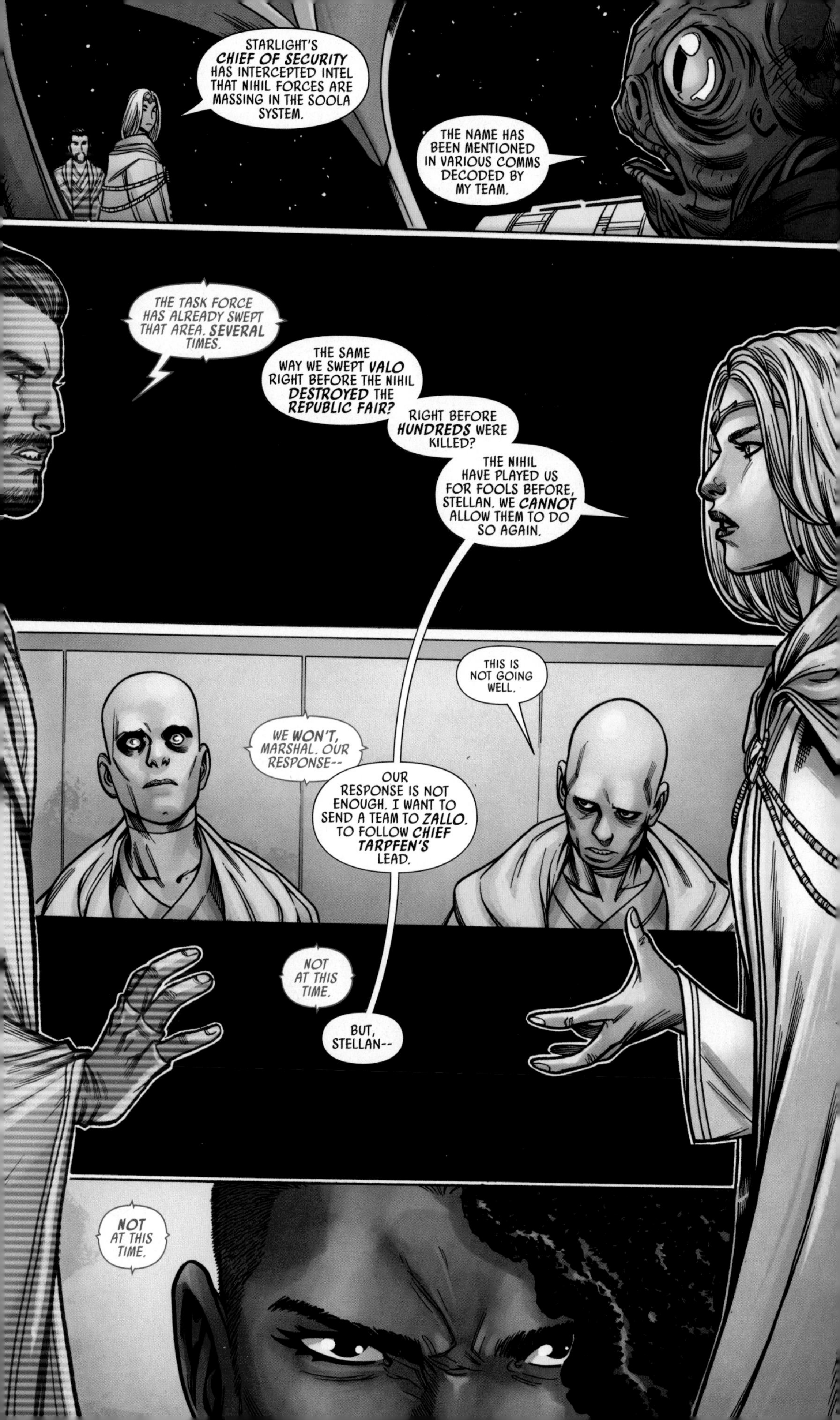
STARLIGHT'S CHIEF OF SECURITY HAS INTERCEPTED INTEL THAT NIHIL FORCES ARE MASSING IN THE SOOLA SYSTEM.
THE NAME HAS BEEN MENTIONED IN VARIOUS COMMS DECODED BY MY TEAM.
THE TASK FORCE HAS ALREADY SWEPT THAT AREA. SEVERAL TIMES.
THE SAME WAY WE SWEPT VALO RIGHT BEFORE THE NIHIL DESTROYED THE REPUBLIC FAIR?
RIGHT BEFORE HUNDREDS WERE KILLED?
THE NIHIL HAVE PLAYED US FOR FOOLS BEFORE, STELLAN. WE CANNOT ALLOW THEM TO DO SO AGAIN.
THIS IS NOT GOING WELL.
WE WON'T, MARSHAL. OUR RESPONSE--
OUR RESPONSE IS NOT ENOUGH. I WANT TO SEND A TEAM TO ZALLO. TO FOLLOW CHIEF TARPFEN'S LEAD.
NOT AT THIS TIME.
BUT, STELLAN--
NOT AT THIS TIME.

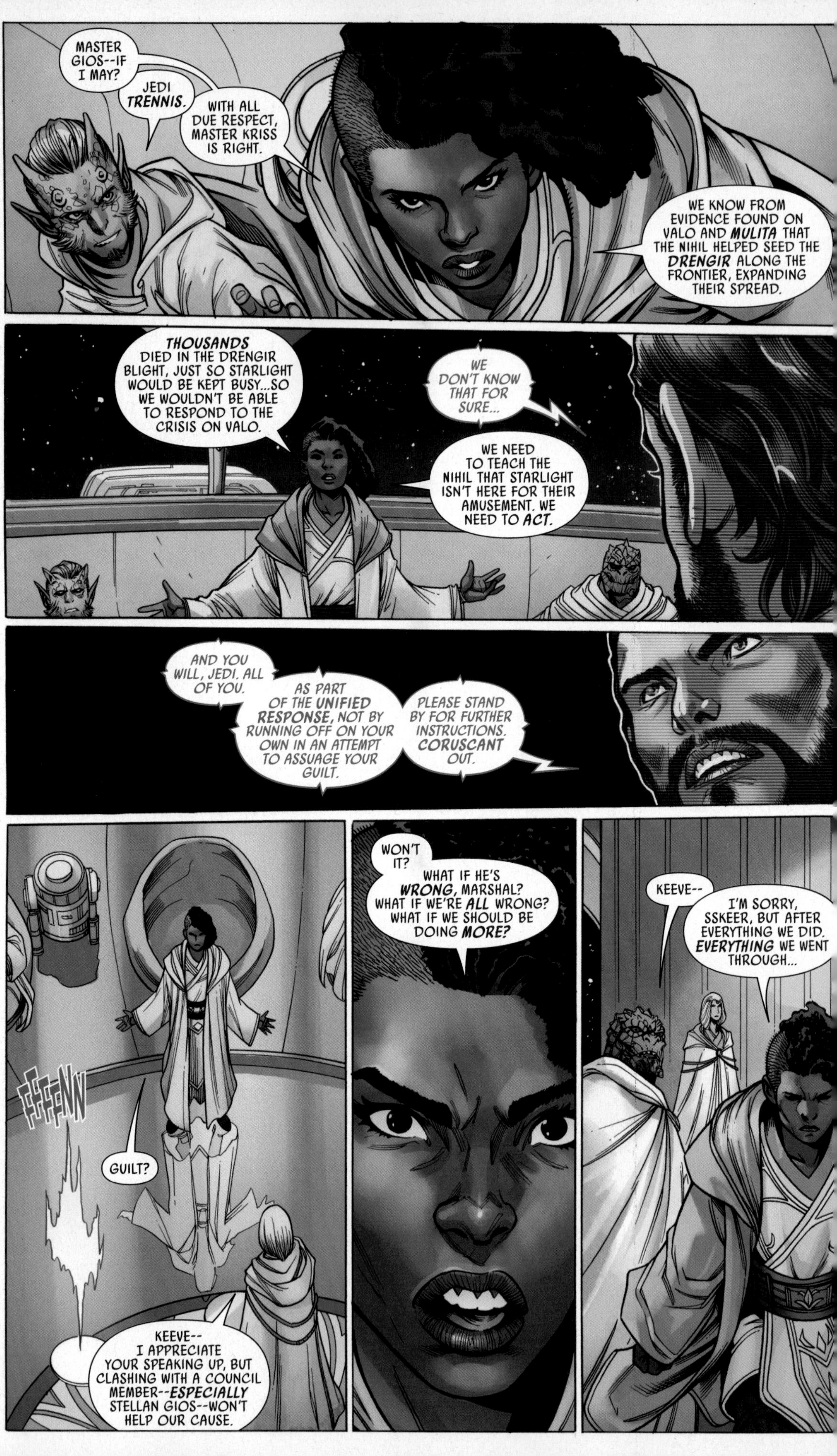
MASTER GIOS--IF I MAY?
JEDI TRENNIS.
WITH ALL DUE RESPECT, MASTER KRISS IS RIGHT.
WE KNOW FROM EVIDENCE FOUND ON VALO AND MULITA THAT THE NIHIL HELPED SEED THE DRENGIR ALONG THE FRONTIER, EXPANDING THEIR SPREAD.
THOUSANDS DIED IN THE DRENGIR BLIGHT, JUST SO STARLIGHT WOULD BE KEPT BUSY...SO WE WOULDN'T BE ABLE TO RESPOND TO THE CRISIS ON VALO.
WE DON'T KNOW THAT FOR SURE...
WE NEED TO TEACH THE NIHIL THAT STARLIGHT ISN'T HERE FOR THEIR AMUSEMENT. WE NEED TO ACT.
AND YOU WILL, JEDI. ALL OF YOU.
AS PART OF THE UNIFIED RESPONSE, NOT BY RUNNING OFF ON YOUR OWN IN AN ATTEMPT TO ASSUAGE YOUR GUILT.
PLEASE STAND BY FOR FURTHER INSTRUCTIONS. CORUSCANT OUT.
FSSSNN
GUILT?
KEEVE-- I APPRECIATE YOUR SPEAKING UP, BUT CLASHING WITH A COUNCIL MEMBER--ESPECIALLY STELLAN GIOS--WON'T HELP OUR CAUSE.
WON'T IT?
WHAT IF HE'S WRONG, MARSHAL? WHAT IF WE'RE ALL WRONG? WHAT IF WE SHOULD BE DOING MORE?
KEEVE--
I'M SORRY, SSKEER, BUT AFTER EVERYTHING WE DID. EVERYTHING WE WENT THROUGH...

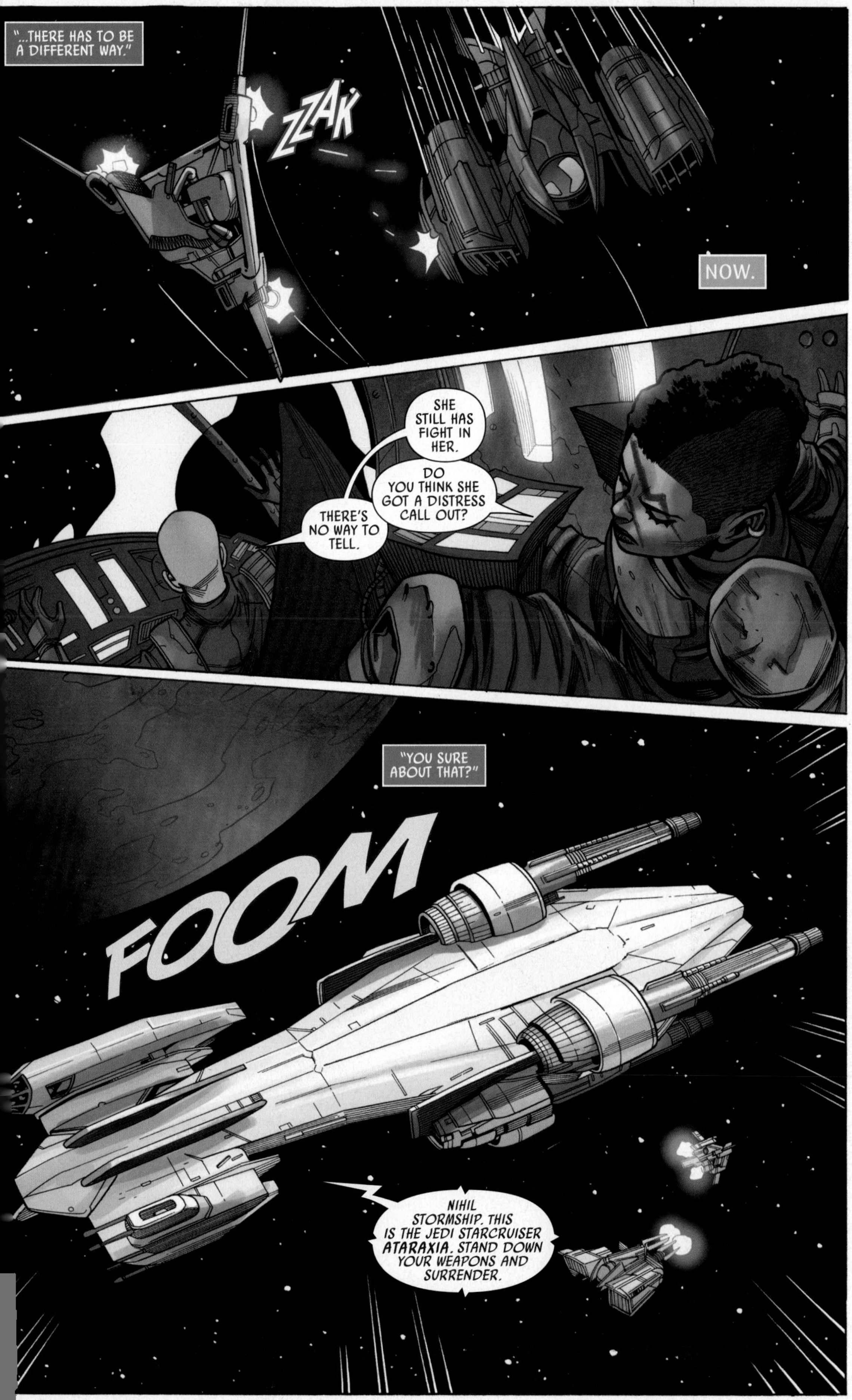
"...THERE HAS TO BE A DIFFERENT WAY."
ZZZAK
NOW.
SHE STILL HAS FIGHT IN HER.
DO YOU THINK SHE GOT A DISTRESS CALL OUT?
THERE'S NO WAY TO TELL.
"YOU SURE ABOUT THAT?"
FOOM
NIHIL STORMSHIP. THIS IS THE JEDI STARCRUISER ATARAXIA. STAND DOWN YOUR WEAPONS AND SURRENDER.

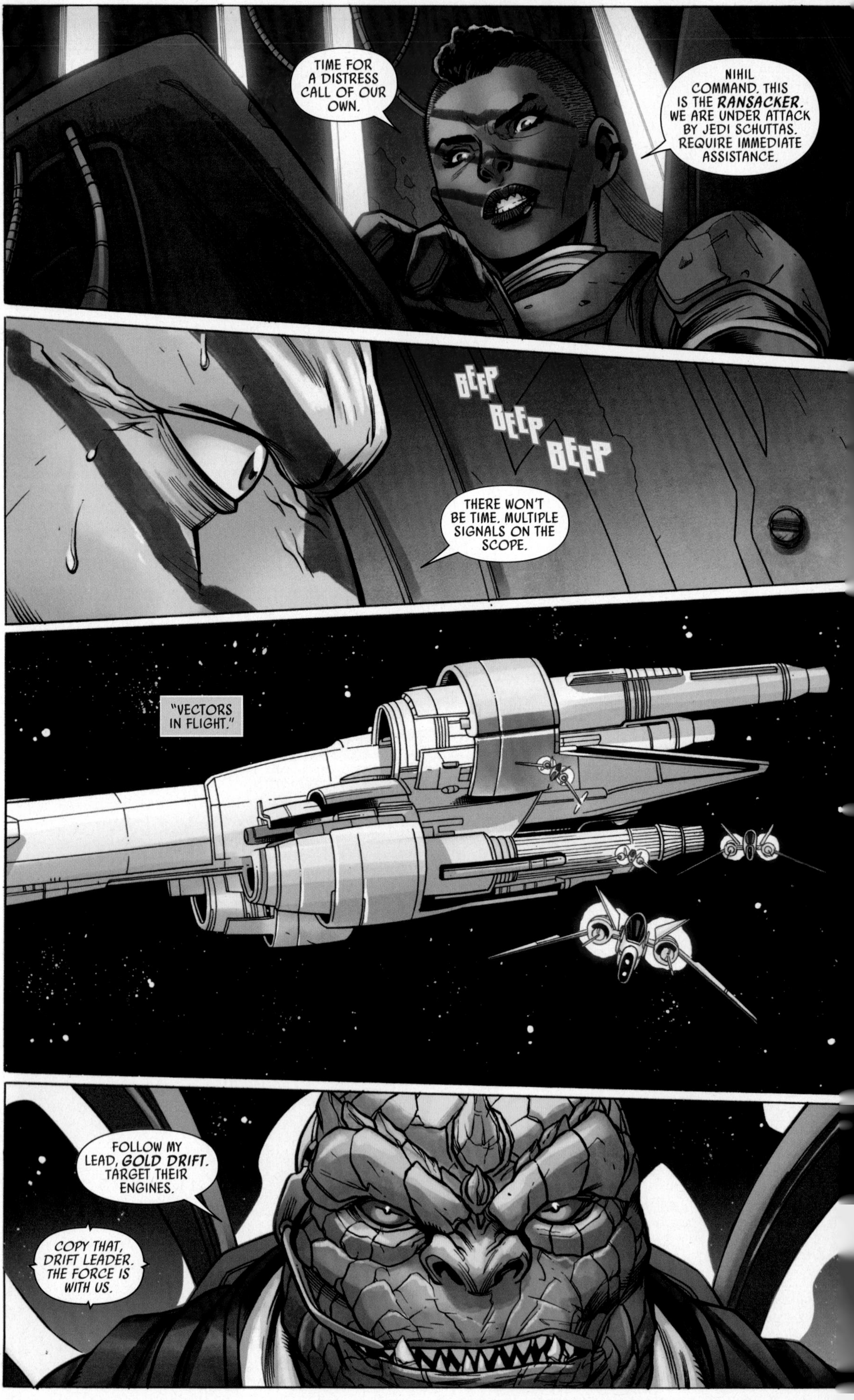
TIME FOR A DISTRESS CALL OF OUR OWN.
NIHIL COMMAND. THIS IS THE RANSACKER. WE ARE UNDER ATTACK BY JEDI SCHUTTAS. REQUIRE IMMEDIATE ASSISTANCE.
BEEP BEEP BEEP
THERE WON'T BE TIME. MULTIPLE SIGNALS ON THE SCOPE.
"VECTORS IN FLIGHT."
FOLLOW MY LEAD, GOLD DRIFT. TARGET THEIR ENGINES.
COPY THAT, DRIFT LEADER. THE FORCE IS WITH US.

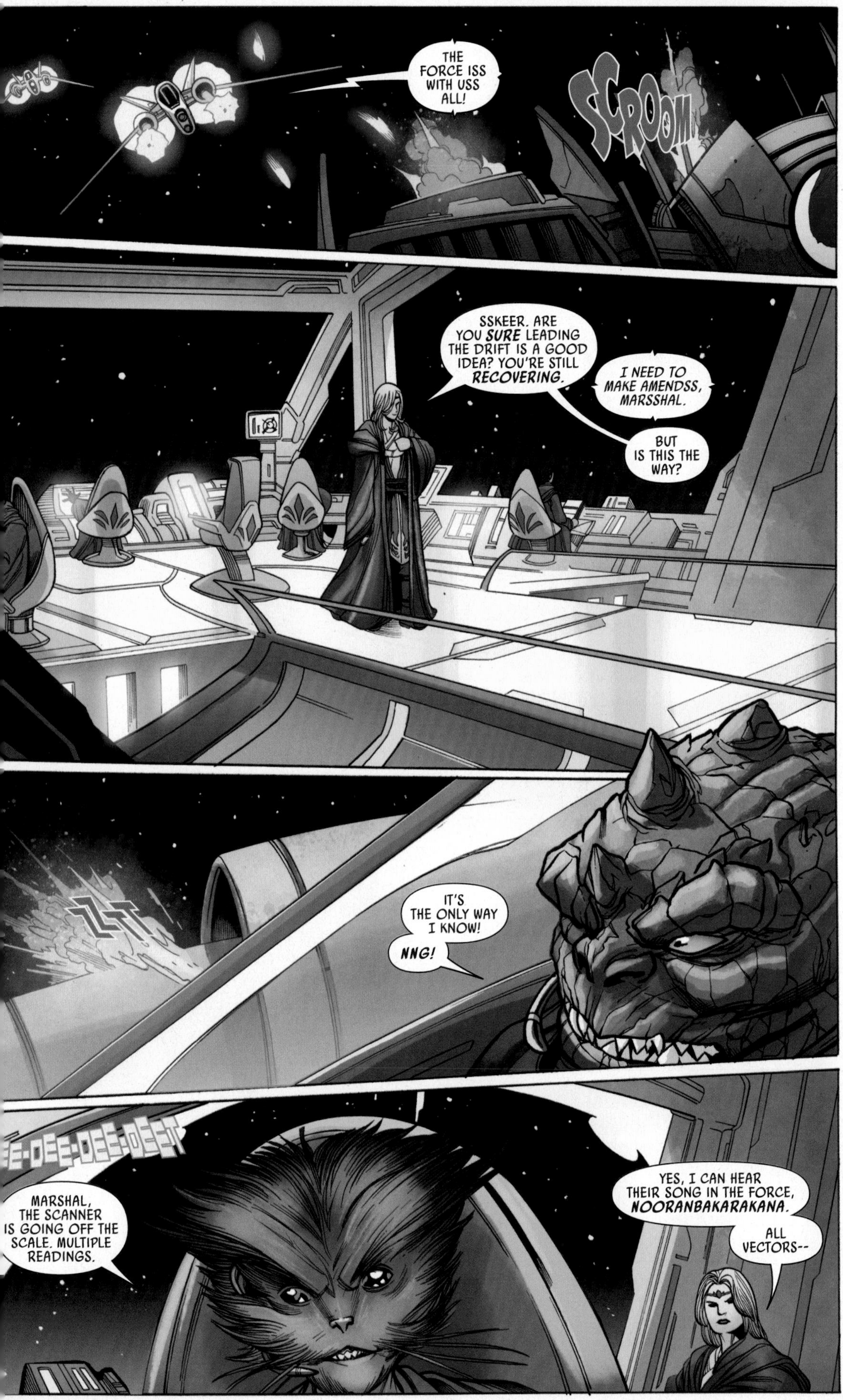
THE FORCE ISS WITH USS ALL!
SCROOM
SSKEER. ARE YOU SURE LEADING THE DRIFT IS A GOOD IDEA? YOU'RE STILL RECOVERING.
I NEED TO MAKE AMENDSS, MARSSHAL.
BUT IS THIS THE WAY?
ZZT
IT'S THE ONLY WAY I KNOW!
NNG!
EE-DEE-DEE-DEET
MARSHAL, THE SCANNER IS GOING OFF THE SCALE. MULTIPLE READINGS.
YES, I CAN HEAR THEIR SONG IN THE FORCE, NOORANBAKARAKANA.
ALL VECTORS--

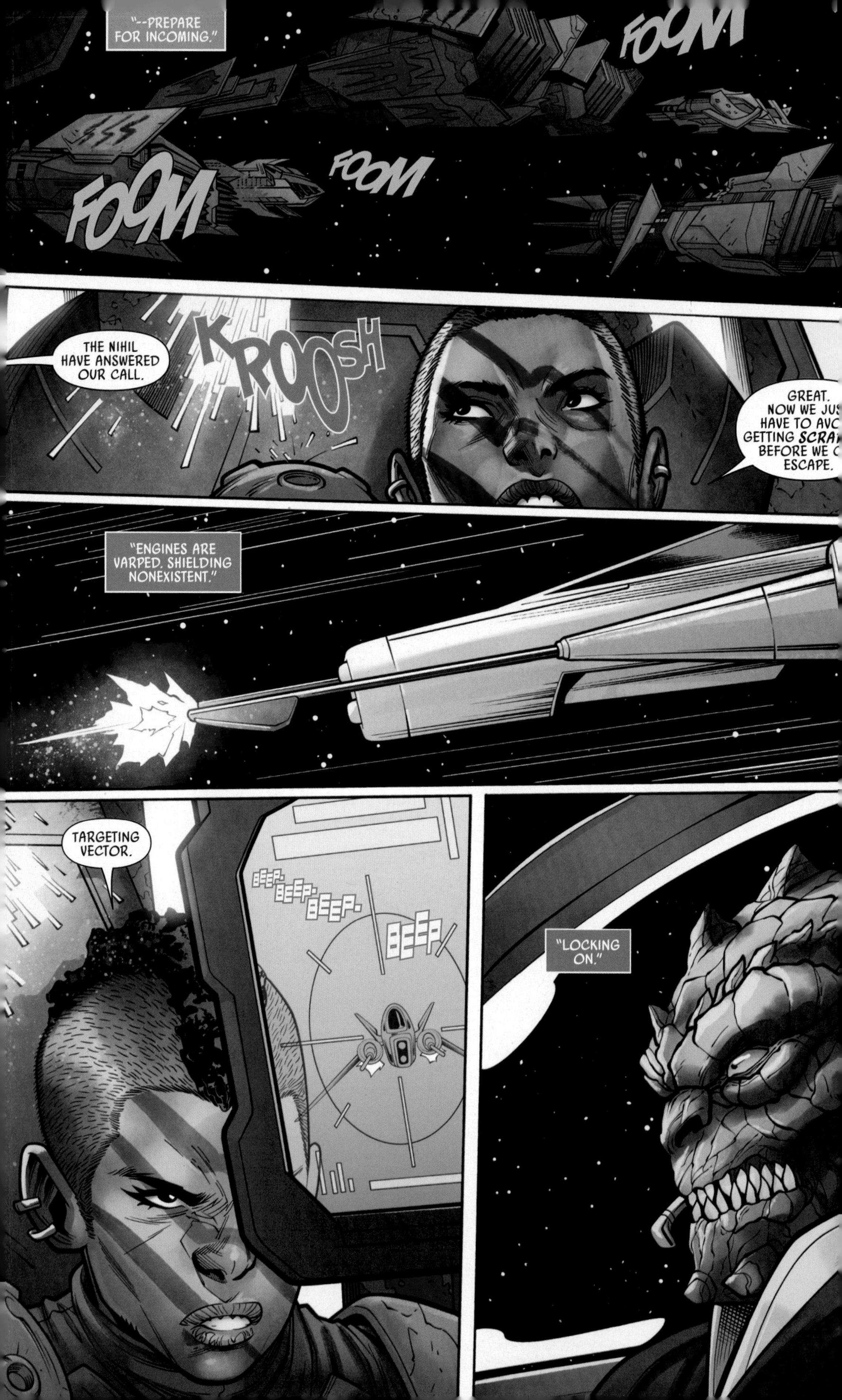
"--PREPARE FOR INCOMING."
FOOM
FOOM
FOOM
THE NIHIL HAVE ANSWERED OUR CALL.
KROOSH
GREAT. NOW WE JUS HAVE TO AVO GETTING SCRA BEFORE WE C ESCAPE.
"ENGINES ARE VARPED. SHIELDING NONEXISTENT."
TARGETING VECTOR.
BEEP- BEEP- BEEP-
BEEP
"LOCKING ON."

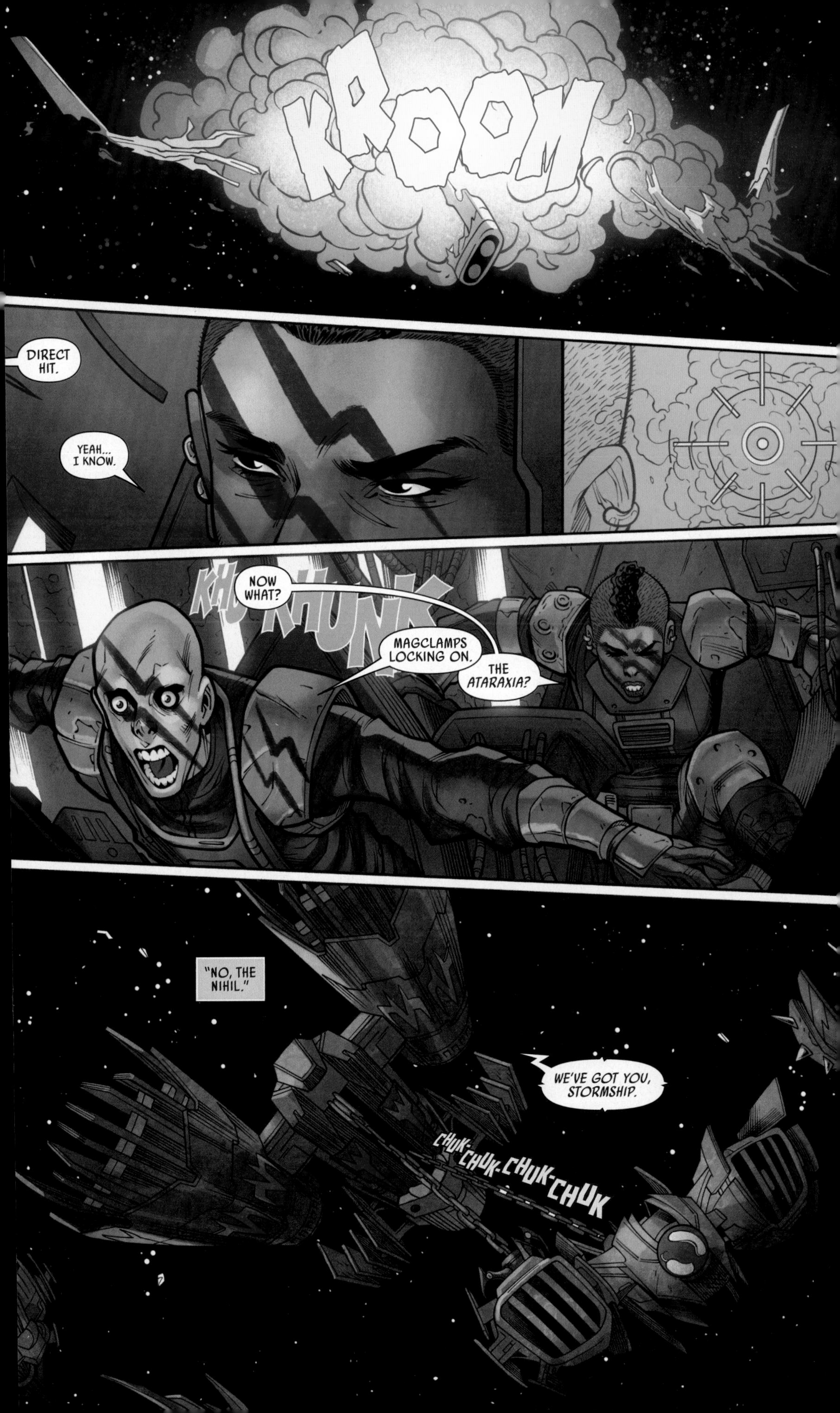
KROOM
DIRECT HIT.
YEAH... I KNOW.
KHUNK KHUNK
NOW WHAT?
MAGCLAMPS LOCKING ON.
THE ATARAXIA?
"NO, THE NIHIL."
WE'VE GOT YOU, STORMSHIP.
CHUK-CHUK-CHUK-CHUK

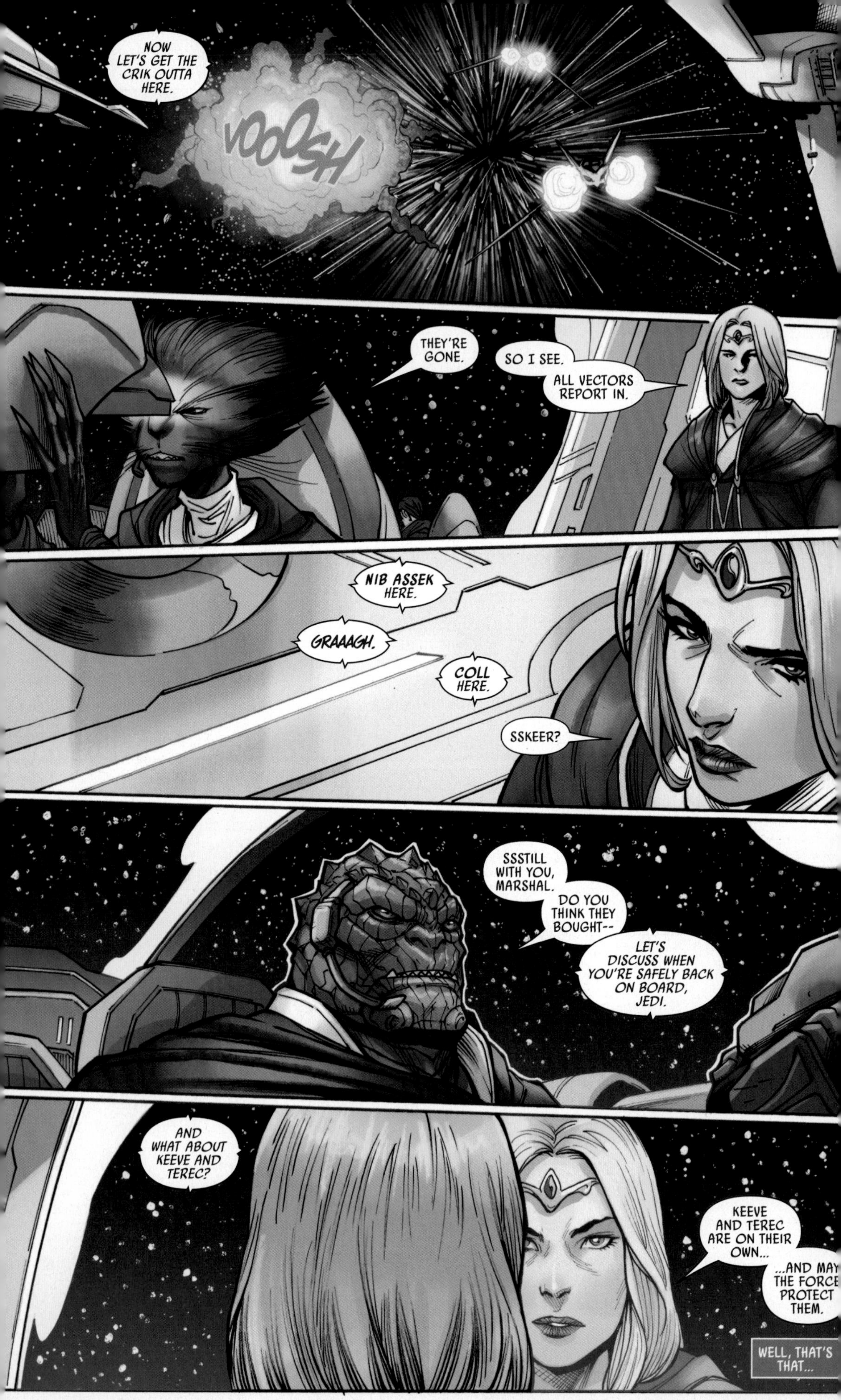

NOW LET'S GET THE CRIK OUTTA HERE.
VOOOSH
THEY'RE GONE.
SO I SEE.
ALL VECTORS REPORT IN.
NIB ASSEK HERE.
GRAAAGH.
COLL HERE.
SSKEER?
SSSTILL WITH YOU, MARSHAL.
DO YOU THINK THEY BOUGHT--
LET'S DISCUSS WHEN YOU'RE SAFELY BACK ON BOARD, JEDI.
AND WHAT ABOUT KEEVE AND TEREC?
KEEVE AND TEREC ARE ON THEIR OWN...
...AND MAY THE FORCE PROTECT THEM.
WELL, THAT'S THAT...

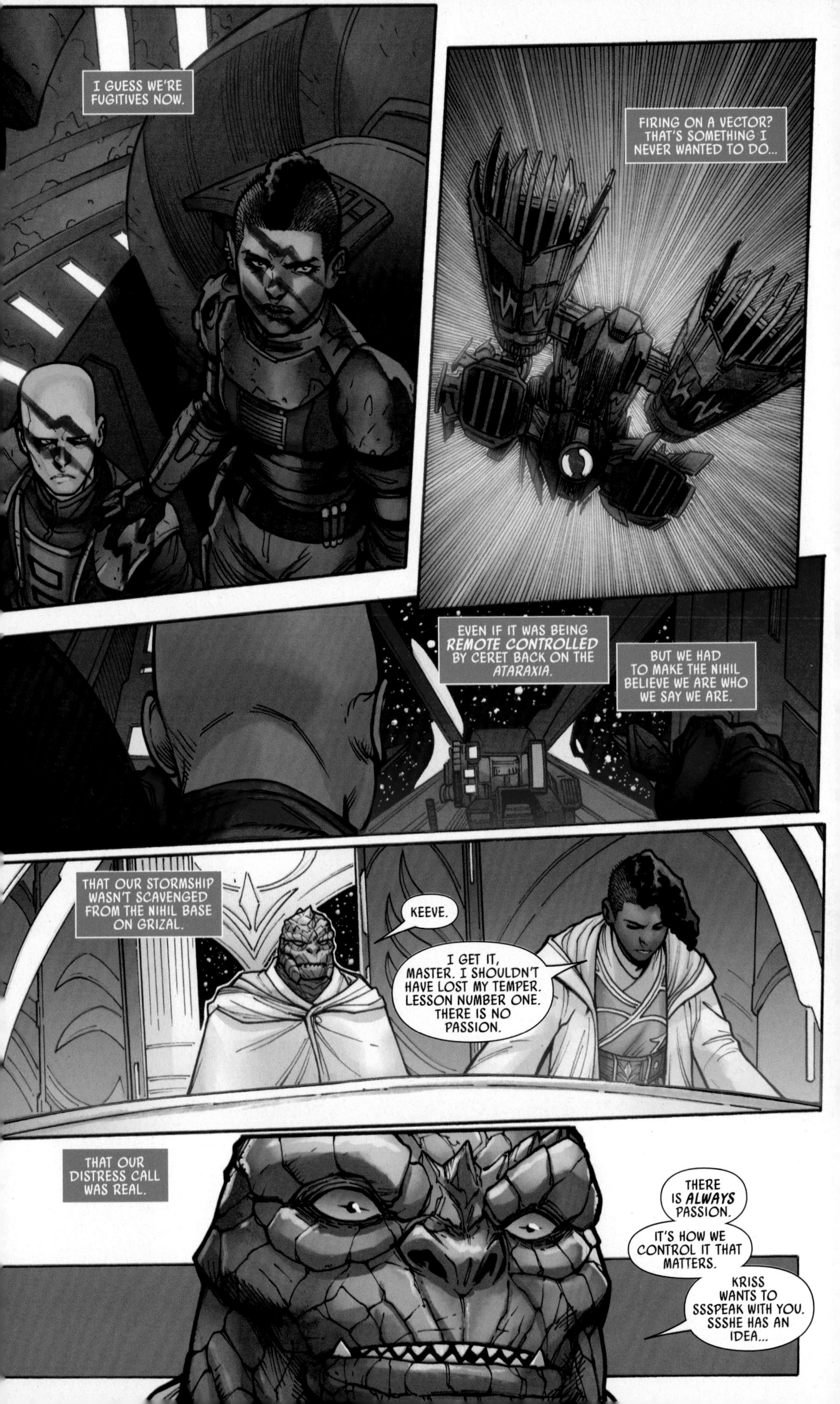
I GUESS WE'RE FUGITIVES NOW.
FIRING ON A VECTOR? THAT'S SOMETHING I NEVER WANTED TO DO...
EVEN IF IT WAS BEING *REMOTE CONTROLLED* BY CERET BACK ON THE *ATARAXIA*.
BUT WE HAD TO MAKE THE NIHIL BELIEVE WE ARE WHO WE SAY WE ARE.
THAT OUR STORMSHIP WASN'T SCAVENGED FROM THE NIHIL BASE ON GRIZAL.
KEEVE.
I GET IT, MASTER. I SHOULDN'T HAVE LOST MY TEMPER. LESSON NUMBER ONE. THERE IS NO PASSION.
THAT OUR DISTRESS CALL WAS REAL.
THERE IS *ALWAYS* PASSION.
IT'S HOW WE CONTROL IT THAT MATTERS.
KRISS WANTS TO SSSPEAK WITH YOU. SSSHE HAS AN IDEA...

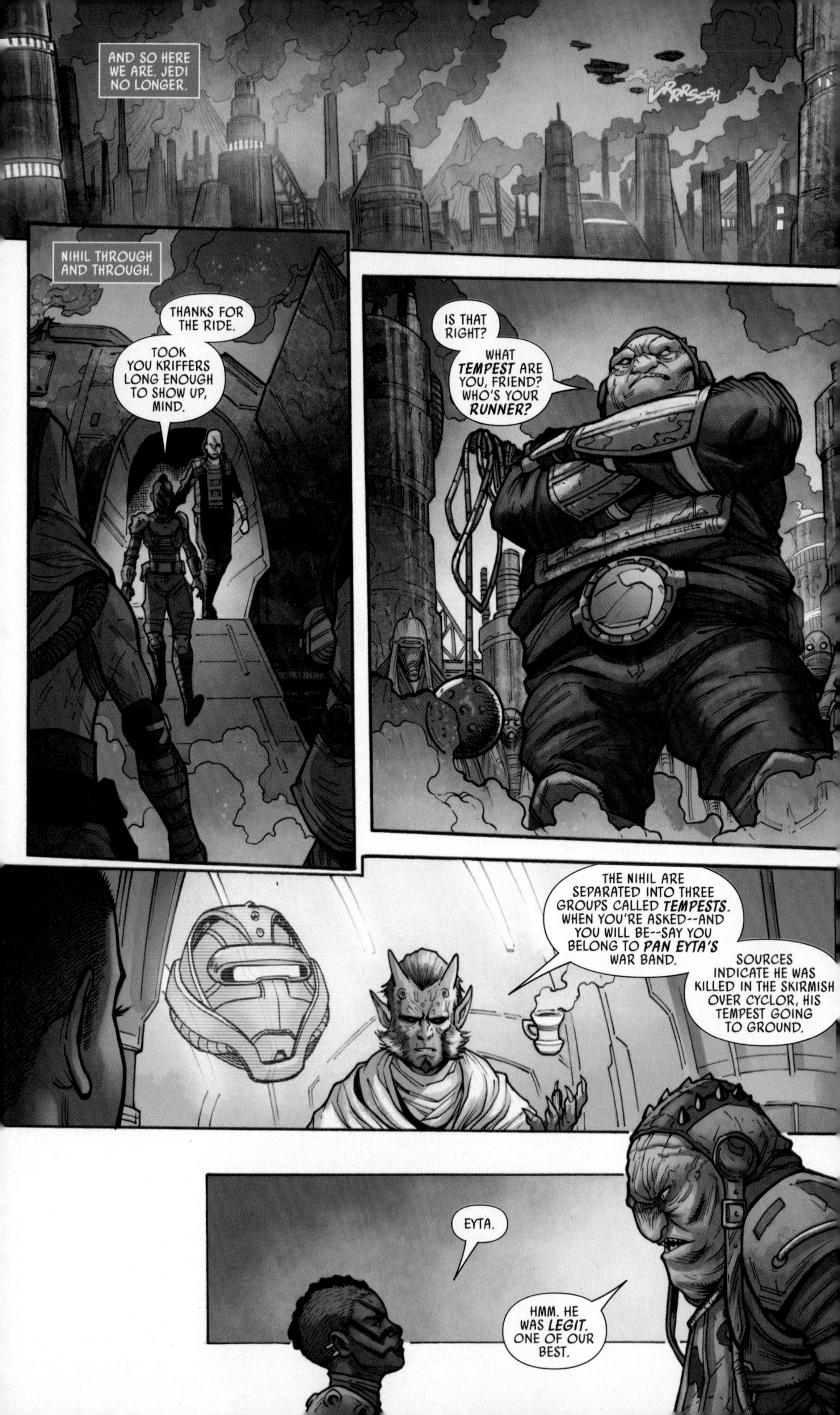
AND SO HERE WE ARE. JEDI NO LONGER.
VRRRSSSH
NIHIL THROUGH AND THROUGH.
THANKS FOR THE RIDE.
TOOK YOU KRIFFERS LONG ENOUGH TO SHOW UP, MIND.
IS THAT RIGHT?
WHAT TEMPEST ARE YOU, FRIEND? WHO'S YOUR RUNNER?
THE NIHIL ARE SEPARATED INTO THREE GROUPS CALLED TEMPESTS. WHEN YOU'RE ASKED--AND YOU WILL BE--SAY YOU BELONG TO PAN EYTA'S WAR BAND.
SOURCES INDICATE HE WAS KILLED IN THE SKIRMISH OVER CYCLOR, HIS TEMPEST GOING TO GROUND.
EYTA.
HMM. HE WAS LEGIT. ONE OF OUR BEST.

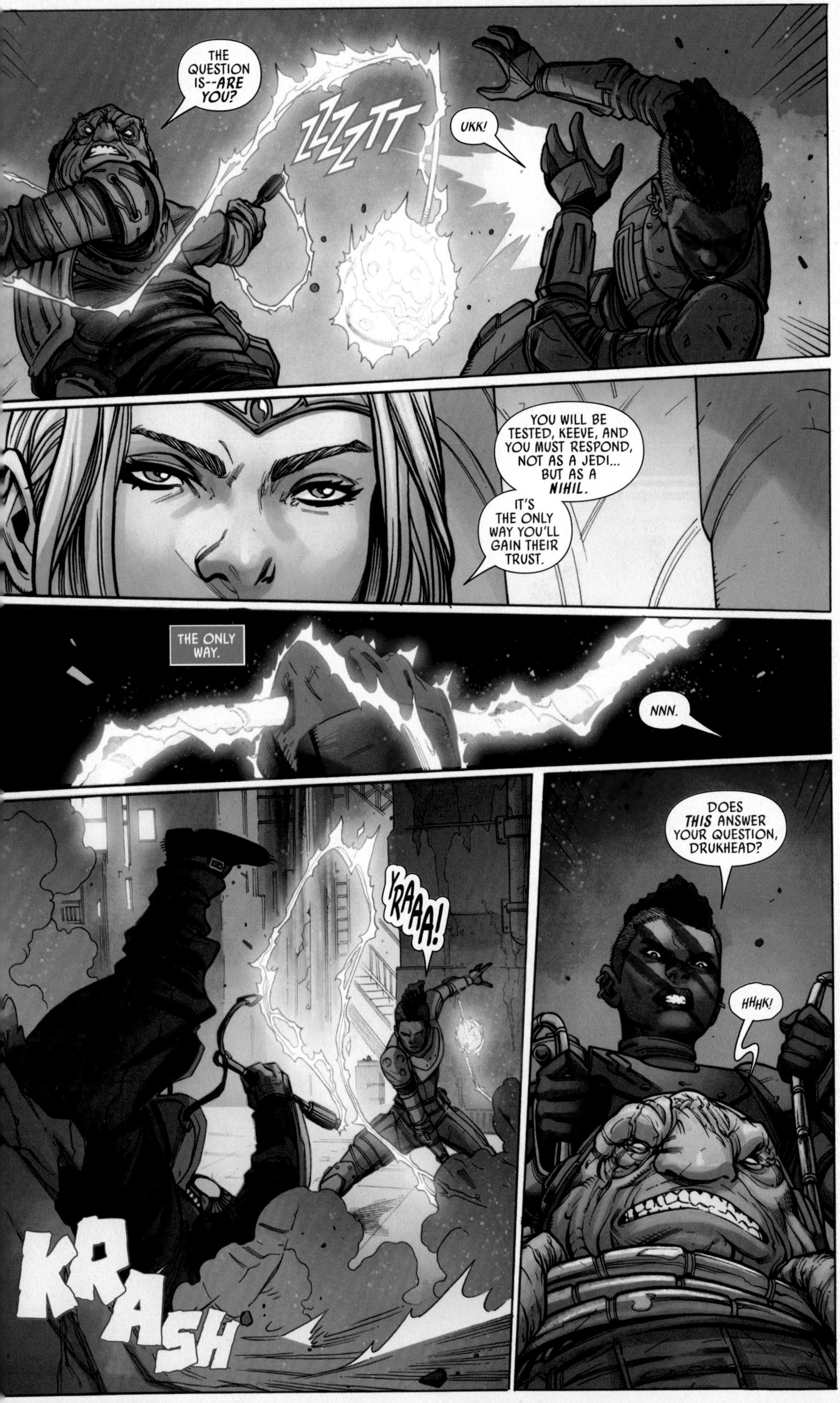
THE QUESTION IS--ARE YOU?
ZZZZTT
UKK!
YOU WILL BE TESTED, KEEVE, AND YOU MUST RESPOND, NOT AS A JEDI... BUT AS A NIHIL.
IT'S THE ONLY WAY YOU'LL GAIN THEIR TRUST.
THE ONLY WAY.
NNN.
YRAAA!
KRASH
DOES THIS ANSWER YOUR QUESTION, DRUKHEAD?
HHHK!

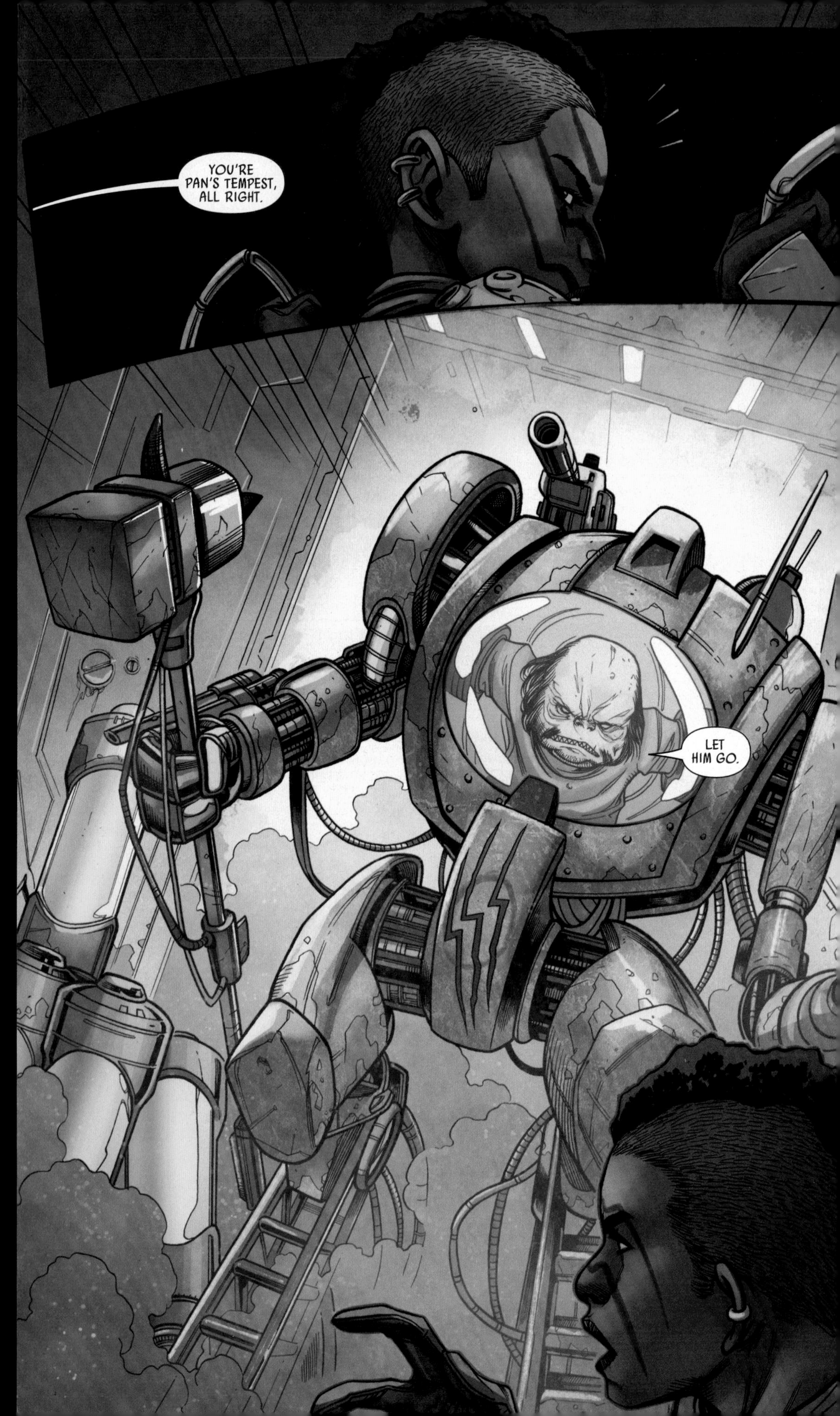
YOU'RE PAN'S TEMPEST, ALL RIGHT.
LET HIM GO.

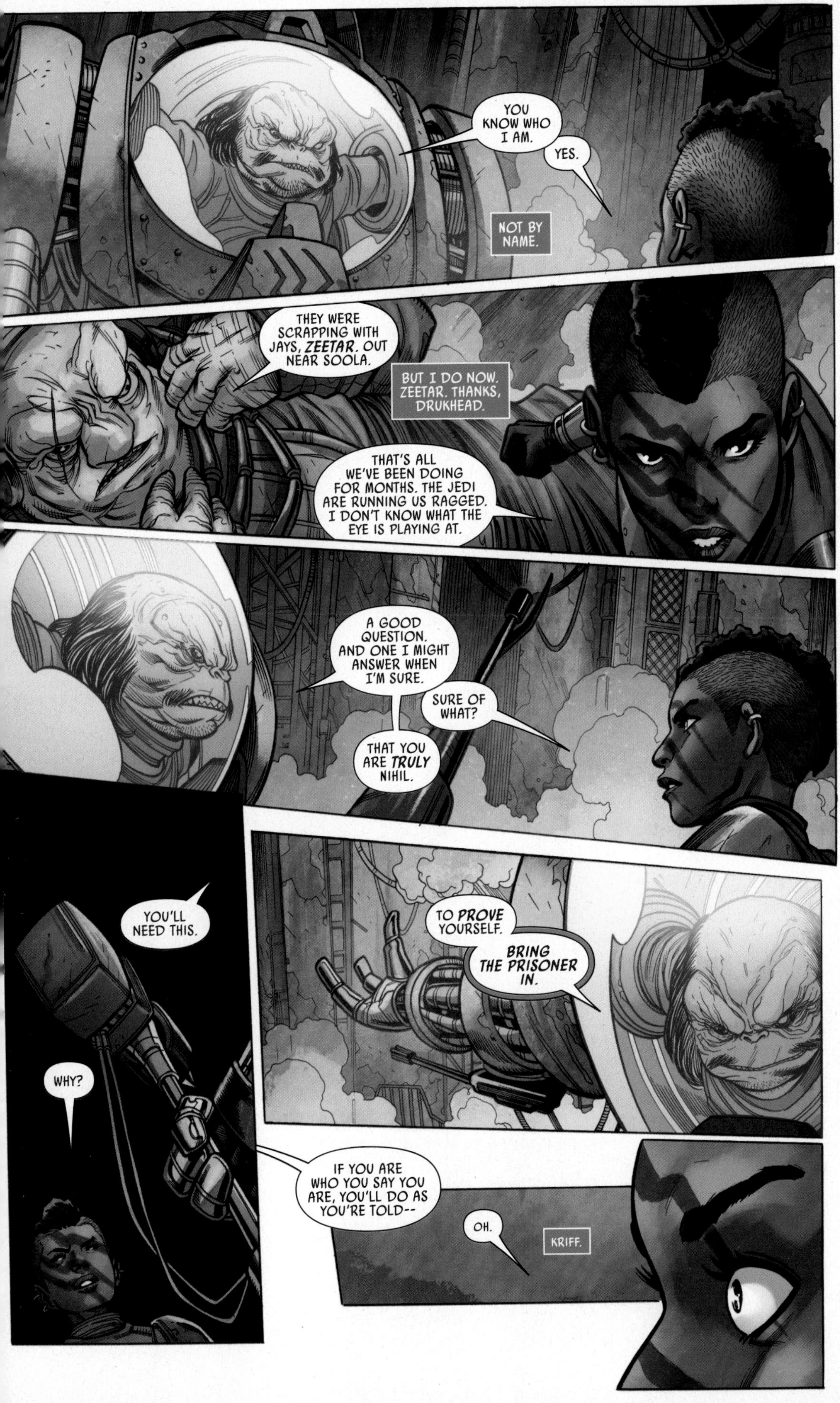
YOU KNOW WHO I AM.
YES.
NOT BY NAME.
THEY WERE SCRAPPING WITH JAYS, ZEETAR. OUT NEAR SOOLA.
BUT I DO NOW. ZEETAR. THANKS, DRUKHEAD.
THAT'S ALL WE'VE BEEN DOING FOR MONTHS. THE JEDI ARE RUNNING US RAGGED. I DON'T KNOW WHAT THE EYE IS PLAYING AT.
A GOOD QUESTION. AND ONE I MIGHT ANSWER WHEN I'M SURE.
SURE OF WHAT?
THAT YOU ARE TRULY NIHIL.
TO PROVE YOURSELF.
BRING THE PRISONER IN.
YOU'LL NEED THIS.
WHY?
IF YOU ARE WHO YOU SAY YOU ARE, YOU'LL DO AS YOU'RE TOLD--
OH.
KRIFF.

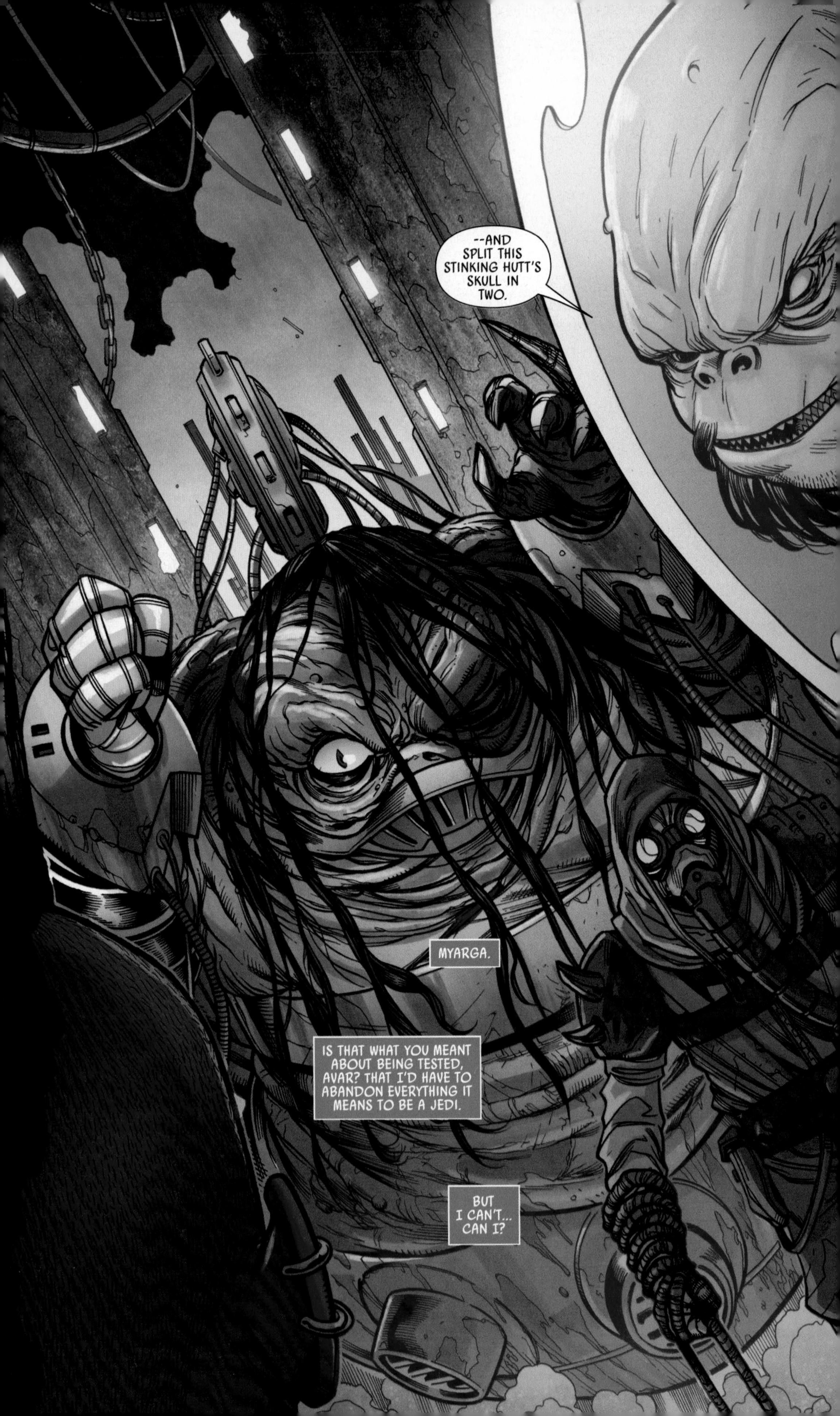
--AND SPLIT THIS STINKING HUTT'S SKULL IN TWO.
MYARGA.
IS THAT WHAT YOU MEANT ABOUT BEING TESTED, AVAR? THAT I'D HAVE TO ABANDON EVERYTHING IT MEANS TO BE A JEDI.
BUT I CAN'T... CAN I?

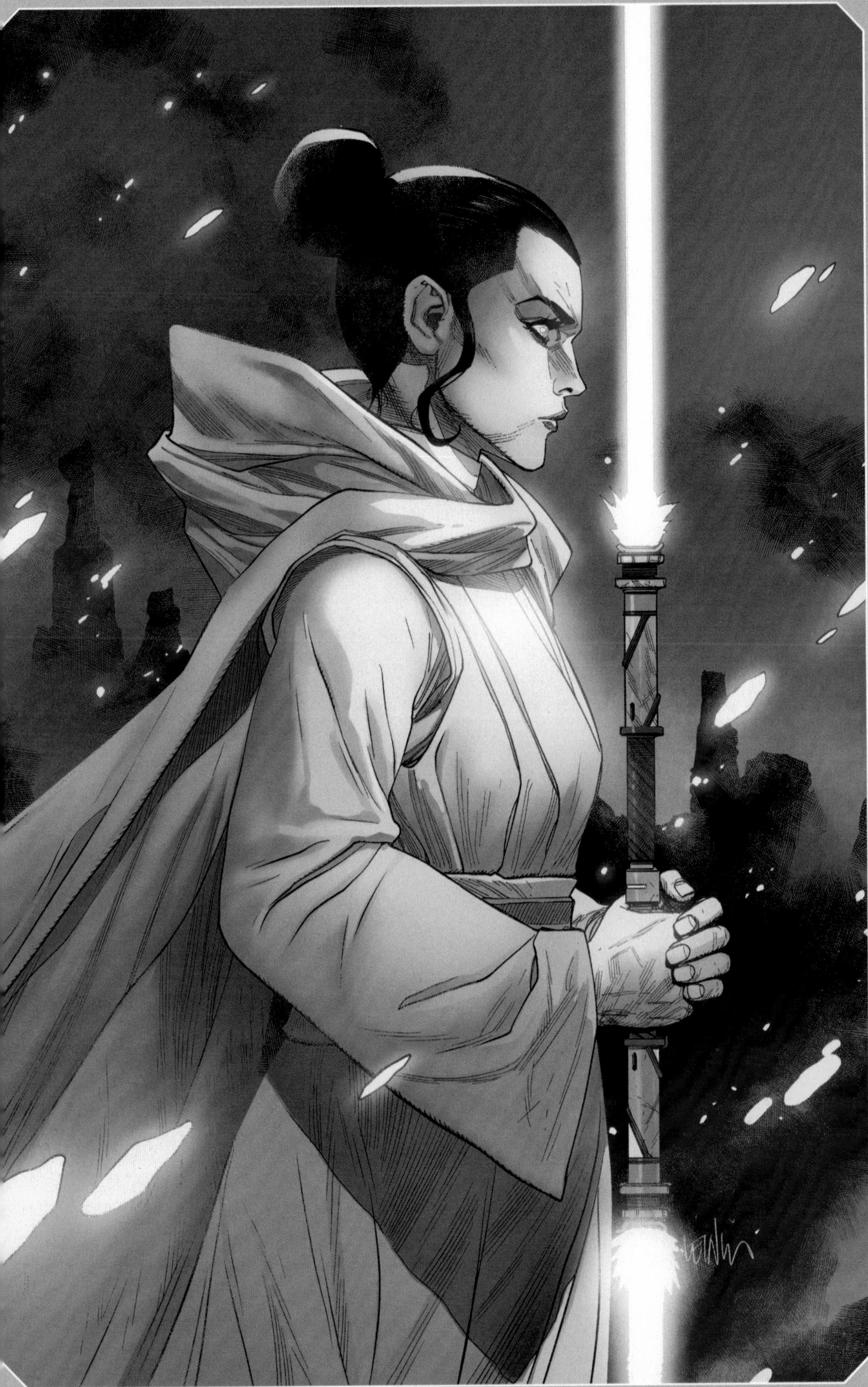

#9 Variant by
LEINIL FRANCIS YU & SUNNY GHO

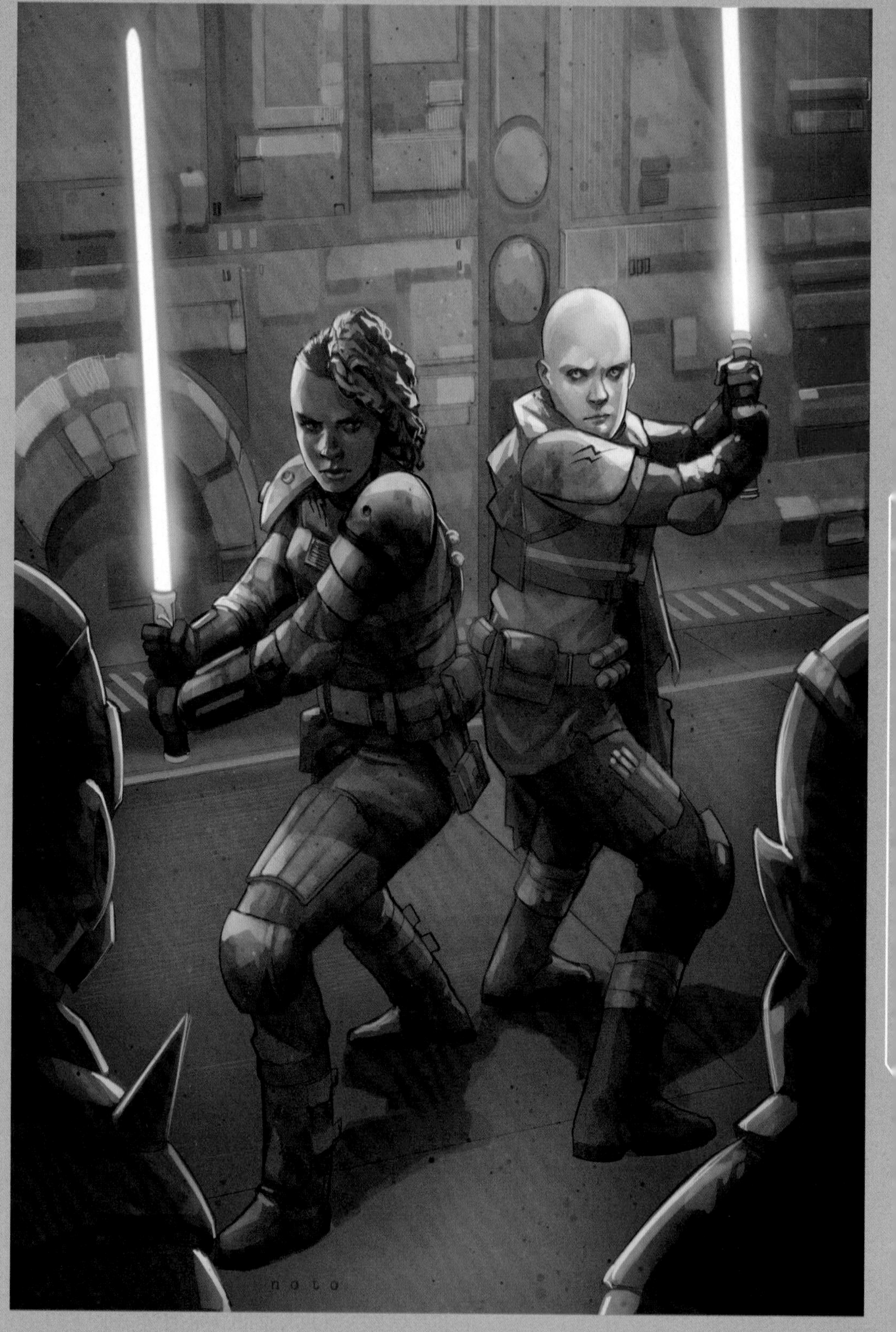

10
OUT OF BALANCE, OUT OF TIME

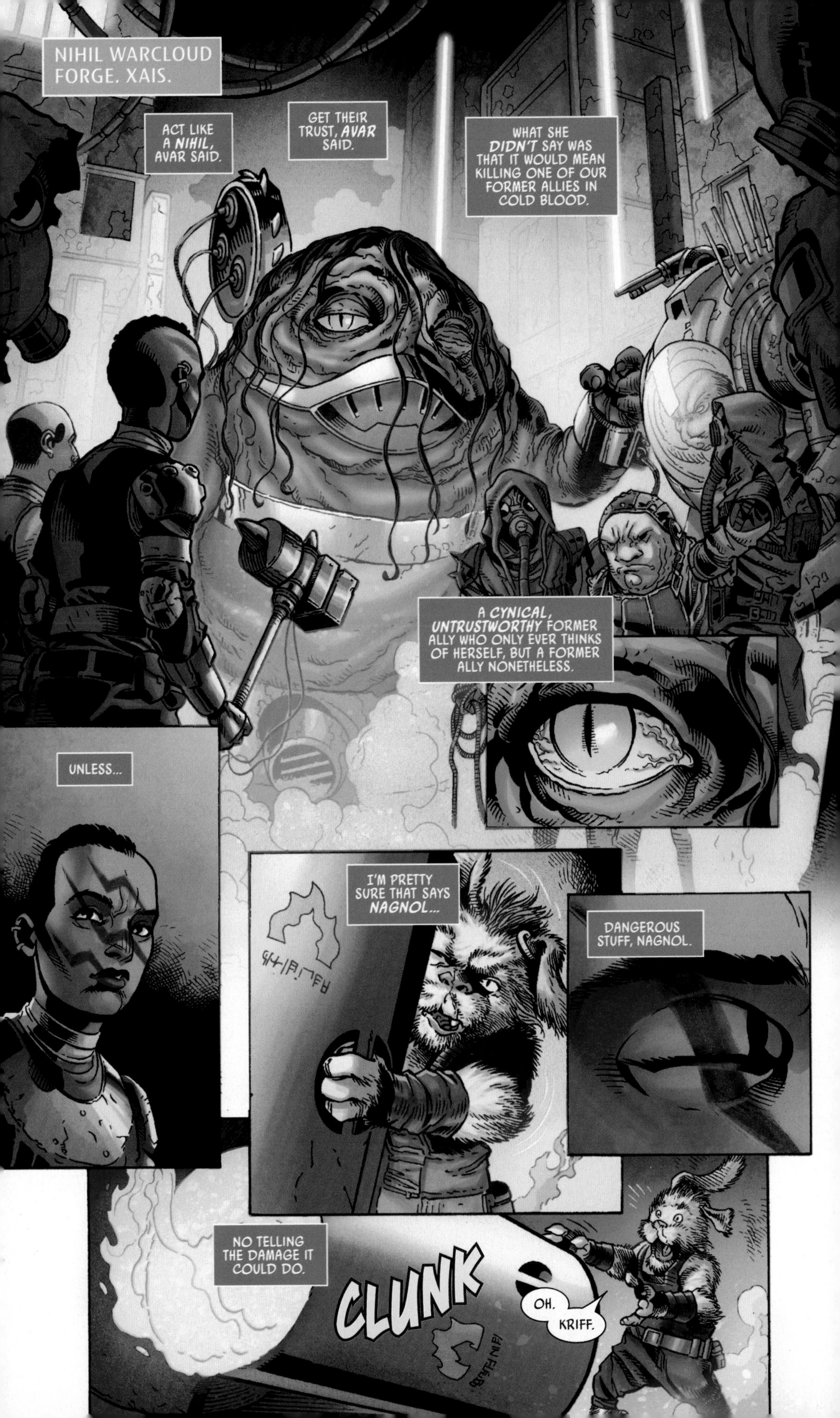
NIHIL WARCLOUD FORGE. XAIS.
ACT LIKE A NIHIL, AVAR SAID.
GET THEIR TRUST, AVAR SAID.
WHAT SHE DIDN'T SAY WAS THAT IT WOULD MEAN KILLING ONE OF OUR FORMER ALLIES IN COLD BLOOD.
A CYNICAL, UNTRUSTWORTHY FORMER ALLY WHO ONLY EVER THINKS OF HERSELF, BUT A FORMER ALLY NONETHELESS.
UNLESS...
I'M PRETTY SURE THAT SAYS NAGNOL...
DANGEROUS STUFF, NAGNOL.
NO TELLING THE DAMAGE IT COULD DO.
CLUNK
OH. KRIFF.

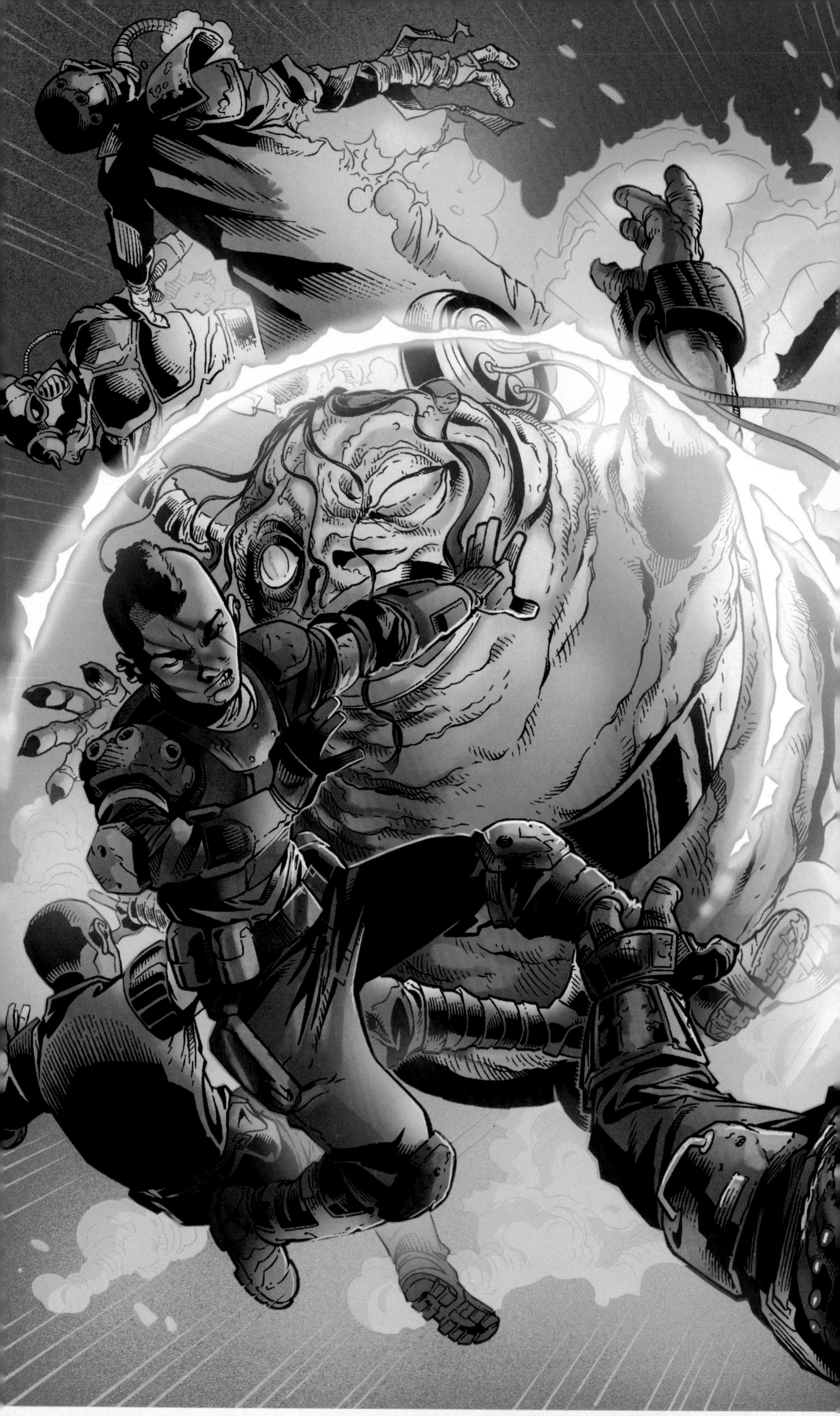

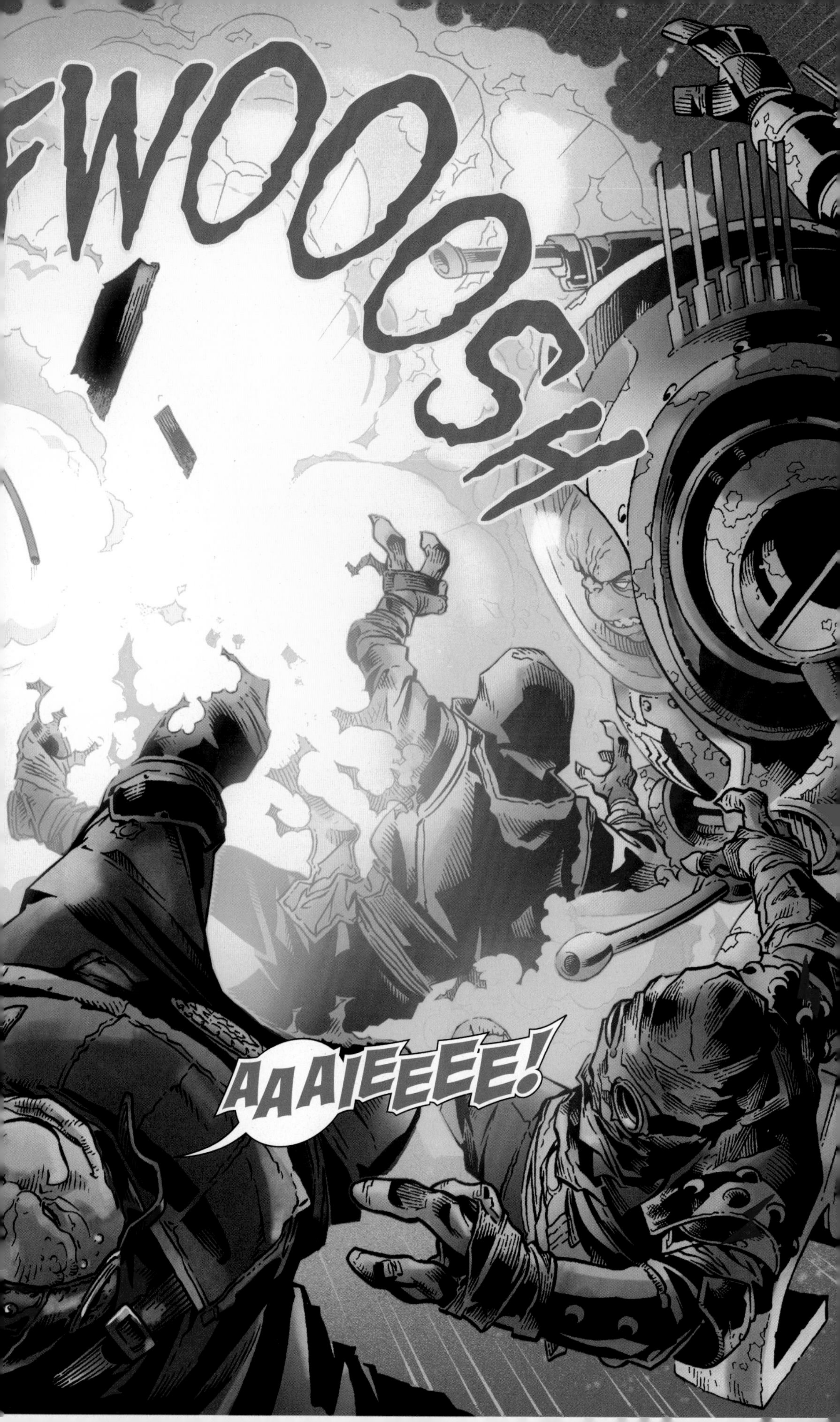
FWOOOSH
AAAIEEEE!

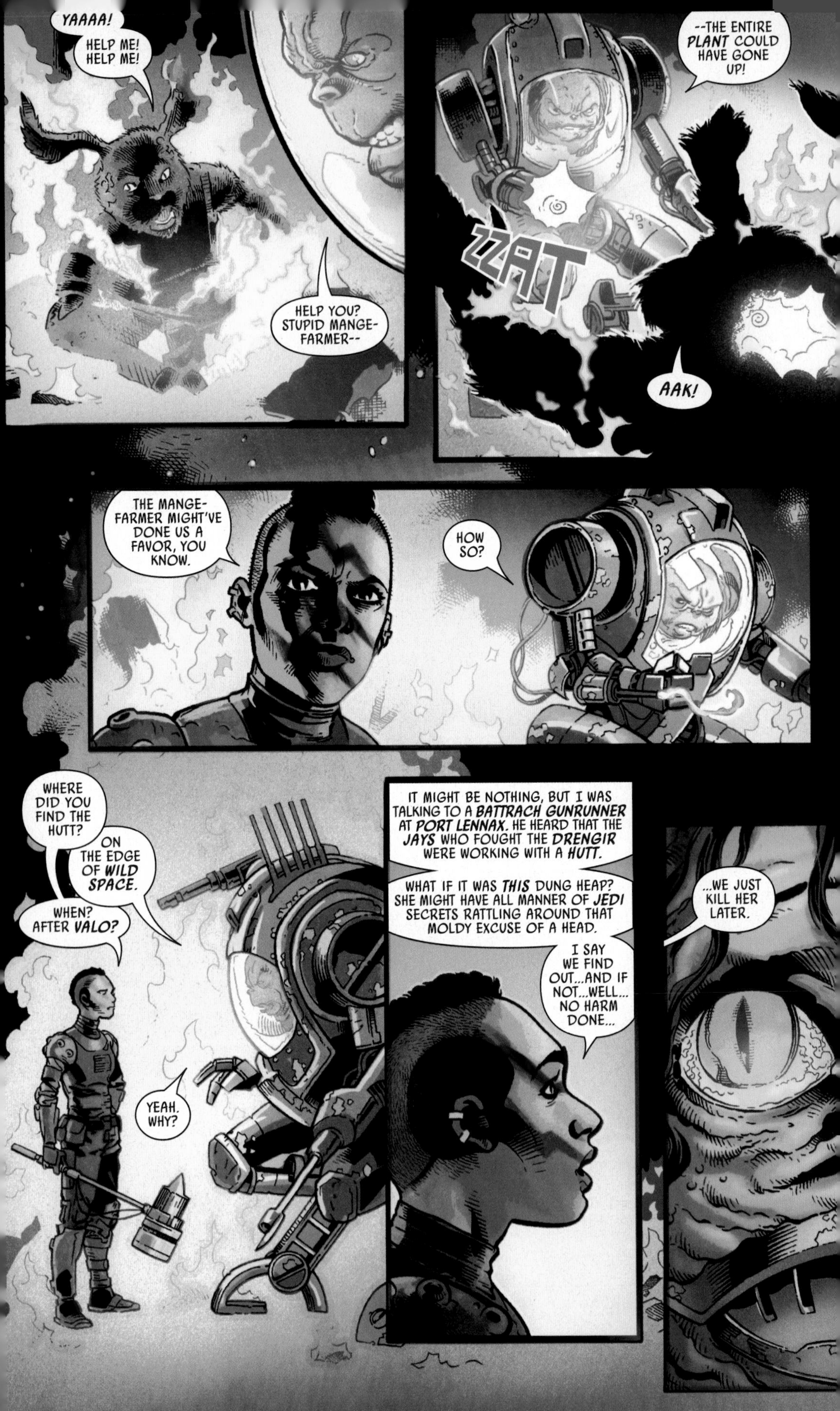
YAAAA!
HELP ME! HELP ME!
HELP YOU? STUPID MANGE-FARMER--
--THE ENTIRE PLANT COULD HAVE GONE UP!
ZZAT
AAK!
THE MANGE-FARMER MIGHT'VE DONE US A FAVOR, YOU KNOW.
HOW SO?
WHERE DID YOU FIND THE HUTT?
ON THE EDGE OF WILD SPACE.
WHEN? AFTER VALO?
YEAH. WHY?
IT MIGHT BE NOTHING, BUT I WAS TALKING TO A BATTRACH GUNRUNNER AT PORT LENNAX. HE HEARD THAT THE JAYS WHO FOUGHT THE DRENGIR WERE WORKING WITH A HUTT.
WHAT IF IT WAS THIS DUNG HEAP? SHE MIGHT HAVE ALL MANNER OF JEDI SECRETS RATTLING AROUND THAT MOLDY EXCUSE OF A HEAD.
I SAY WE FIND OUT...AND IF NOT...WELL... NO HARM DONE...
...WE JUST KILL HER LATER.

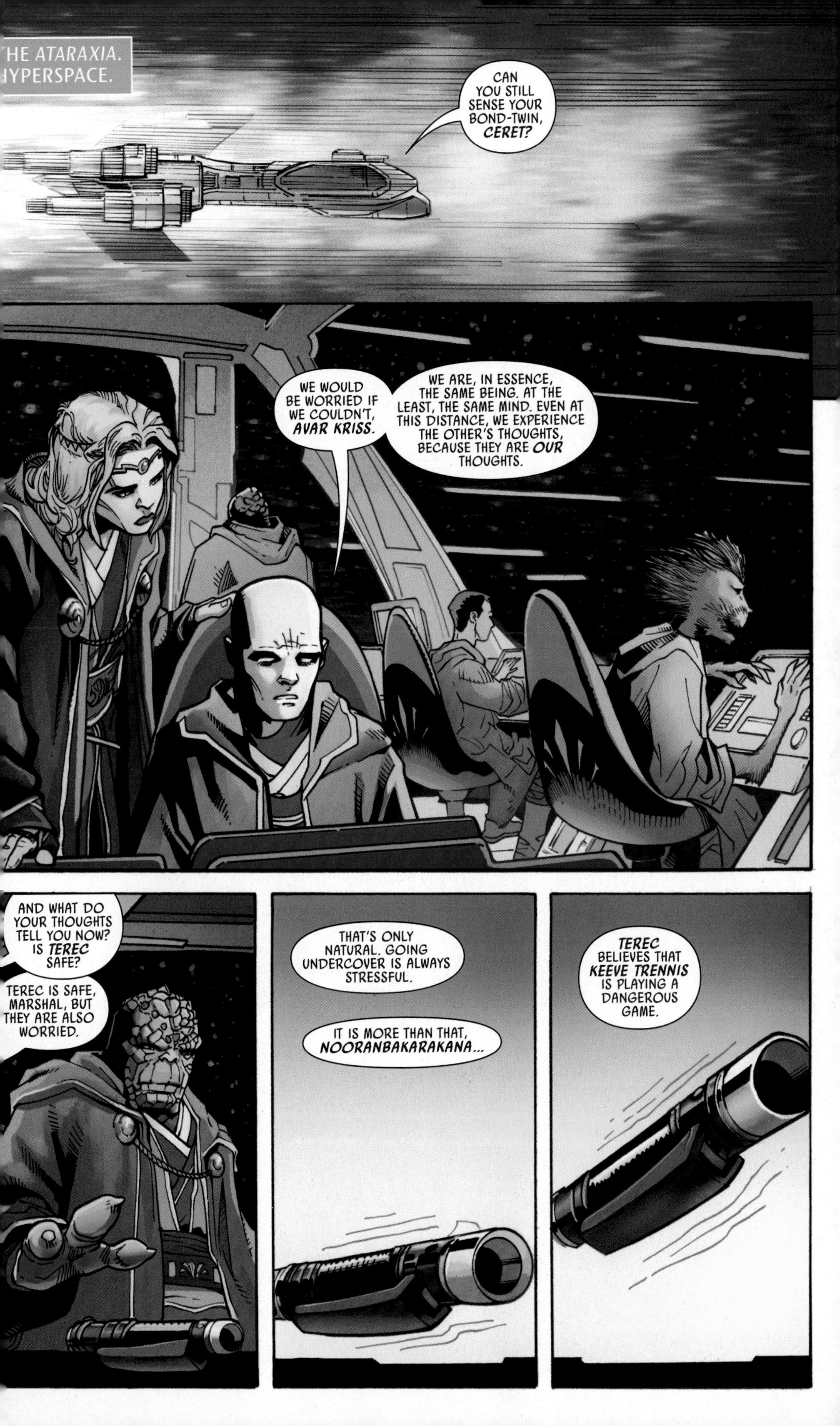
THE ATARAXIA.
HYPERSPACE.
CAN YOU STILL SENSE YOUR BOND-TWIN, CERET?
WE WOULD BE WORRIED IF WE COULDN'T, AVAR KRISS.
WE ARE, IN ESSENCE, THE SAME BEING. AT THE LEAST, THE SAME MIND. EVEN AT THIS DISTANCE, WE EXPERIENCE THE OTHER'S THOUGHTS, BECAUSE THEY ARE OUR THOUGHTS.
AND WHAT DO YOUR THOUGHTS TELL YOU NOW? IS TEREC SAFE?
TEREC IS SAFE, MARSHAL, BUT THEY ARE ALSO WORRIED.
THAT'S ONLY NATURAL. GOING UNDERCOVER IS ALWAYS STRESSFUL.
IT IS MORE THAN THAT, NOORANBAKARAKANA...
TEREC BELIEVES THAT KEEVE TRENNIS IS PLAYING A DANGEROUS GAME.

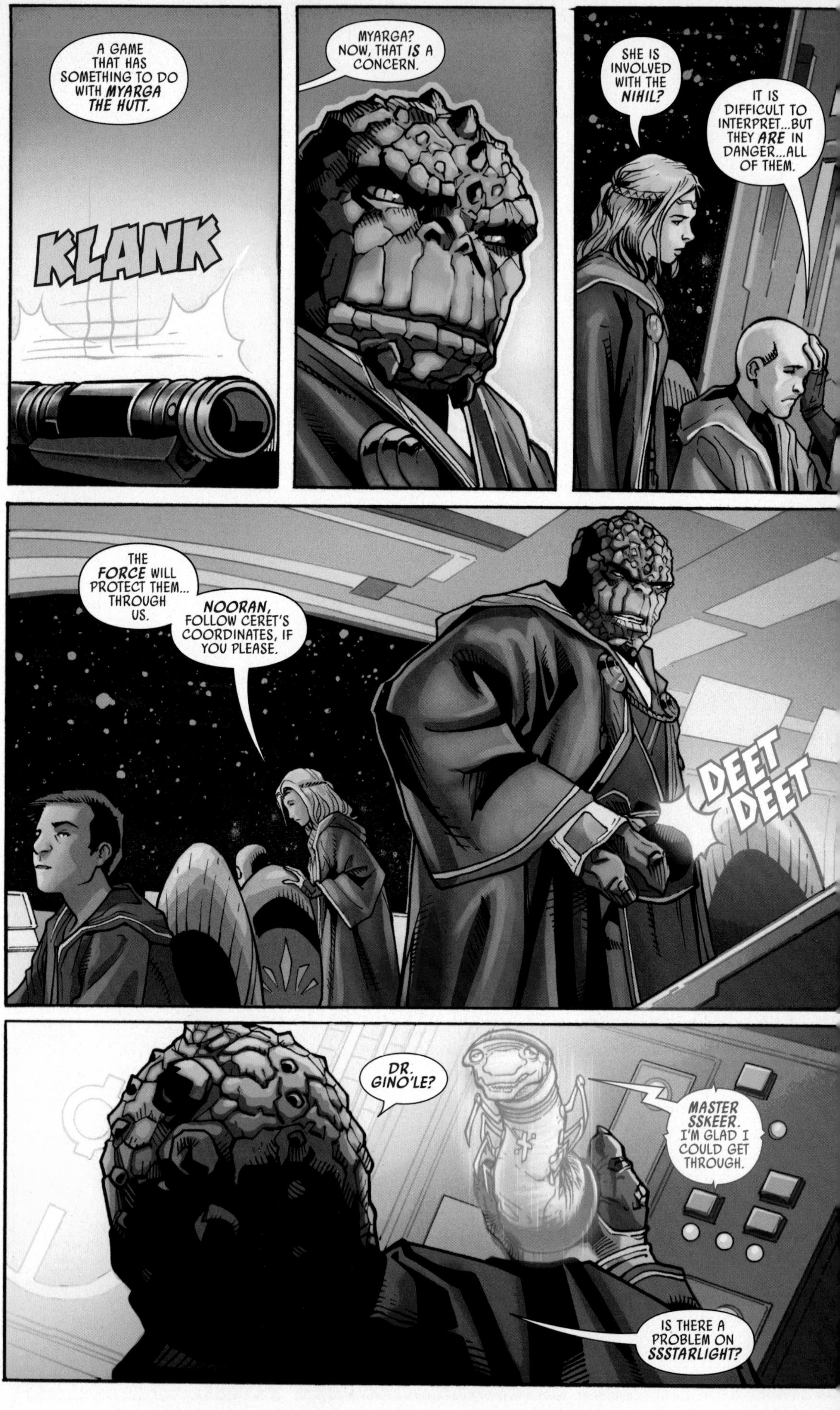
A GAME THAT HAS SOMETHING TO DO WITH MYARGA THE HUTT.
KLANK
MYARGA? NOW, THAT IS A CONCERN.
SHE IS INVOLVED WITH THE NIHIL?
IT IS DIFFICULT TO INTERPRET...BUT THEY ARE IN DANGER...ALL OF THEM.
THE FORCE WILL PROTECT THEM... THROUGH US.
NOORAN, FOLLOW CERET'S COORDINATES, IF YOU PLEASE.
DEET DEET
DR. GINO'LE?
MASTER SSKEER. I'M GLAD I COULD GET THROUGH.
IS THERE A PROBLEM ON SSSTARLIGHT?

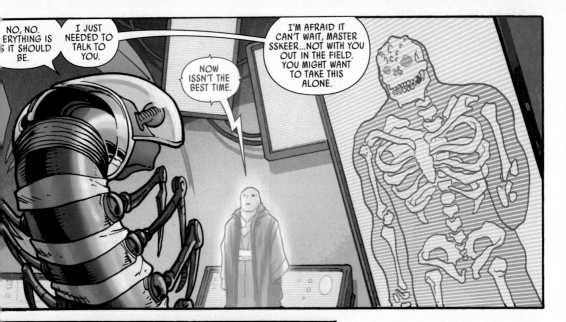

NO, NO. EVERYTHING IS AS IT SHOULD BE.

I JUST NEEDED TO TALK TO YOU.

NOW ISSN'T THE BEST TIME.

I'M AFRAID IT CAN'T WAIT, MASTER SSKEER...NOT WITH YOU OUT IN THE FIELD. YOU MIGHT WANT TO TAKE THIS ALONE.

I HAVE NO SSECRETS FROM MY FELLOW JEDI.

IF YOU INSIST--ALTHOUGH I'M AFRAID IT ISN'T GOOD NEWS.

I'VE RECEIVED THE RESULTS FROM THE TESTS WE RAN--

--AND WE KNOW WHY YOU ARE LOSING YOUR CONNECTION TO THE FORCE.

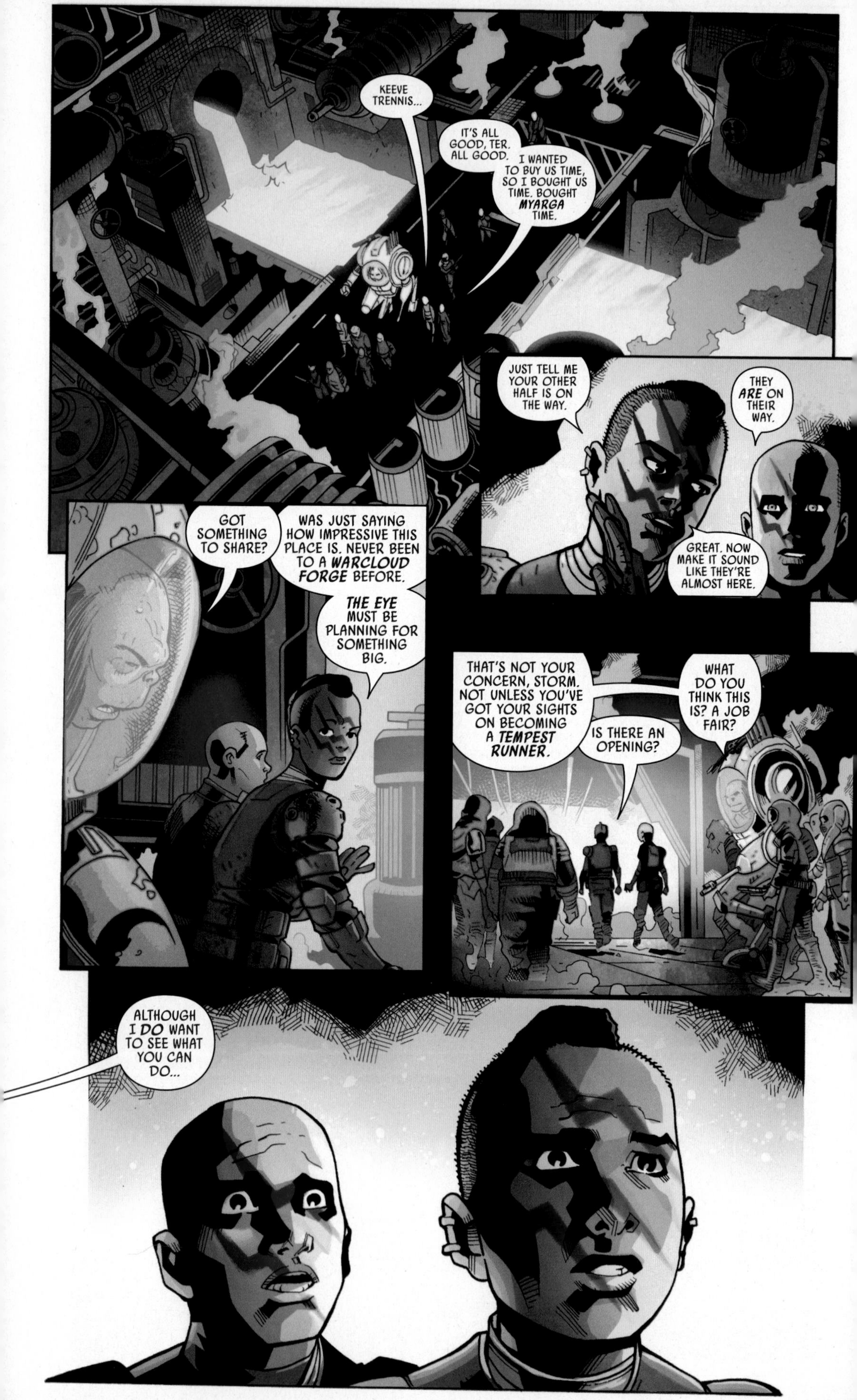
KEEVE TRENNIS...
IT'S ALL GOOD, TER. ALL GOOD.
I WANTED TO BUY US TIME, SO I BOUGHT US TIME. BOUGHT MYARGA TIME.
JUST TELL ME YOUR OTHER HALF IS ON THE WAY.
THEY ARE ON THEIR WAY.
GREAT. NOW MAKE IT SOUND LIKE THEY'RE ALMOST HERE.
GOT SOMETHING TO SHARE?
WAS JUST SAYING HOW IMPRESSIVE THIS PLACE IS. NEVER BEEN TO A WARCLOUD FORGE BEFORE.
THE EYE MUST BE PLANNING FOR SOMETHING BIG.
THAT'S NOT YOUR CONCERN, STORM. NOT UNLESS YOU'VE GOT YOUR SIGHTS ON BECOMING A TEMPEST RUNNER.
IS THERE AN OPENING?
WHAT DO YOU THINK THIS IS? A JOB FAIR?
ALTHOUGH I DO WANT TO SEE WHAT YOU CAN DO...

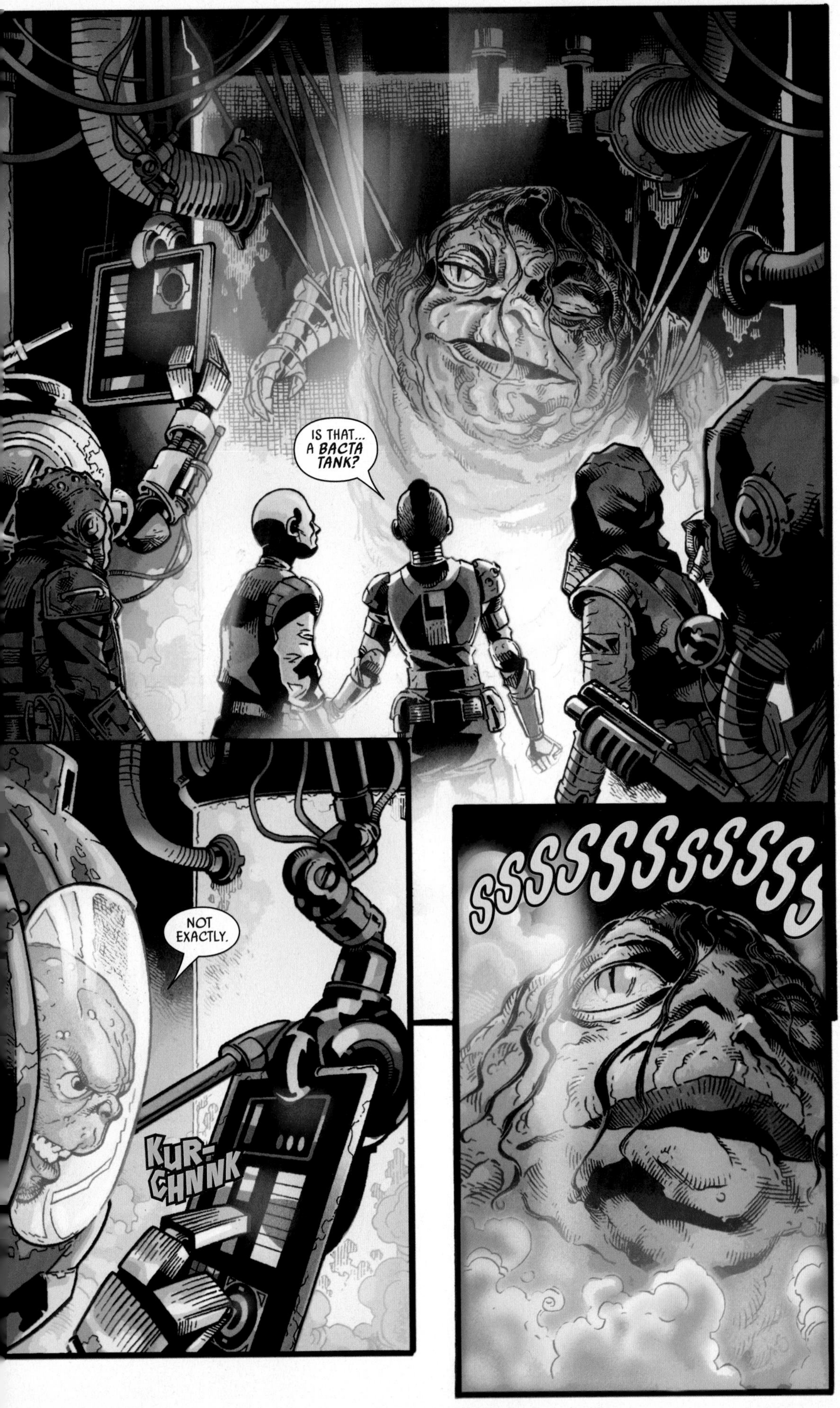
IS THAT... A BACTA TANK?
NOT EXACTLY.
KUR-CHNNK
SSSSSSSSSSS

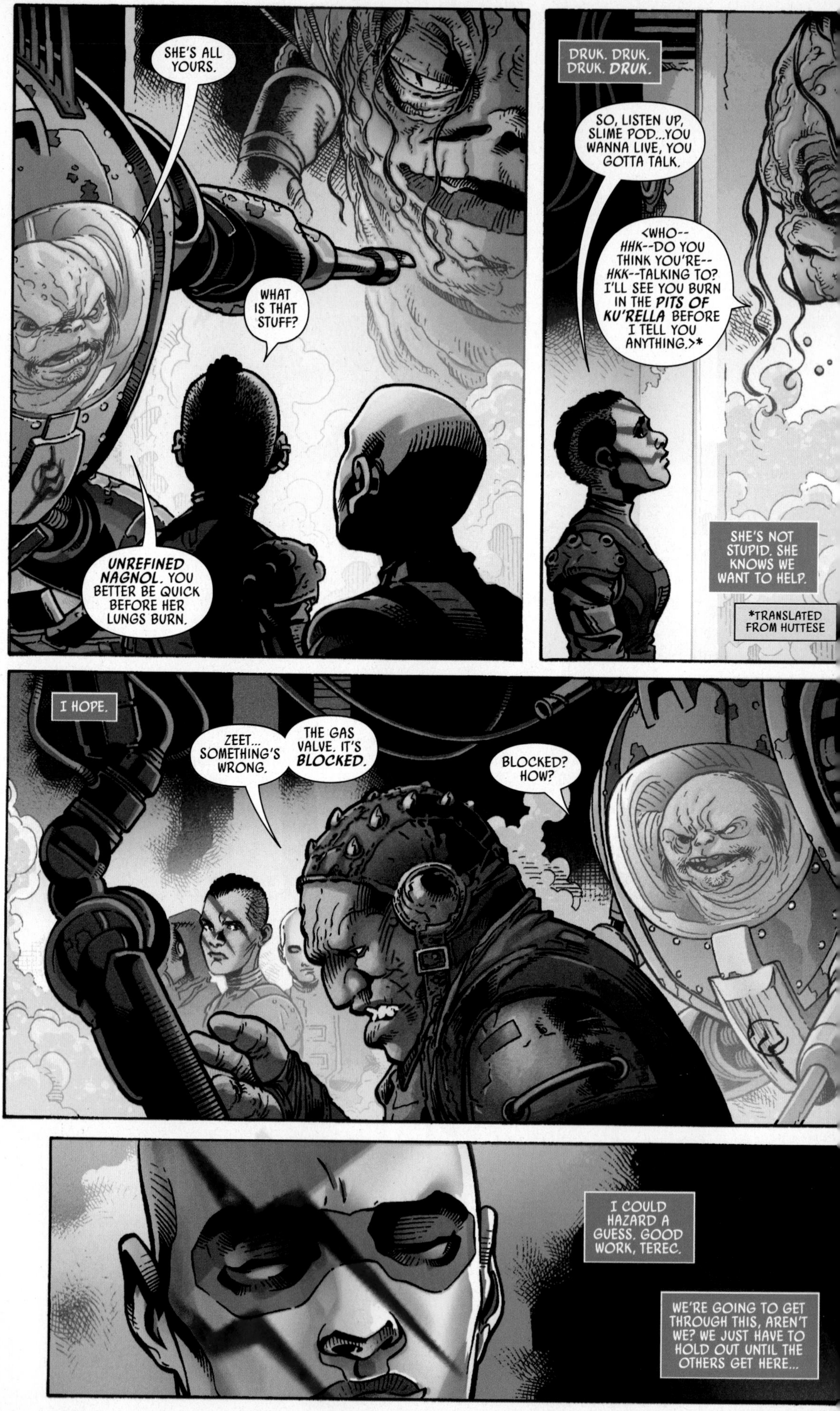
SHE'S ALL YOURS.
WHAT IS THAT STUFF?
UNREFINED NAGNOL. YOU BETTER BE QUICK BEFORE HER LUNGS BURN.
DRUK. DRUK. DRUK. DRUK.
SO, LISTEN UP, SLIME POD...YOU WANNA LIVE, YOU GOTTA TALK.
<WHO--HHK--DO YOU THINK YOU'RE--HKK--TALKING TO? I'LL SEE YOU BURN IN THE PITS OF KU'RELLA BEFORE I TELL YOU ANYTHING.>*
SHE'S NOT STUPID. SHE KNOWS WE WANT TO HELP.
*TRANSLATED FROM HUTTESE
I HOPE.
ZEET... SOMETHING'S WRONG.
THE GAS VALVE. IT'S BLOCKED.
BLOCKED? HOW?
I COULD HAZARD A GUESS. GOOD WORK, TEREC.
WE'RE GOING TO GET THROUGH THIS, AREN'T WE? WE JUST HAVE TO HOLD OUT UNTIL THE OTHERS GET HERE...

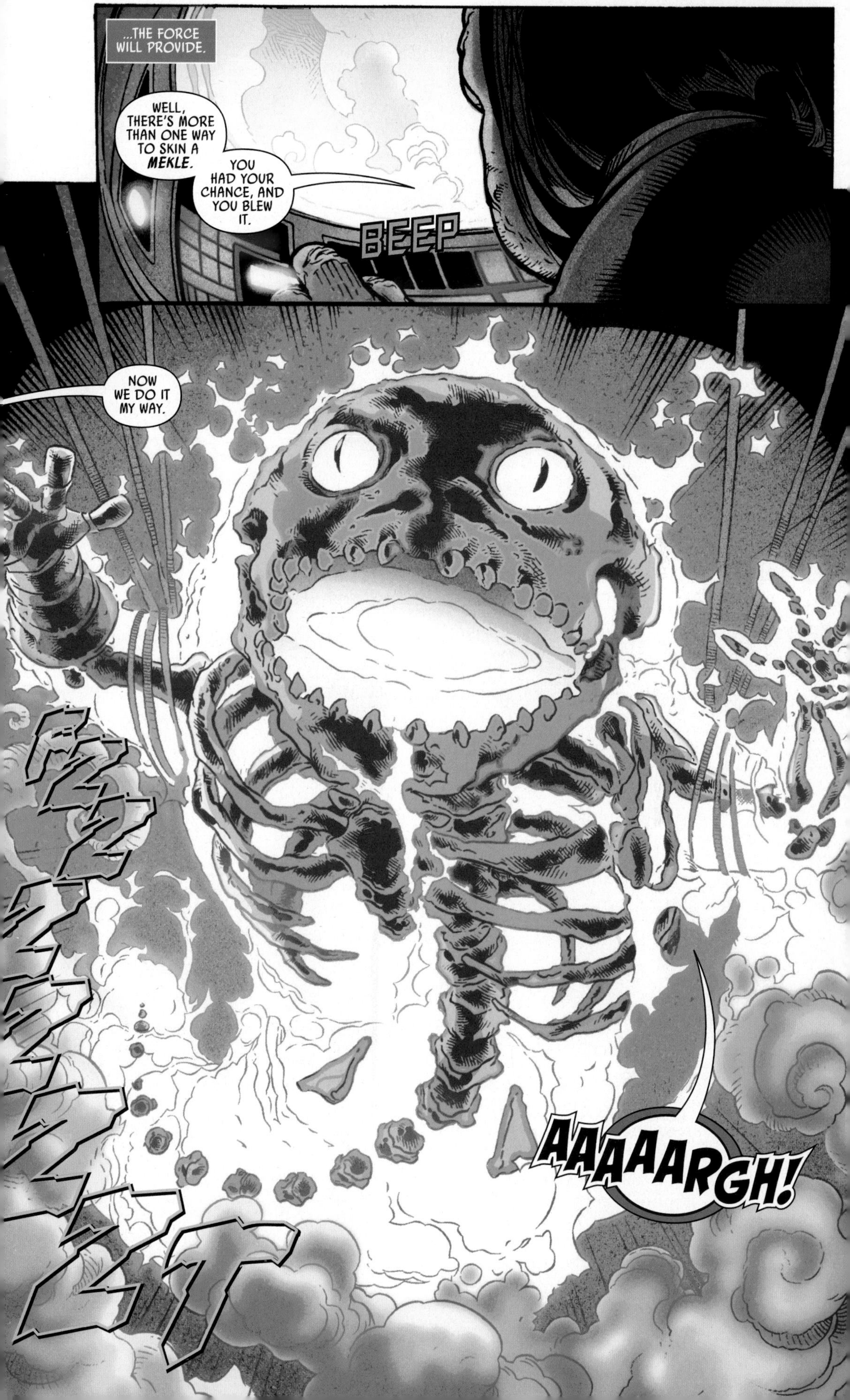

...THE FORCE WILL PROVIDE.
WELL, THERE'S MORE THAN ONE WAY TO SKIN A MEKLE.
YOU HAD YOUR CHANCE, AND YOU BLEW IT.
BEEP
NOW WE DO IT MY WAY.
AAAAARGH!

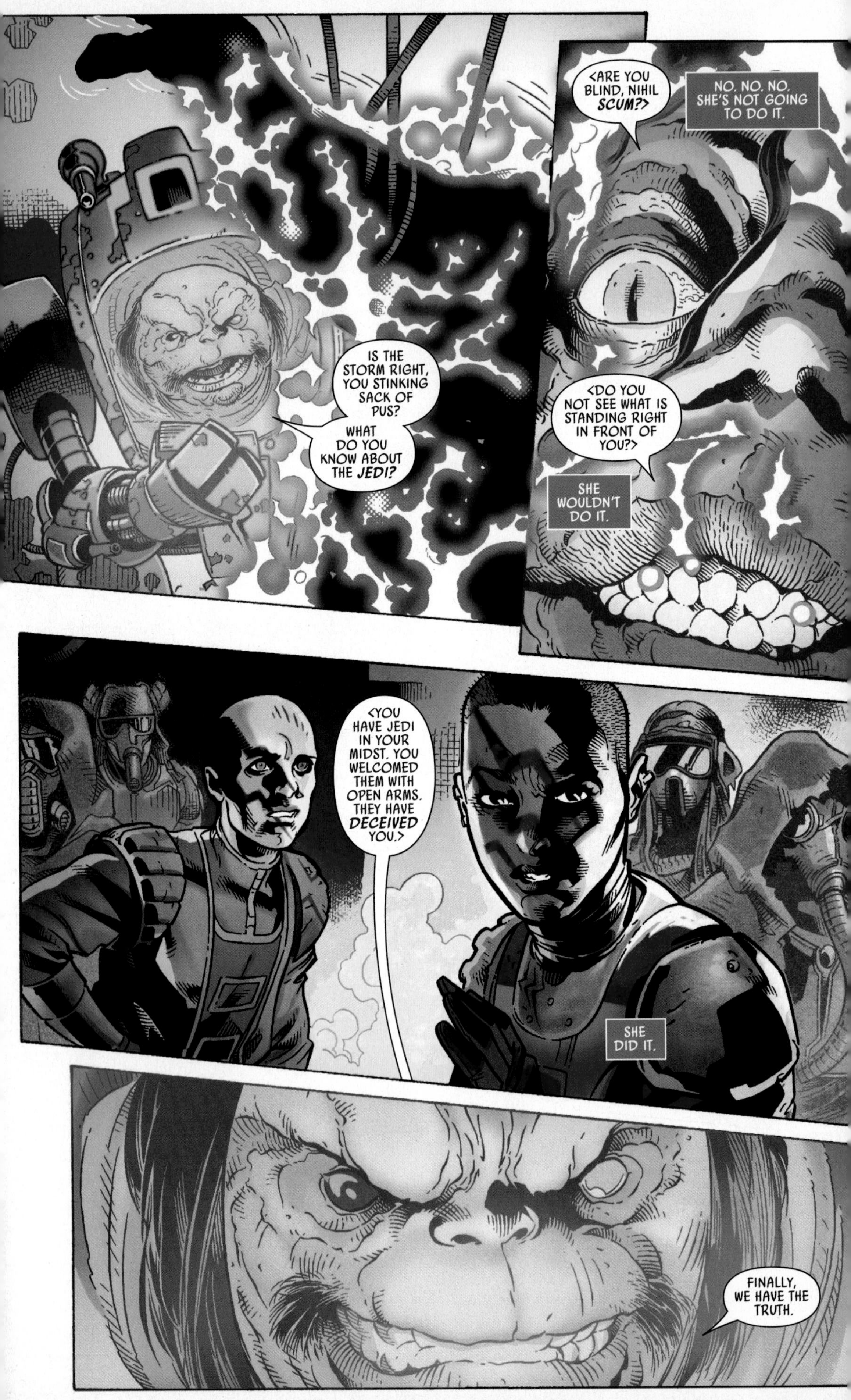

IS THE STORM RIGHT, YOU STINKING SACK OF PUS?
WHAT DO YOU KNOW ABOUT THE JEDI?
<ARE YOU BLIND, NIHIL SCUM?>
NO. NO. NO. SHE'S NOT GOING TO DO IT.
<DO YOU NOT SEE WHAT IS STANDING RIGHT IN FRONT OF YOU?>
SHE WOULDN'T DO IT.
<YOU HAVE JEDI IN YOUR MIDST. YOU WELCOMED THEM WITH OPEN ARMS. THEY HAVE DECEIVED YOU.>
SHE DID IT.
FINALLY, WE HAVE THE TRUTH.

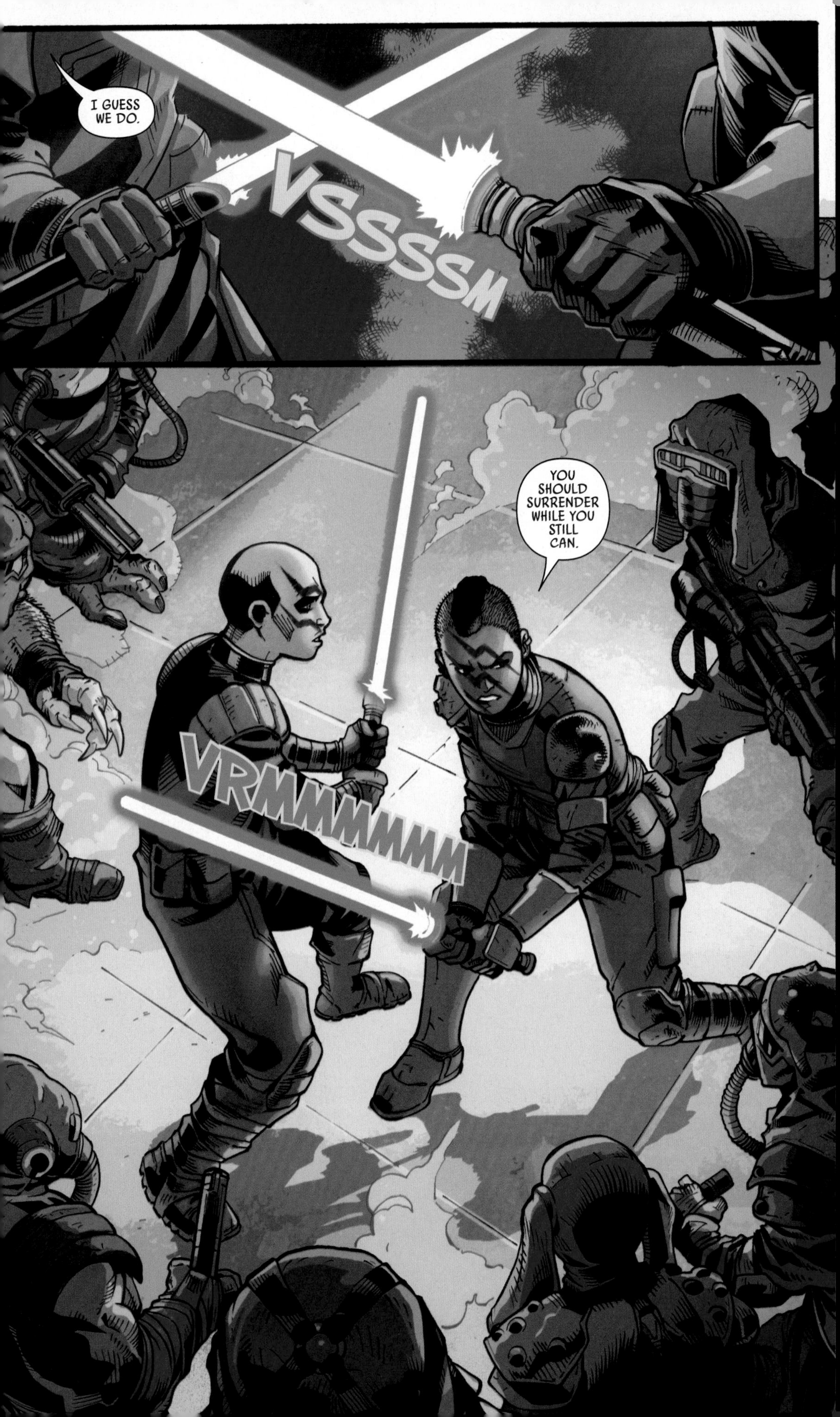

I GUESS WE DO.
VSSSSM
YOU SHOULD SURRENDER WHILE YOU STILL CAN.
VRMMMMMMM

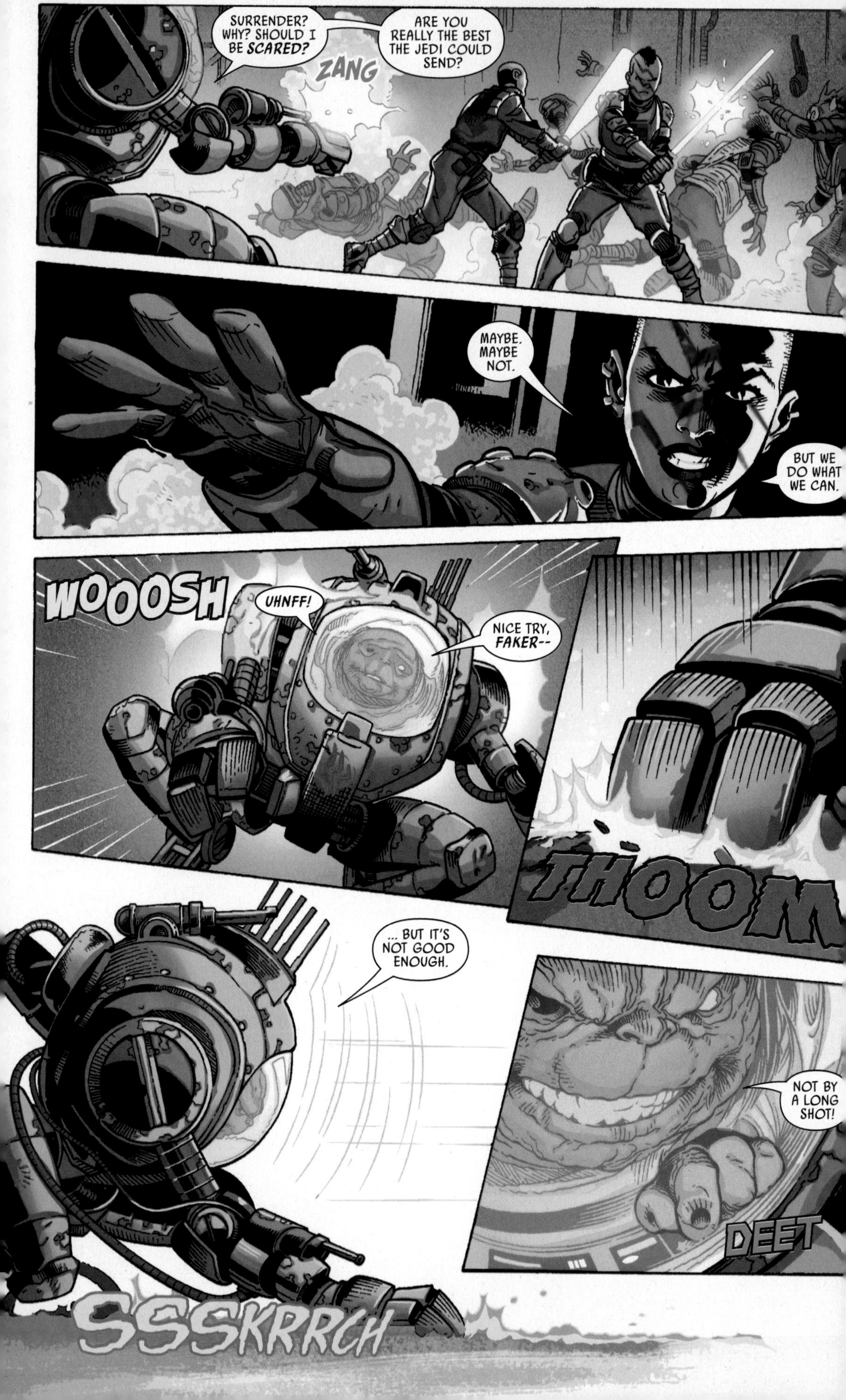
SURRENDER? WHY? SHOULD I BE SCARED?
ARE YOU REALLY THE BEST THE JEDI COULD SEND?
ZANG
MAYBE. MAYBE NOT.
BUT WE DO WHAT WE CAN.
WOOOSH
UHNFF!
NICE TRY, FAKER--
THOOM
... BUT IT'S NOT GOOD ENOUGH.
NOT BY A LONG SHOT!
DEET
SSSKRRCH

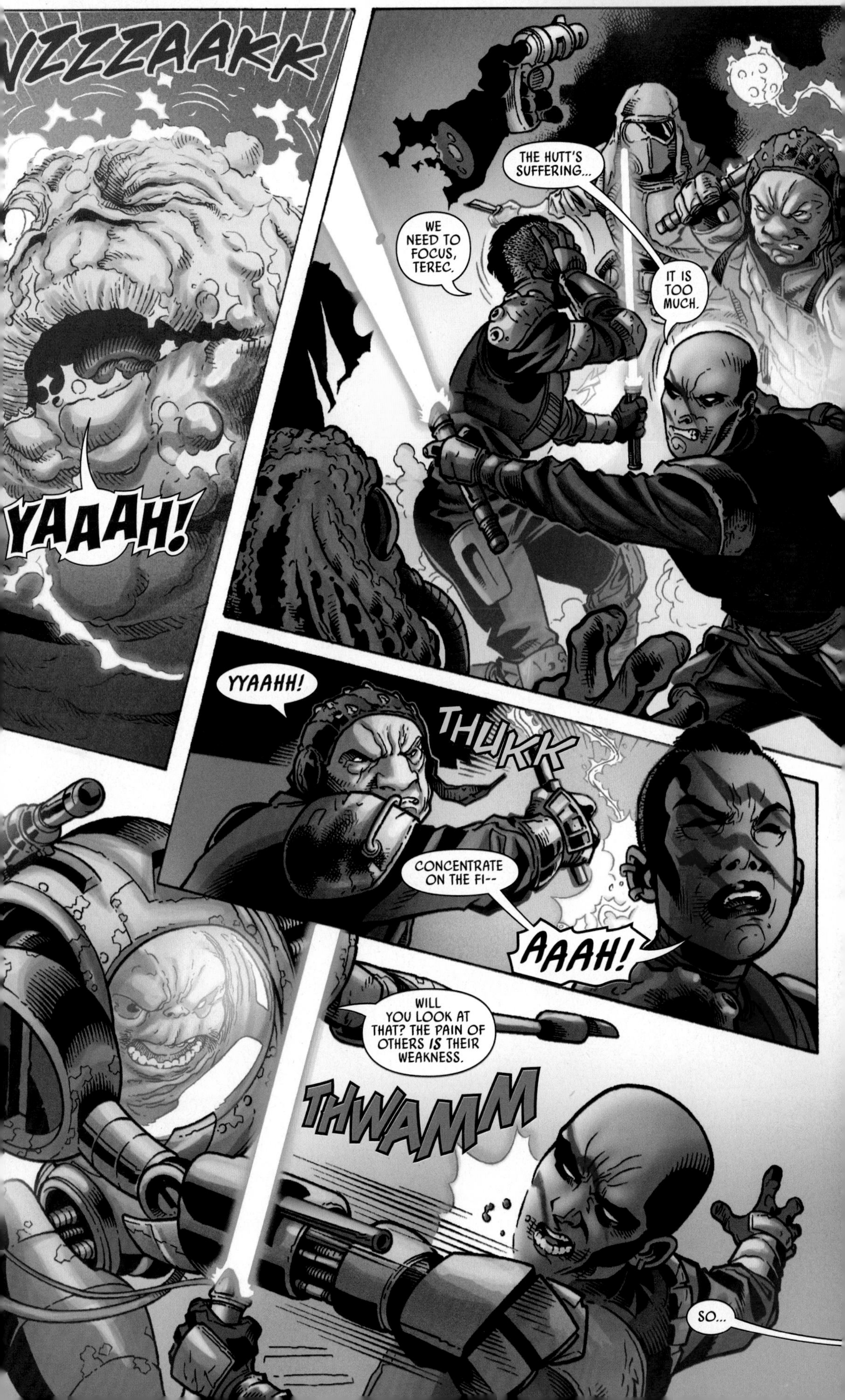
VZZZAAKK
YAAAH!
THE HUTT'S SUFFERING...
WE NEED TO FOCUS, TEREC.
IT IS TOO MUCH.
YYAAHH!
THUKK
CONCENTRATE ON THE FI--
AAAH!
WILL YOU LOOK AT THAT? THE PAIN OF OTHERS *IS* THEIR WEAKNESS.
THWAMM
SO...

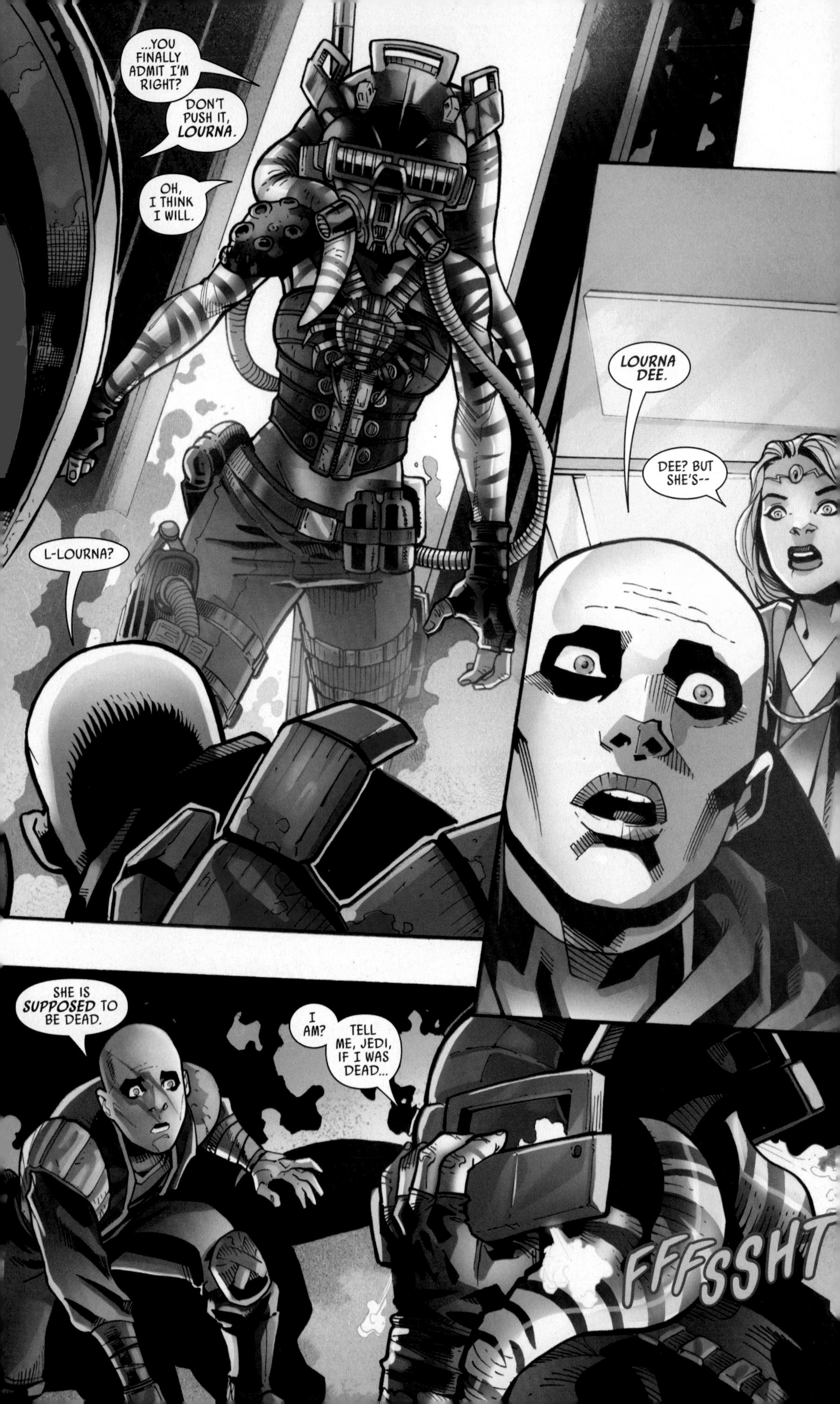

...YOU FINALLY ADMIT I'M RIGHT?
DON'T PUSH IT, LOURNA.
OH, I THINK I WILL.
LOURNA DEE.
DEE? BUT SHE'S--
L-LOURNA?
SHE IS SUPPOSED TO BE DEAD.
I AM?
TELL ME, JEDI, IF I WAS DEAD...
FFFSSHT

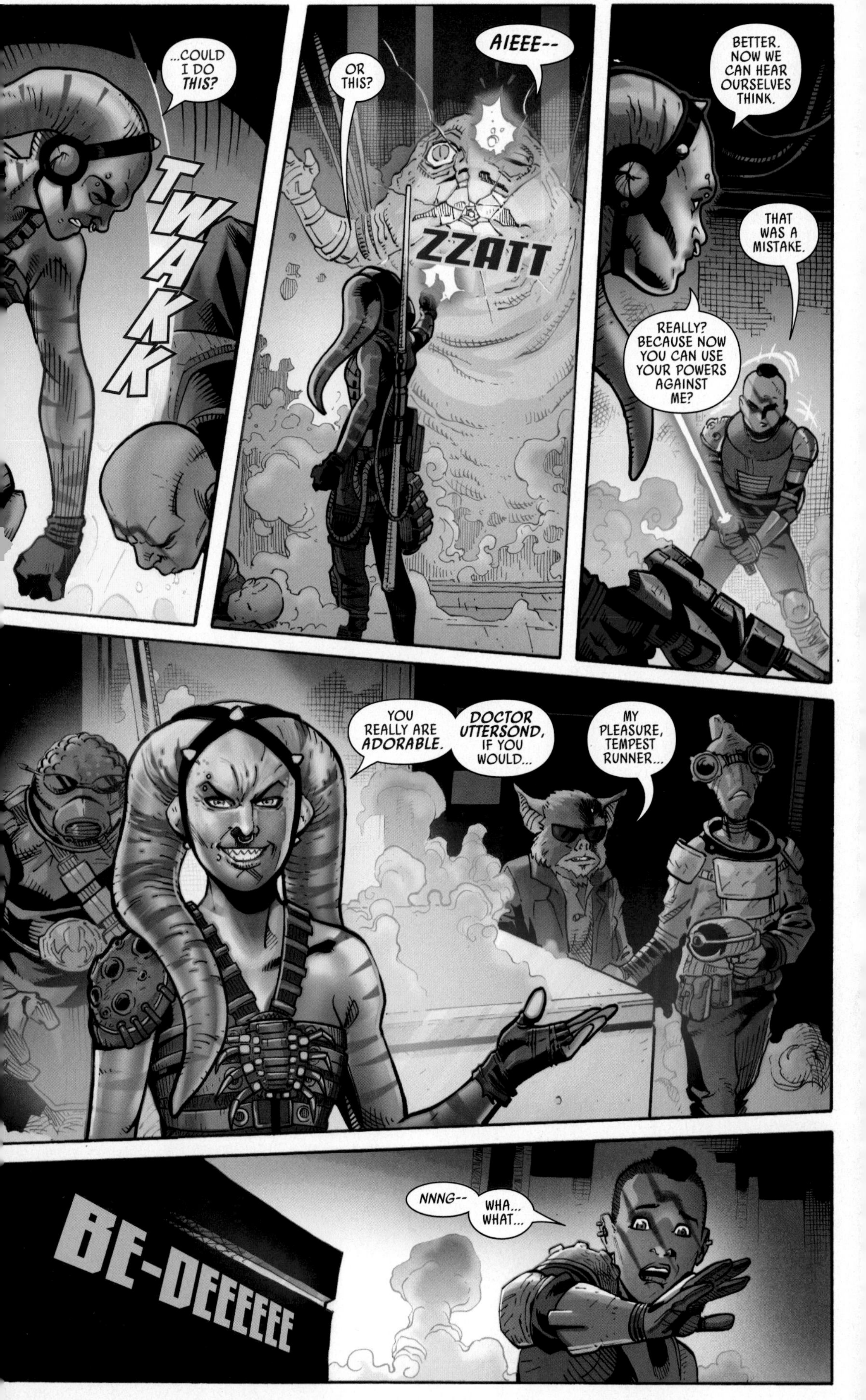
...COULD I DO THIS?
TWAKK
OR THIS?
AIEEE--
ZZATT
BETTER. NOW WE CAN HEAR OURSELVES THINK.
THAT WAS A MISTAKE.
REALLY? BECAUSE NOW YOU CAN USE YOUR POWERS AGAINST ME?
YOU REALLY ARE ADORABLE.
DOCTOR UTTERSOND, IF YOU WOULD...
MY PLEASURE, TEMPEST RUNNER...
BE-DEEEEEE
NNNG--
WHA... WHAT...

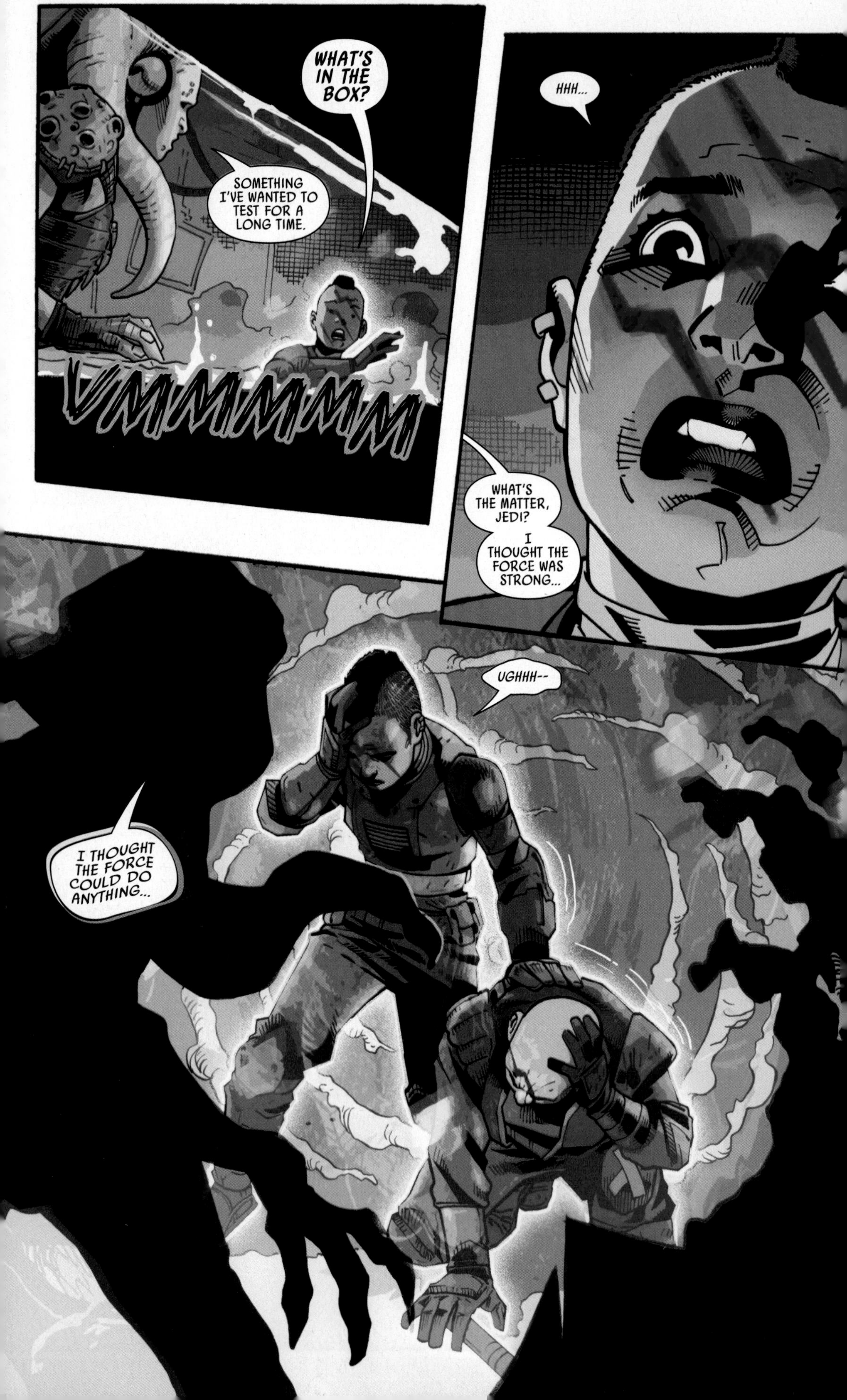

WHAT'S IN THE BOX?
SOMETHING I'VE WANTED TO TEST FOR A LONG TIME.
VMMMMMM
HHH...
WHAT'S THE MATTER, JEDI?
I THOUGHT THE FORCE WAS STRONG...
UGHHH--
I THOUGHT THE FORCE COULD DO ANYTHING...

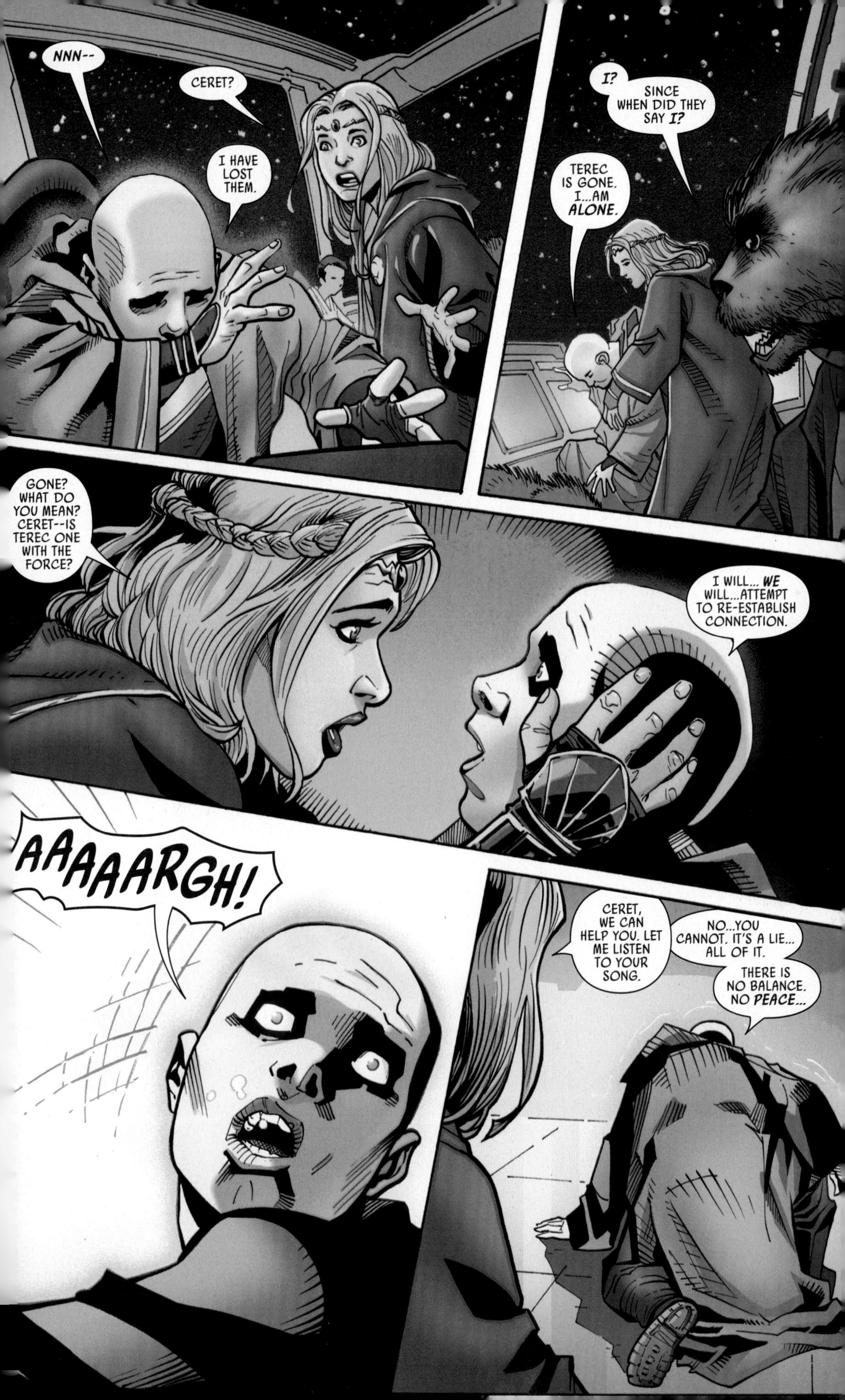
NNN--
CERET?
I HAVE LOST THEM.
I?
SINCE WHEN DID THEY SAY I?
TEREC IS GONE. I...AM ALONE.
GONE? WHAT DO YOU MEAN? CERET--IS TEREC ONE WITH THE FORCE?
I WILL... WE WILL...ATTEMPT TO RE-ESTABLISH CONNECTION.
AAAAARGH!
CERET, WE CAN HELP YOU. LET ME LISTEN TO YOUR SONG.
NO...YOU CANNOT. IT'S A LIE... ALL OF IT.
THERE IS NO BALANCE. NO PEACE...

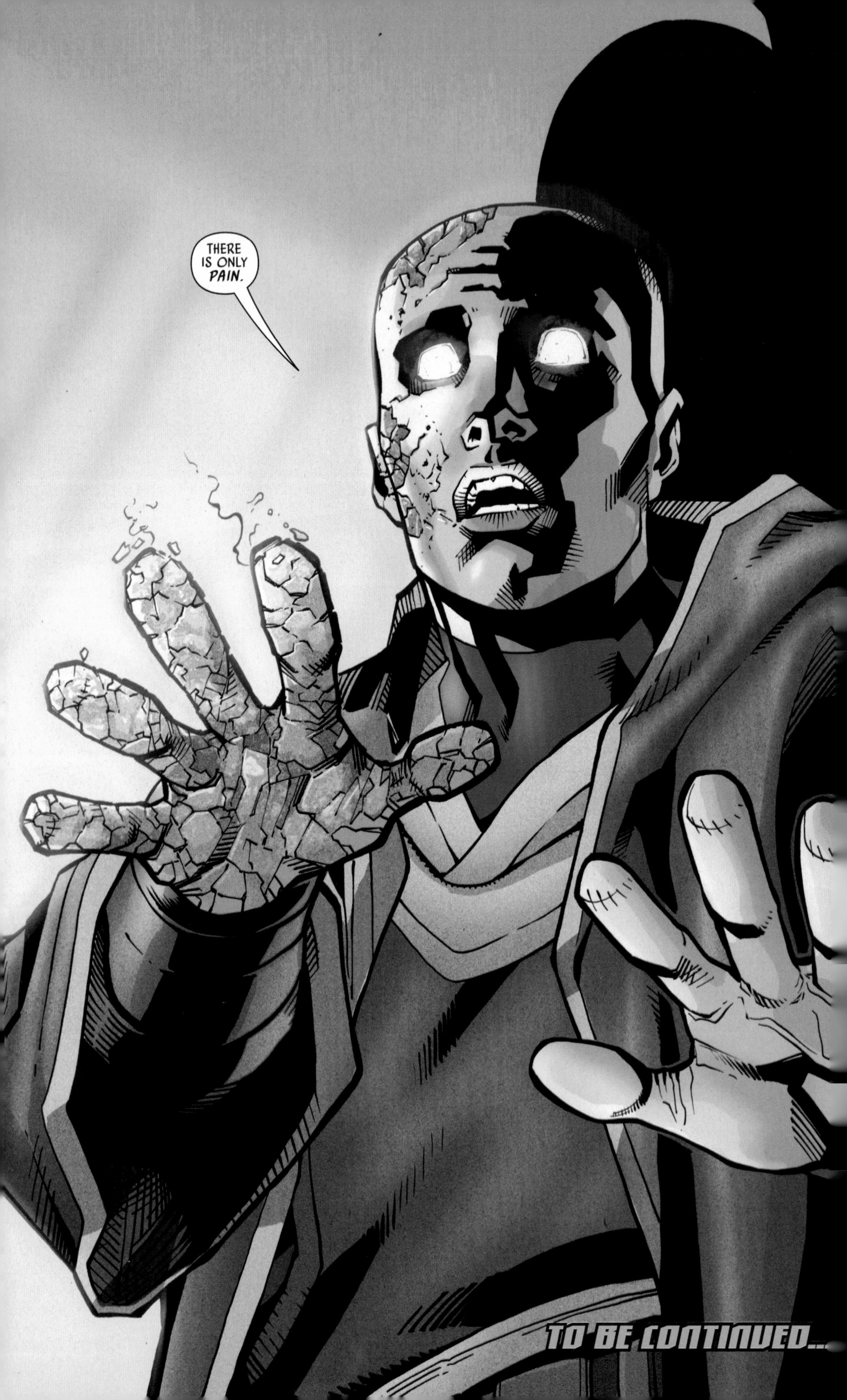
THERE IS ONLY PAIN.
TO BE CONTINUED...

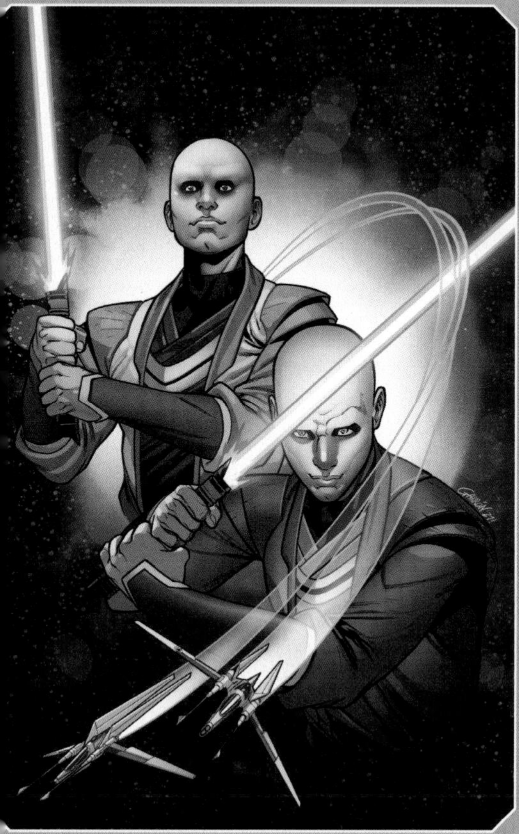

#6 Pride Variant by
JAVIER GARRÓN & MARTE GRACIA

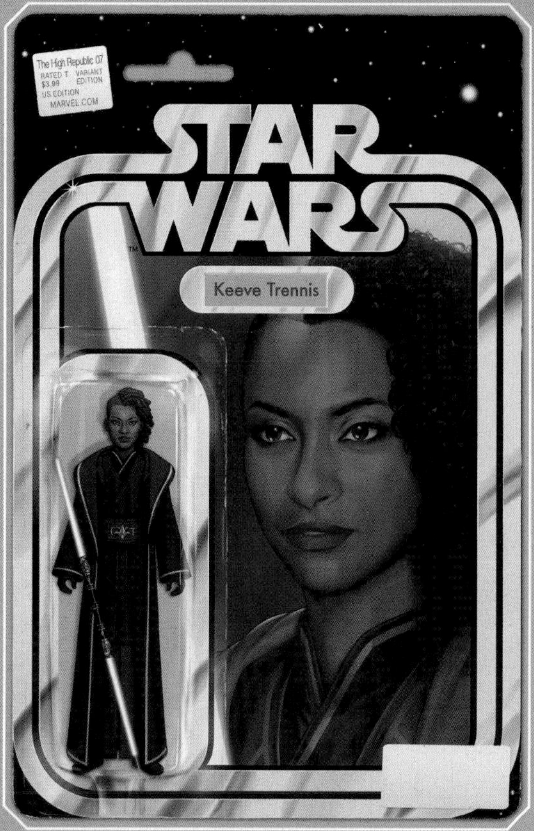
The High Republic 07
RATED T VARIANT
$3.99 EDITION
US EDITION
MARVEL.COM
STAR WARS
Keeve Trennis

#7 Action Figure Variant by
JOHN TYLER CHRISTOPHER

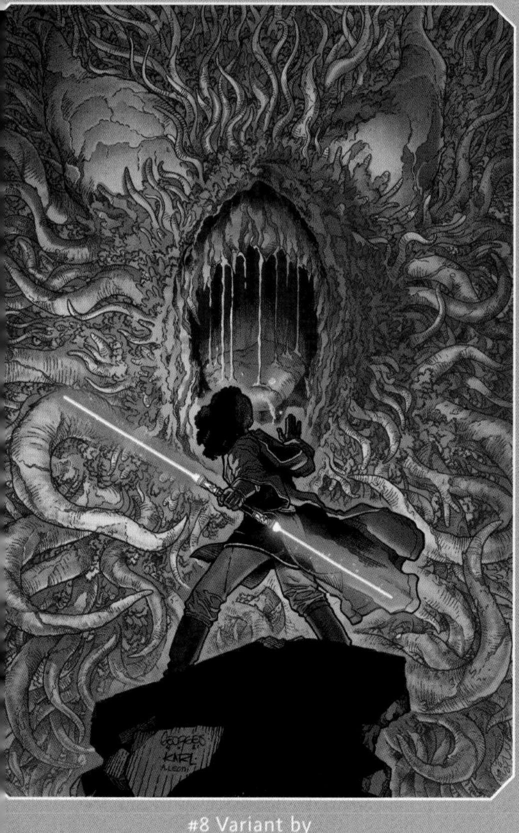

#8 Variant by
GEORGES JEANTY, KARL STORY & ANNALISA LEONI

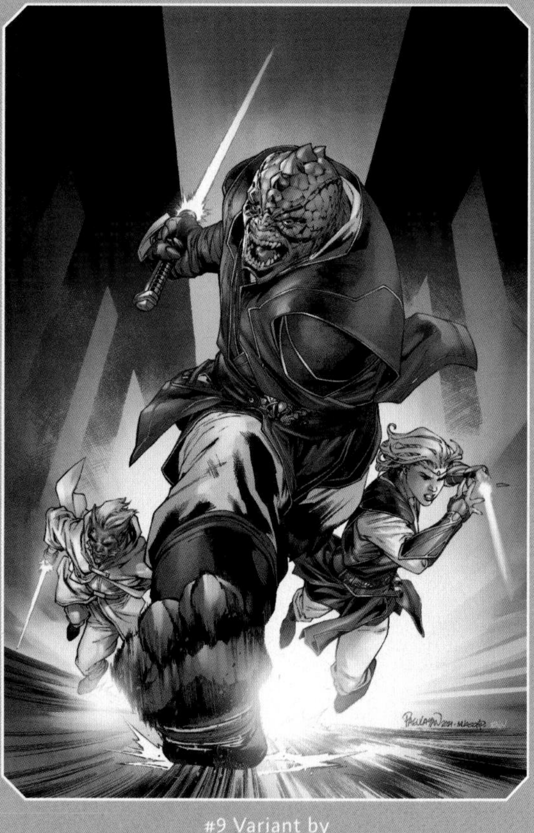

#9 Variant by
CARLO PAGULAYAN, JASON PAZ & RAIN BEREDO

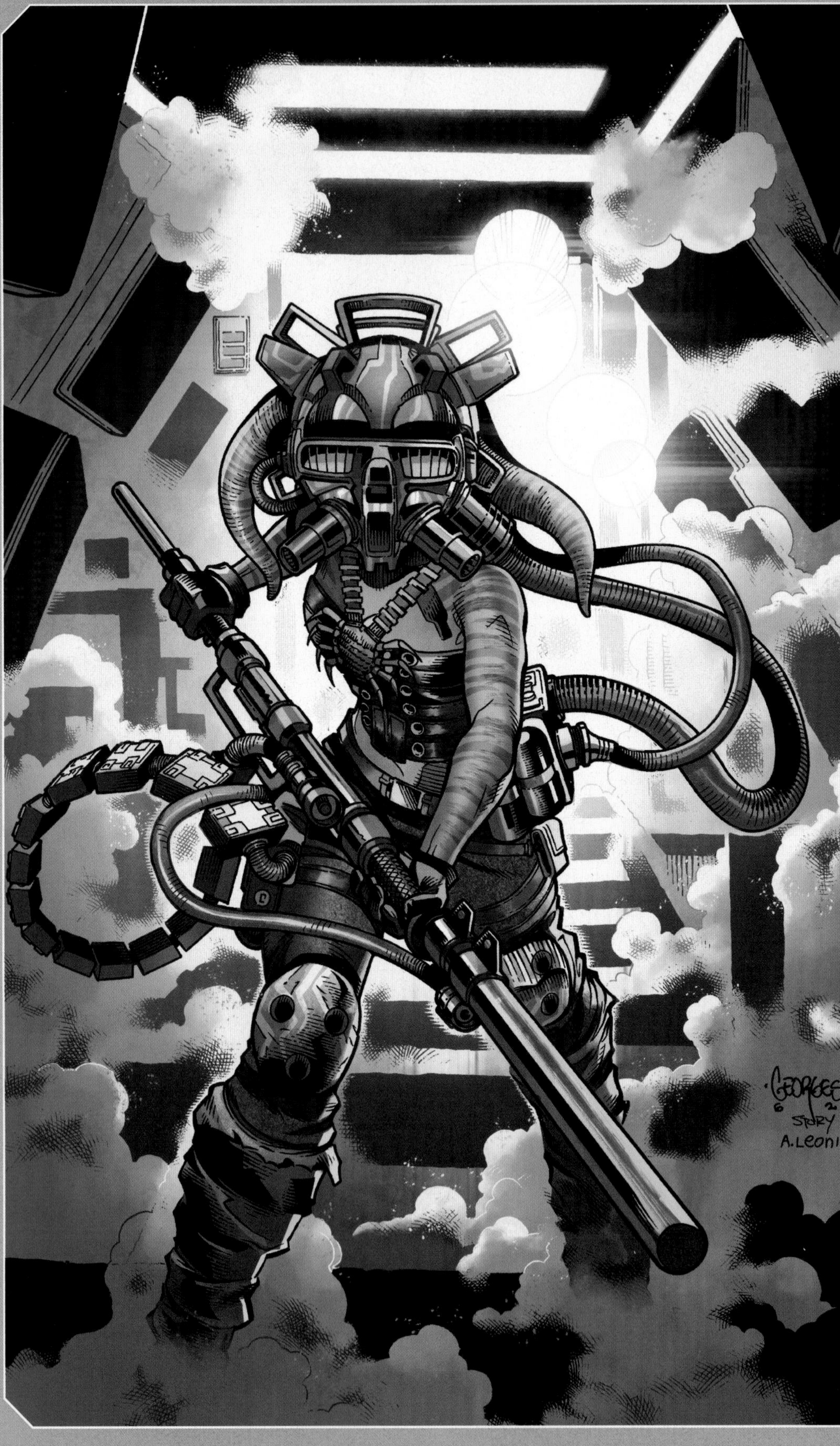
GEORGES
6 21
STORY
A.LEONI

#10 Variant by
GEORGES JEANTY, KARL STORY & ANNALISA LEONI

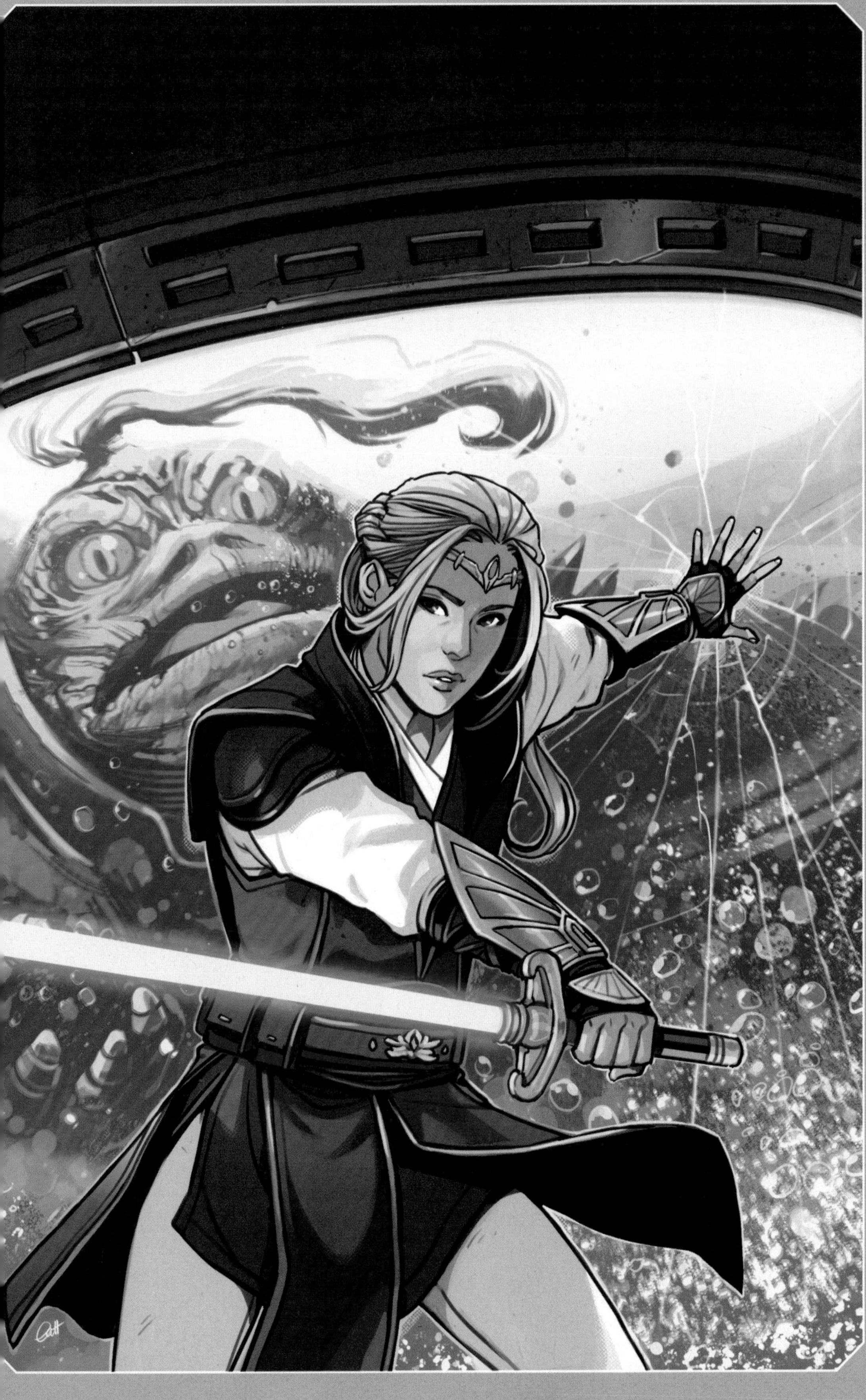

#10 Variant by
CASPAR WIJNGAARD

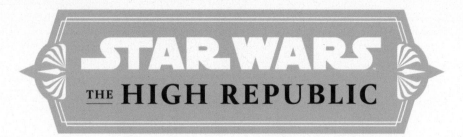

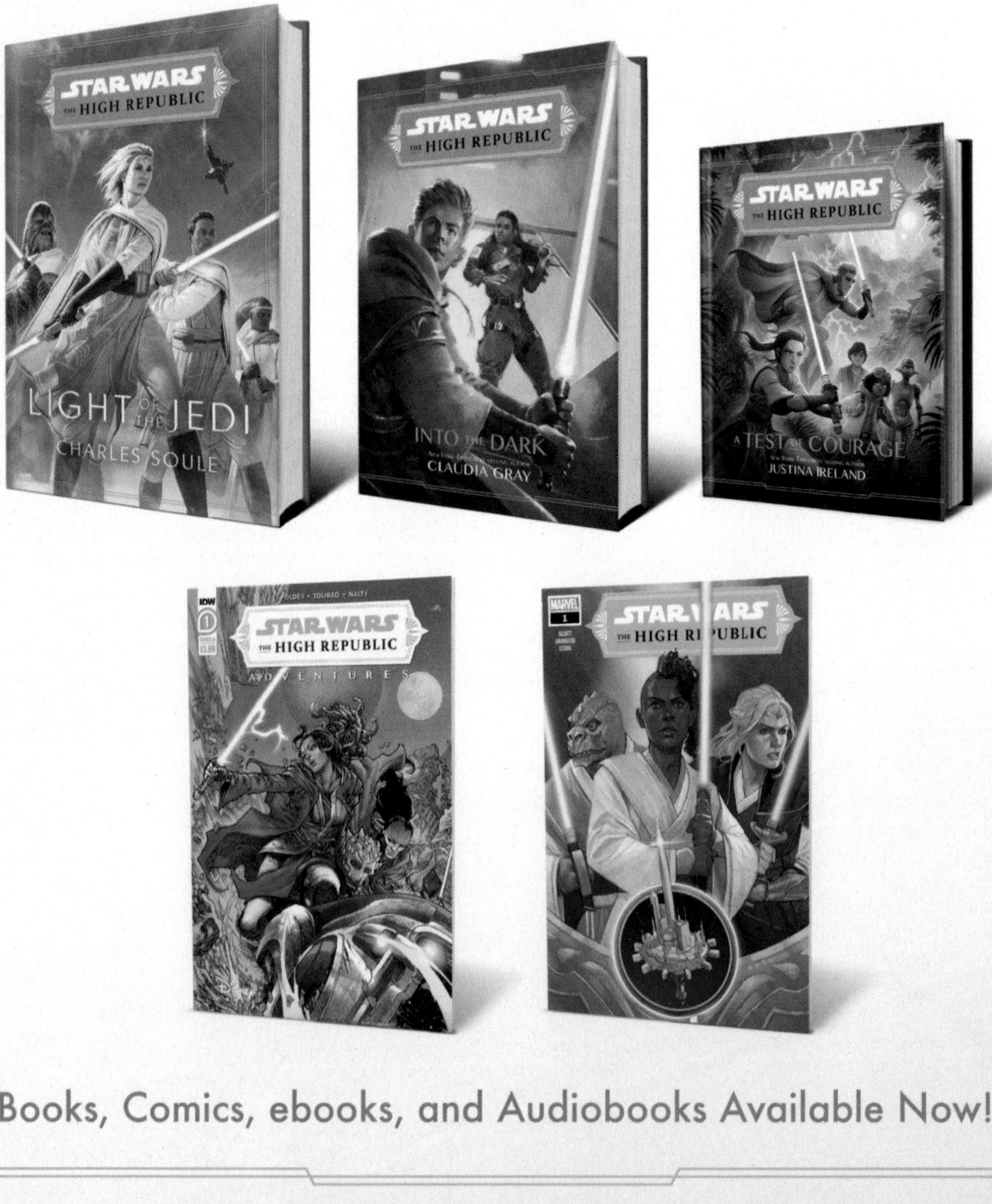
STAR WARS
THE HIGH REPUBLIC
LIGHT OF THE JEDI
CHARLES SOULE
STAR WARS
THE HIGH REPUBLIC
INTO THE DARK
CLAUDIA GRAY
STAR WARS
THE HIGH REPUBLIC
A TEST OF COURAGE
JUSTINA IRELAND
IDW
STAR WARS
THE HIGH REPUBLIC
ADVENTURES
MARVEL
STAR WARS
THE HIGH REPUBLIC

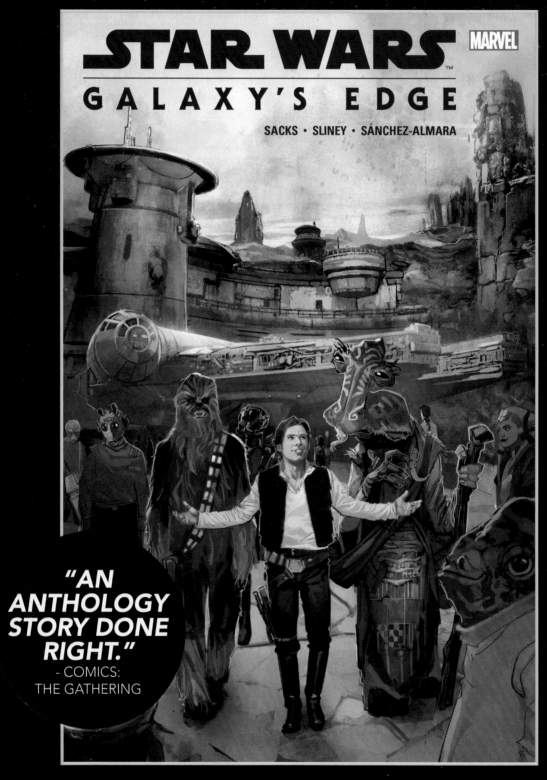